❧ Vanished History ❧

MAKING SENSE OF HISTORY
Studies in Historical Cultures
General Editor: Stefan Berger
Founding Editor: Jörn Rüsen

Bridging the gap between historical theory and the study of historical memory, this series crosses the boundaries between both academic disciplines and cultural, social, political and historical contexts. In an age of rapid globalisation, which tends to manifest itself on an economic and political level, locating the cultural practices involved in generating its underlying historical sense is an increasingly urgent task.

VANISHED HISTORY

The Holocaust in Czech and Slovak Historical Culture

Tomas Sniegon

berghahn
NEW YORK · OXFORD
www.berghahnbooks.com

First published in 2014 by
Berghahn Books
www.berghahnbooks.com

©2014 Tomas Sniegon

Library of Congress Cataloging-in-Publication Data

Sniegon, Tomas, author.
  Vanished history: the Holocaust in Czech and Slovak historical culture /
Tomas Sniegon.
        pages cm. -- (Making sense of history; v. 18)
  Includes bibliographical references.
  ISBN 978-1-78238-294-2 (hardback: alk. paper) -- ISBN 978-1-78238-
295-9 (ebook)
1. Jews--Czech Republic--History. 2. Holocaust, Jewish
(1939-1945)--Czech Republic--Influence. 3. Jews--Slovakia--History.
4. Holocaust, Jewish (1939-1945)--Slovakia--Influence. 5. Jews--
Czechoslovakia--History. 6. Holocaust, Jewish (1939-1945)--Czechoslovakia-
-Influence. 7. Czech Republic--Ethnic relations. 8. Slovakia--Ethnic
relations. 9. Czechoslovakia--Ethnic relations. I. Title.
  DS135.C95S57 2014
  940.53'18094371--dc23

                                                          2013044572

British Library Cataloguing in Publication Data
A catalogue record for this book is available from the British Library

Printed on acid-free paper.

ISBN: 978-1-78238-294-2 (hardback)
ISBN: 978-1-78238-295-9 (ebook)

Contents

Illustrations

Figure 1 The suitcase of the Czech Jewish woman prisoner Zdena Fantlová
exhibited at the Museum in Auschwitz. Fantlová was deported to Auschwitz with her
entire family but was the only one who survived the Holocaust. After the victory of
the communist regime in Czechoslovakia she emigrated first to Australia in 1949 and
later to the United Kingdom. Photo: Tomas Sniegon

Introduction

Czechoslovak history's velvet awakening

This book is an analysis of the Holocaust's position in Czech and Slovak historical culture during 'the long 1990s', a period which commenced with the radical political changes in Europe of 1989 and developed towards the Czech Republic's and Slovakia's entry into the European Union in 2004. In a broader perspective the book concerns the role of history during the two societies' development from dictatorship to democracy, when both were forced to redefine themselves both internally and in relation to the wider world. It deals with questions surrounding values and expectations that were reflected at a national Slovak and Czech level, and their relation to, primarily, a supranational, European historical culture that was being created in parallel. It is precisely this European historical culture and its relation to certain selected national historical cultures that has been the focus for the project, *The Holocaust and European Historical Culture*, within whose frame this work has been written.[1]

In concrete terms, I focus on the Czech and Slovak manifestations of historical consciousness in relation to the Holocaust or Shoah: the genocide perpetrated by the Nazis against Jews and certain other ethnic/religious groups during the Second World War. This event has not been randomly selected. The Holocaust struck and deeply affected both of the countries that are at the centre of this book. At the same time the genocide against the Jews during the period of this study has attained a broader significance in terms of its European and universal symbolic value. Because the Czech Republic and Slovakia have endeavoured to become part of an international context in the post-communist era, it has been an urgent matter for them to deal with their painful history.

At the end of the Cold War, the political situation in Central Europe changed dramatically. Until 1989 Czechoslovakia was a communist state, strongly dependent on the Soviet Union. Towards the end of 1989 communist

Notes for this section begin on page 23.

rule was replaced by a newly born democracy during a peaceful process called the 'Velvet Revolution'. But as early as 1 January 1993 Czechoslovakia split into two independent states: the Czech Republic and Slovakia. The Velvet Revolution culminated in a peaceful 'velvet divorce', which ended the velvet process and initiated a wholly new period in the development of both countries.

Even if the disintegration of the Czechoslovak state was not totally unexpected, many were surprised by the speed of the process. The radical changes affected almost all aspects of life. The old system disappeared after several decades of stagnation. The newly won freedom of the press and other forms of expression, freedom to travel, freedom of commerce and freedom to choose different political parties offered people in Czechoslovakia new possibilities, but at the same time increased competition, social stress and confrontation with the surrounding world. In such an atmosphere, old and established values were challenged and continuously redefined, while new ones were still waiting to be born or developed. Thus the Velvet Revolution was not only a political, ideological and socioeconomic revolution, but a cultural and mental one as well.

In this turbulent situation, where hopes of a brighter future were strong, history did not just become a passive remnant. While in 1990 the Slovak historian, Lubomír Lipták, described the fall of communism in Czechoslovakia in November 1989 as a radical change without precedent, as 'a change that needed neither historical attire nor sweeping slogans',[2] another historian, Vilém Prečan, spoke just a few years later about 'a surplus of history'.[3] History had great and sometimes even decisive significance for orientating individuals and collectives in the Czech Republic and Slovakia in the direction of something perceived as a better society and a happier situation in life. Historical consciousness, which every human being develops in order to mentally be able to move between yesterday's questions, today's tasks and tomorrow's promises, therefore came to function as an active and mobilising power in this transformation.

Many historical disclosures began to be served as the 'truth' that had at last arrived to replace the communists' 'lies' and 'fallacies'. Suddenly there was not only one, but two, three or even more 'truths' that conflicted with each other. They were supported by previously suppressed historical facts and, moreover, often claimed to be 'scientifically proven'. But which historical arguments was a person to accept as his or her own, and how was that person to find a standpoint in this argumentation? Which historical events did he or she most want to forget and which, conversely, were to be highlighted? And why? Should the Holocaust belong to the first or the second category?

During the Cold War a relative silence regarding the history of the Holocaust prevailed, particularly in Eastern Europe, where the suffering of the Jews was not allowed to compete with the communists' suffering and heroism. After the fall of the Berlin Wall, the Holocaust began to be held up on an increasingly broad front. The British historian, Tony Judt, enthusiastically describes the new attention paid to the Holocaust in Europe as 'the very definition and guarantee of the continent's restored humanity'.[4] The Holocaust has become a phenomenon that now reaches far beyond Europe's borders; some researchers even talk about the Holocaust as the foundation for a new global or 'cosmopolitan' memory, the function of which is to create a basis for the defence of human rights.[5] Irrespective of whether one regards these claims as exaggerated or not, it is not possible to ignore that the Holocaust in our particular era has been given emphasis, especially in Western societies, more than any other historical event. How was this emphasis concretely manifested during the intensive transformation of the two Central European states of this study?

From Cold War to peace, from Hiroshima to Auschwitz

Among the historical events most often noted in Czechoslovakia during the early post- communist development were the most decisive moments from the communist period: the victory of communism in 1948, the terror of the Stalin era until the mid-1950s, and the invasion of Czechoslovakia by the Soviet Union and the Warsaw Pact which halted the reform process that became known internationally as the Prague Spring of 1968. Second World War traumas can be added to these.[6] Despite the Second World War having ended forty-five years earlier, it was only following the cessation of the Cold War that it became possible to freely discuss all its aspects. For example, in 1990 the Czechs were able to celebrate for the first time since 1948 that their part of Czechoslovakia had been liberated not only by the Red Army but also by American troops.

Discussions about pre-1945 history became in certain respects even more important than debates about the just-concluded communist epoch, particularly in debates concerning foreign policy and events and processes, such as the reunification of Germany or European integration. The period up to 1945 represented, namely, a time when Czechoslovakia, far more than later, had contacts with the well-developed democratic countries in the West, which at this stage were seen simultaneously as Czechoslovakia's new and old allies. This did not, however, mean that the memories were only positive. Thoughts about the Munich Agreement of 1938 and the Western powers' so-called *appeasement* politics, which left Czechoslovakia to Hitler, had left a bitter aftertaste for many Czechs and Slovaks. But the memory of the Second World War, the most traumatic event in twentieth-century Europe, was no longer there to serve as a cut off between separate countries and rival ideologies.

As the Swedish historian Klas-Göran Karlsson points out, the traumatic war history after the fall of the Berlin Wall has not only been the focus of national historical accounts, it is instead treated in a way which is thought to answer to 'European' values.[7] The process of reconciliation between old enemies, which at one time was the basis for Western Europe's integration, was now expanded to the other side of the former Iron Curtain. The memory of the Second World War was put to use to avoid violent conflicts in the future, but served also as a building block for the new European identity which as early as 1992 was formally decided in the so-called Maastrich Treaty.[8] The political will to overcome old conflicts between East and West was manifest both during the process of reuniting Germany in 1990 and at the celebrations of important, positive junctures in the Second World War, such as the Fiftieth Anniversary of the Allied invasion of Normandy in 1944 and the surrender of the Third Reich in 1945. Despite neither Germany nor Russia being invited to Normandy in 1994, and despite many Western statesmen boycotting the military parade at the celebrations in Moscow in May 1995 as a protest against Russia's ongoing war in Chechnya, the victory over Nazism was still unanimously presented as a new springboard for Europe's united future.

Now that the immediate threat of a global nuclear war between the world's dominating military superpowers has disappeared, Hiroshima has lost some of its political-symbolic significance. Instead it is the Holocaust that has become the strongest symbol of absolute evil, the lowest point in history. As the Israeli Holocaust historian of Czech-Jewish descent, Yehuda Bauer, observed in 2000 at the opening ceremony of the 'Stockholm International Forum on the Holocaust', the Holocaust has become a universal concern and one that, according to him, is politically expressed: 'Major politicians, wrongly but characteristically, compare Saddam Hussein to Hitler, or the tragedy in Kosovo to the Holocaust'.[9] Another proof he submitted for the increasing global significance of the Holocaust is an Auschwitz museum now being built near Hiroshima, and the fact that a department for teaching about the Holocaust has been opened at Shanghai University.

But did the Holocaust play any role whatsoever in the Czech and Slovak historical debates? Were there strong tendencies towards remembering or, perhaps, an interest in forgetting? Who wanted to remember and who wanted to forget?

The tragedy of the Czech and Slovak Jews

Before presenting my theoretical points of departure and my analytical tools, I would like to briefly discuss the course of the Holocaust in the area which after 1918 had become Czechoslovak territory and which during the Second World War was divided into two parts: the occupied Protectorate of Bohemia and Moravia on the one side and the Slovak Republic on the other.

The number of Czechoslovak citizens who lost their lives during the Second World War is estimated at 360,000. Even though the old numbers from the early post-war period have been re-examined and partly modified since 1989, all kinds of evidence show that most of these victims were Jews. According to statistical records about 270,000 Czechoslovak Jews were murdered, which means that as many as three out of four Czechoslovak victims of Second World War violence were killed in the Holocaust as a result of anti-Jewish politics.[10] Almost 80,000 Jewish victims came from the Protectorate of Bohemia and Moravia, i.e., the area of the Czech Lands with the exclusion of the Sudetenland, the territory annexed by Hitler's Third Reich after the 1938 Munich Agreement.[11] Roughly 70,000 were Jews from Slovakia. The rest of the victims came from territories that were taken away from Slovakia by Hungary shortly after the Munich Agreement: southern and eastern Slovak regions (approx. 42,000 victims) and the poorest eastern province of Ruthenia (approx. 80,000 victims).[12] Among the victims of the Nazi genocide were also around 5,500 Czech and 2,000 Slovak gypsies.[13]

In the Czech territory, i.e., the Protectorate of Bohemia and Moravia, the occupying power, Germany, was responsible alone for 'the final solution'. In Slovakia, however, the domestic regime, led by the Catholic priest, Jozef Tiso, organised the forcible measures and deportations with their own forces and in that way took over a great part of the responsibility from Germany. At the end of the war, Tiso's Slovak regime stood among the losers, side by side with its main ally, Germany, while Bohemia and Moravia were liberated and thus situated on the winning side.

Slovakia was never forced into openly dealing with its war history on the international stage. As early as 1945, Slovakia ceased to exist as an international entity and was once again included in Czechoslovakia. The stance of the Allied great powers, in particular that of the USA, was of decisive importance. The USA never recognised Slovakia as an independent state and viewed Czechoslovakia's exile government in London, with Edvard Beneš at its head, as the country's sole official representative during the war. In December 1941 the USA even ignored the declaration of war by Slovakia.[14] The reunification of the Czech and Slovak parts was part of the Beneš government's plan to reconstruct the first Czechoslovak Republic within its pre-war borders and in this way cancel the results of the Munich Agreement with regard to constitutional law. Thus even the trial of Jozef Tiso and his close collaborators in 1947 was seen as an internal Czechoslovak matter rather than part of the international post-war judicial processes.[15] At the end of the war Tiso fled to German Bavaria, where he was captured by American troops and shortly thereafter handed over to the Czechoslovak authorities. In April 1947 Tiso was sentenced to death in accordance with Czechoslovak law and executed just three days later. The trial was characterised by an intensive political power struggle in Slovakia and the whole of Czechoslovakia. This fact made it easier for those who wanted to interpret the sentence as a communist or Czech revenge against the man who had become the main symbol of the Slovak state.[16]

Despite the fact that the communists could have had reason to use Tiso ideologically as a frightening example of Nazi collaboration in their historical propaganda, they did so only to a limited degree during their time in power. They probably feared that giving too much voice to historical problems would threaten the sensitive relations between Czechs and Slovaks and increase the opposition to communism in Slovakia. Why the same regime that had defined itself as being consistently anti-Nazi and anti-fascist avoided a debate of the Holocaust is something I will discuss in more detail later, as this question is central for this study.

The organisation of this study

At the core of this study are four concrete examples of history's position in Czech and Slovak societies where Holocaust history directly or indirectly stands at the centre. These examples are intended to reflect different attitudes to 'the final solution' and the memory of it among Czechs and Slovaks during the period of transition from communism to democracy. However, the study does not strive to present a complete list of all the cases touching upon the Holocaust in Czech and Slovak development after 1989. Instead, it focuses on those situations where the post-communist constructions of meaning with regard to Czech and Slovak history were confronted with the process of making sense of the Holocaust. Thus, the selected cases, over and above other situations, can be argued to reflect the essential features of Czech and Slovak historical cultures in relation to the Holocaust.

In the following part, the theoretical, conceptual and analytical starting points will be explained. Thereafter, a survey of the use of Holocaust history in Czechoslovakia between 1945 and 1989 will be presented as an empirical background description. During this period history was first and foremost decided by the dictates of communist ideology.

The subsequent four empirically orientated chapters will, from a main principle of chronology, illuminate the historical-cultural development in the Czech Republic and Slovakia.

The first of these chapters will focus on the Czech and Slovak historical debate against the background of Czechoslovakia's division in 1990–1992. It was at this time that the first Slovak nation state or, alternatively, the German satellite of the Second World War, was primarily debated. The reason for putting focus on this particular period is that nationalistic sentiments were most strongly expressed during this time, while the old Czechoslovak communist historical narrative was being replaced by new ones.

The second empirical chapter is concerned with the Czech reaction to the American film, *Schindler's List*, perhaps the most well-known and influential historical-cultural product about the Holocaust. Directed by Steven Spielberg, it portrays a former Czechoslovak citizen, the Sudeten German, Oskar Schindler, paying tribute to his heroic action in saving more than 1,000 Jewish prisoners.

Here the Czech reactions are placed in relation to the Americanisation of the Holocaust.

In the third empirical chapter another Czech debate will be analysed: the debate concerning two memorial sites, *Lety* and *Hodonín u Kunštátu*, where during the Second World War there were two concentration camps for Roma from the Protectorate of Bohemia and Moravia who were threatened with extermination. At these sites the Czechs, after the war, constructed a pig farm and a holiday establishment, a fact that during the 1990s drew significant attention and protests. As will be shown, the process described as the Europeanisation of the Holocaust meant that the genocide of the Jews and that of the Roma were coupled together without consideration of the differences between the two operations, a concept whose problems become evident when viewed through the lens of the Czech actions.

In the final empirical chapter the main question is how the Holocaust has been presented in a Slovak museum, which during the communist era was the most prominent museum about the Second World War in Slovakia. The establishment was later converted into the first museum in the country to also include the history of the Holocaust. It was above all this museum that was given the task of adjusting the memory of the war and the Holocaust to the needs of the new Slovakia: a Slovakia which had introduced a democratic system and strengthened its ties with the European Union and NATO. Thus the complications surrounding the Europeanisation of Slovak history and the Second World War are given particular attention in this chapter. Lastly, a concluding discussion with a summary of my findings will be presented.

Theoretical and conceptual starting points

The concept of historical consciousness is of fundamental theoretical significance for this book. The function of historical consciousness is to orientate people in a flow of time by relating the comprehension of their own present situation to, on the one hand, experiences and memories of the past, and on the other hand, expectations and fears in relation to the future. Historical consciousness places all human beings in a context of meaning which is greater than their own clearly defined lives. The concept is meaningful when dealing with individual as well as collective contexts of significance, but it is in the latter sense as a mental tool, which to a high degree is determined by collective experiences and memories, and which incorporates us into a collective context, that it will be used in the present work. In practice this collective context has often comprised a national unity, but in our era this is challenged by both regional and transnational unities. As has already been stated, this study highlights a European historical context of meaning that competed with or complemented the Czech and Slovak context.

It has to be mentioned, however, that the concept of historical consciousness as used here is different from the traditional usage of the term historical consciousness in the Czech and Slovak scholarly contexts. Some Czech and Slovak historians, among them, Miroslav Hroch, had used the term (*historické vědomí*) already during the 1960s, i.e., before the definition of historical consciousness which was established by Karl-Ernst Jeismann in 1979 and which is used here.[17] However, they did not understand the term in the same way as Jeismann did later. According to Hroch, the term reflected the level of historical knowledge and common awareness about (especially national) history.[18] This interpretation was questioned in 1995 by another Czech historian, Zdeněk Beneš.[19] However, it is only now, in very recent years, that the concept of historical consciousness has been approached on a broader bases that is closer to Jeismann's original definition.[20]

Historical consciousness is, to a great extent, connected to different social and cultural developments in a society and a state, but it can also be triggered by various political interest groups which have the capacity and will to create meaning from the past, as well as the power and possibility to reach out to large parts of the population with their message. In such situations, historical consciousness can be transformed into an effective weapon in the struggle for political power in a country.

Hence, it may be presumed that historical consciousness is most often mobilised in times of rapid change, turbulence and crisis. It is then that our need for and interest in orientating ourselves and creating meaning in time increases. The period of Central European history examined in this book was definitely such a time.

An important aspect of the term historical consciousness is that it helps us to see that history is so much more than a subject of science and teaching. The historical dimension has links to problems concerning existence and identity, moral-judicial decisions, political and ideological questions of contention, and so much more. Those wishing to examine historical consciousness are, however, faced with the problem that the object, as such, cannot be analysed. Analyses can only be directed towards the concrete manifestations of historical consciousness, which will here be described as aspects of a historical culture. At the centre of this culture stands a historical artefact or product, which can consist of a scientific monograph or history textbook for teaching use, but which may also be a film, a monument or a debate relating to a current historical question. Such historical-cultural products will be analysed in the separate empirical chapters to follow.

A historical culture has been described as a communicative context, linked to the historical products mentioned.[21] These can consequently be analysed in terms of sender/production, intermediary/communication and recipient/consumption. The following account will not be purely historiographical, i.e., focused on how and under which conditions historical products are depicted, but will also show how history is communicated in the Czech Republic and Slovakia in political debates, film reviews and museum exhibitions. The question of how historical-cultural artefacts are received is difficult to assess. It is in all likelihood partly dependent on the effectiveness of the communicative process, and partly traditions and conceptions regarding historical development, which brings us back to the primary cultural question of which history a society believes to be worth saving, debating, celebrating or forgetting.

An adjacent perspective on historical culture has to do with power. The research questions that are related to power and influence are multiple: Which groups in a society have the power to choose which historical perspectives are promoted or withheld? What role does the state play as a conveyor of history? What importance do domestic actors have in highlighting and mobilising crucial questions, and to what extent is the historical-cultural debate influenced in a country of international actors, questions and trends? What power functions does history exercise in a society?

Historical culture has traditionally been framed in a national manner and has often had a strongly homeland-focused and patriotic stamp. During the communist era it had a special character particularly with regard to modern history, as 'national values' were coupled with a class perspective. The national framework was, even so, constantly among the decisive criteria. Books and museum exhibitions have had Czechoslovak, Czech or Slovak history as a focal point. Interpretations of historical phenomena such as war have been built around 'national' actors and structures even more than those of domestic political events.

Against this background it has seemed reasonable to base this book upon national historical cultures. The term 'nationalising' signifies in this context that a historical phenomenon is 'written into' a national interpretative context sanctioned by long usage and is adapted to the values seen as characterising it. This does not, however, mean that historical cultures cannot be connected to other categories than the nation and state. Among those that become visible in this book are professional groups, regions and ethnic groups. Above all, as has been mentioned, the national historical-cultural context over the past decades has been challenged by a European-wide interpretative context. In this work, the 'Europeanisation' of history will signify the communicative process by which a historical-culturally interesting phenomenon is placed in relation to what is perceived and portrayed as European interpretations and values.

Historical narrative

One method of analysing historical culture is by positioning the narrative at the centre. This will be further explained later in this introductory chapter. First, it is necessary to present an analytical framework for the narrative concept.

A narrative is always a story about something. The communicative element is prominent: there is always someone who narrates, and someone who takes in the story. A historical narrative concerns our relationship with the past; it is a presentation of how selected, mutually dependent events follow upon one another in a temporal perspective.

The narrative, which has a beginning, a middle section and a conclusion, is bound together by a plot. A plot ties together the story's different stages and therefore contributes to creating context, wholeness and meaning around questions regarding what happened, how it happened and why it happened. A historical narrative emphasises the totality and not the separate event that stands out as important, because it is precisely the plot that decides the choice of events in different historical narratives and not the opposite. The same events can, however, be included in different historical narratives when they are presented with different plots in focus.

Notions such as goals and means, actors, intentions and motives become particularly important in a storyline of this kind, while structural, impersonal conditions end up in the background.[22] This close link to dimensions such as identity, morality and power illustrates the narrative's close relation to historical consciousness.

In the narrative two extreme positions are often placed against each other to create excitement and conflict, and the story frequently ends with the antagonisms being solved – or culminating. Clearly, not everything we relate can qualify as a narrative in a deeper sense. Nor can all stories be described as having the same historical significance. Some are strictly individual and particular, while others are common goods and function in a unifying or separating manner.

In historical culture, narratives are constructed, chosen and valued. In a competitive situation, some are seen as useful and important while others are not. In the historical-cultural context we often adapt our interpretation of the past and formulate our stories in connection to already formulated narratives, placing them in the more general themes that characterise them.[23] Researchers sometimes use the term *grand narratives* or *master narratives*, which are defined as stable conveyors of meaning that ideologically and culturally support and legitimise whole institutions or societies. Attempting to find these kinds of slow-moving narratives in Czechoslovakia's changeable history is far from unproblematic. Despite this, I will be focusing on such hegemonic narratives, which fulfil the necessary criteria more than all the others.

The use of history

Every historical culture has a procedural aspect. This concerns questions on how historical consciousness is expressed and how historical culture is created.

Historical culture is a product of individuals and collectives who actively use history. They mobilise and activate their historical consciousness and transform it into concrete texts and actions. Individuals and groups use history to satisfy different needs and interests, and to attain diverse goals.

As Klas-Göran Karlsson has shown, it is possible when considering these needs and goals, and in addition different historical and societal contexts, to distinguish between at least several different types of history usage. These include scientific, existential, moral, ideological and political use, as well as non-use.[24] A typology of this kind conflicts with the traditional understanding of our attitude towards history that developed during the professionalisation of the history discipline, namely, that scientific historians are the only 'true' users of history, while all others more or less abuse it. However, as Friedrich Nietzsche demonstrated as early as the end of the 1800s, traditionally understood historical science cannot deal with and satisfy all the historical dimensions concerned with history as a necessity of life.[25]

Karlsson's thought is that the typology can be analytically applied to different societies and ages to provide knowledge about similarities and differences in regard to the use of history. The presented uses of history comprise analytical categories or ideal types. Several of the uses can overlap and strengthen each other, which in this book is most clearly shown in the chapter on the Holocaust of the Roma, the Porrajmos. Sometimes a use of history is instead weakened by another. As the borders between these attitudes are not always exactly clear, and as different ways of using history can be combined, the typology is not intended to be used in a normative way. However, with its help it is possible to better understand the main actors' needs and intentions.

Existential history usage helps its practitioners to seek answers to questions about existence and identity. It is triggered by a need to remember in order to orientate oneself in a society characterised by uncertainty and crisis, a society in the process of rapid change or under strong pressure. This use is often found in groups struggling against amnesia, unconscious forgetting, and striving for cultural homogenisation.

Moral history usage expresses thoughts about questions of right and wrong in history, about good and bad. History becomes a moral-political power in a time when political liberalisation or another radical change makes it possible to bring previously unnoticed or consciously suppressed historical questions into the political-cultural agenda. The main practitioners of this method, often intellectual and cultural elites, are eager for forgotten and previously denied, even banal and trivialised history to be accepted, rehabilitated and reinstated. Their goal can generally be described as settling things, with the functional state power restoring the situation that prevailed before this power's encroachment on history.

Political and ideological history usage arises in connection with questions about power and legitimacy. The political use is metaphoric, analogical, instrumental and comparative. The intention here is to invoke historical phenomena to support a current issue and by this means bring about a political debate. Similarities are strongly emphasised to the detriment of differences, which makes the relationship between then and now both simple and unproblematic. The objects used in such comparisons are not selected randomly; what is important is that they possess strong emotional, moral and political power. The ideological use of history is connected to those systems of ideas that exploit history in order to justify a position of power. Its main practitioners who, like those of the political use of history are political and intellectual elites, invoke 'historical laws' and 'objective needs' in order to construct a relevant contextual meaning which legitimises a certain power position, and which rationalises it by portraying history in such a way that mistakes and problems on the road to power are toned down, trivialised or ignored.

A special form of the ideological use of history is the *non-use of history*. This refers to the desire not to be 'disturbed' by history in situations where it is deemed important to focus on the present and the future. Intentional non-use of history thus does not comprise temporary and unintentional forgetting. Rather, it represents a conscious tendency not to legitimise the existing society with the aid of history or cultural heritage, or parts thereof, but instead to refer to specific socioeconomic conditions in the present or to a bright future. The historical dimension is deliberately ignored and suppressed.

Scientific history usage has developed around the question of what is true or false in the interpretation of the past. It is based on a professional and theoretical-analytical and methodological system of rules within the scientific discipline and history as a taught subject. In contrast to the political use of history, the scientific use consciously distances the historical dimension from present interests and needs. The past is to be studied in itself and unique aspects and differences, rather than similarities, between historical phenomena are emphasised. This genetic, prospective view generally represents history as a science.

A boundary between the scientific and the ideological use of history is also important, though not always completely clear. In both cases interpretation and the creation of meaning play a central role, and in both cases intellectual groups are the main actors. In Karlsson's opinion the main difference should be seen in the aims of both uses: while history as a science is normally carried out with the intention of creating new knowledge and thereby contributing to intra-scientific research development, ideological history is used to convince and to mobilise large groups of people for the great ideological task. Practitioners of scientific history often place emphasis on parts of the context of historical meaning, whereas ideological practitioners tend to underline the whole.[26]

The Holocaust's Americanisation and Europeanisation

It has already been stated that nationalisation and Europeanisation belong to those historical-cultural processes which since 1989 have most influenced the question of what position the Holocaust is given in the Czech and Slovak historical cultures. However, it must also be noted that the Holocaust's Americanisation has also influenced the Holocaust debate, particularly in the Czech case.

Both the Americanisation and Europeanisation of the Holocaust became prominent and analytically relevant processes within the context of the Cold War's end, but despite their being generally accepted as important, researchers still have problems defining what the Americanisation and Europeanisation of the Holocaust actually entail. It is particularly the Americanisation of the Holocaust, which has been developing since the 1970s, that is difficult to see as a clearly formulated narrative that might pose long-term challenges for the main Czech and Slovak historical narratives.

The Holocaust's Americanisation can be perceived in two ways. The first concerns how the Holocaust is incorporated into the domestic American historical culture and how it finds its place in the historical consciousness of Americans, i.e., what role it is given in relation to American values and in American conceptions about the future of the USA. Researchers have pointed out that the Holocaust's positioning in an American- meaning context can primarily be connected to leading elements in American societal life, such as multiculturalism and ethnicity, while at the same time the Holocaust's representation in an American context is adapted to 'traditional' American values, such as positive and forward-orientated thinking, a striving for 'happy endings', a focus on strong individual heroes and the toning down of brutality, despair and a tragic view of life.[27] The American historian and linguist Alvin Rosenfeld associates the Holocaust's Americanisation with 'a tendency to individualize, heroize, moralize, idealize and universalize'.[28]

The second perception in regard to the Americanisation of the Holocaust is linked to the question of whether the USA with the help of the Holocaust's 'American' representation has influenced other countries and cultures both through political activities and by the distribution of popular culture produced by the American film and television industry, and American mass media with its global reach.

Both perceptions are, of course, closely connected to each other. In this study I wish to draw attention to the 'outwardly directed' Americanisation in relation to the Czech and Slovak historical cultures after the fall of communism. However, it must be pointed out that despite the significant influence of the USA in regard to both political and economic contacts and the export of popular culture, it is still unclear and unascertained how much and in which ways this political and cultural Americanisation of the Holocaust has influenced the democratic process in the Eastern and Central European region since 1989.

A concrete sign of American influence is, firstly, that the term *Holocaust* itself initially only came to be used in Czechoslovakia at the beginning of the 1990s. Prior to this the Holocaust was denoted either with a Czech or Slovak translation of the German term 'the final solution' or as 'race reprisals' – though without information connecting these terms to the Jews. After the demise of communism the American term was finally adopted; it had been used in the USA since the end of the 1960s and particularly since 1978, when the American television series of the same name was broadcast, firstly in the USA in April 1978 and later in Western Europe.[29]

The formation of the President's Commission on the Holocaust by US President James Carter in the same year can be seen as another important milestone here, since one of the most important goals of this commission was to create a new *American* definition and understanding of the Holocaust – even though an originally non-American phenomenon. Created at a time 'when the Holocaust had moved not only from the periphery to the center of American Jewish consciousness, but to the center of national consciousness as well',[30] the mechanical transplantation of this definition back into the European and especially Central European context of the early post-Cold-War era was far from problem-free.[31] While the first breakthrough of the parallel cultural and political interest in the Holocaust in the USA in 1978 did not affect Czechoslovakia at all, the following wave in 1993, dominated by the opening of the United States Holocaust Memorial Museum in Washington D.C. and the worldwide success of the film *Schindler's List,* became much more relevant, especially for the newly formed Czech Republic.

There were also political activities that can be linked to the role of the USA in NATO and to NATO's expansion, which also came to encompass different uses of the Holocaust term. In this book I demonstrate historical-cultural manifestations of these activities in connection to the mid-1990s Czech debate on the genocide of the Roma. The political initiative on the part of the USA was, however, never as great as for example in Romania, which in 2003, less than one year before the country became a NATO member, established the American-Romanian International Commission on the Holocaust in Romania – also known as 'The Wiesel Commission'. This Commission was initiated by then-Romanian President, Ion Iliescu, and led by American professor, Elie Wiesel, a Nobel Peace Prize winner who had himself survived the Holocaust and who moreover had his roots in Transylvania. The Commission's two most important aims were to include the Holocaust in Romanian historical culture and, with the help of this inclusion, prove to the world at large that the new post-communist Romania respected human rights on a historical basis and was therefore developing in the right direction, as seen from a Western perspective.[32]

With regard to the influence of American popular culture one can, above all, discuss Steven Spielberg's film, *Schindler's List*, which had a special connection to the Czech Republic. This movie was not a clear guide to how the Holocaust should be written into Czech and Slovak historical narratives, a guide that could be perceived as American. In connection with *Schindler's List,* the nationalisation of the Holocaust became more than problematic, as I will demonstrate in the chapter devoted to this subject. All this being said, *Schindler's List* was followed in both the Czech Republic and Slovakia by a further American initiative: Steven Spielberg's, Survivors of the Shoah Visual History Foundation. Focused on interviews with those who had survived the Holocaust, this activity also came without a clear American message, i.e. without being framed into what could be described as an American meaning.[33]

The Holocaust's Europeanisation can, on the other hand, be interpreted much more unequivocally. Because European institutions began to use the Holocaust to give historical legitimacy to the ongoing European integration process in the 1990s, one can first and foremost perceive the process of Europeanisation as an attempt to create a common European historical narrative, or at least a common European view of the Holocaust that would be able to compete with established national narratives and induce the EU members and candidate countries to concur. What is meant by the Holocaust's Europeanisation is therefore a historical-cultural process stemming from the EU goal of including the Holocaust as a cultural aspect of the current process of European integration.[34]

As previously mentioned, it was initially the Second World War and not specifically the Holocaust that was used in this process shortly after the end of the Cold War, the aim being to bridge the differences between East and West. One could not, however, speak of either a united or centralised view of the Second World War. It was only when the Holocaust had been put forth as the war's most significant component that the Europeanisation process gained a historical foundation stone which could assist the EU in developing a cultural counterpart to the member states' common political decisions and common European market.[35] The Holocaust has, as one of the European institutions concluded, 'driven the EU's founders to build a united and peaceful Europe and thus been at the very root of the European integration project'.[36]

The relationship between the memory of the Holocaust and respect for human rights in Europe after the Cold War began to receive attention first when the EU was set to expand eastwards while simultaneously fearing the radical growth of post-communist nationalist and religious hatred in the former Yugoslavia, which grew into the most violent conflict in Europe since the end of the Second World War. This can be illustrated by the fact that in 1995, during the first expansion after the fall of the Berlin Wall, there were no special EU demands placed upon the new member countries of Finland, Sweden and Austria. This was particularly interesting in Austria's case, as it was exactly the situation regarding the memory of the Holocaust that led to the country's international isolation both shortly prior to and soon after its attachment to the EU. In the first case, the crisis started in 1985 when former UN Secretary-General and later Austrian President, Kurt Waldheim, was disclosed as an intelligence officer of the Wehrmacht during the Second World War. At the centre of the second crises stood Jörg Haider, the leader of the extreme-right Freiheitliche Partei Österreichs (FPÖ) party which, after its success in the 1999 parliamentary elections, became part of the Austrian coalition government in 2000.[37]

Shortly after the expansion from twelve to fifteen EU member states in 1995, the three aforementioned countries that interestingly enough were all neutral during the Cold War were included in 'old Europe'. After 1995, however, there were ten more countries, eight of them post-communist, which were depicted as 'the new Europe' standing at the top of the EU waiting list. At a top meeting of the EU in Vienna in December 1998, during the Austrian presidency, the Holocaust was used to urge the new candidates to combat racism and tendencies towards national hate.[38]

Among the individual member countries that actively contributed to the process of cultural Europeanisation by political means, while using the Holocaust as the main part of the European Canon, newly 'Europeanised' Sweden played a specific role. After discovering how little the younger generations in this country actually knew about the Holocaust and how uncertain they were about whether or not the Holocaust had actually taken place, the Prime Minister of Sweden, Göran Persson, himself a former minister of education and as such actually partly responsible for the prevailing lack of knowledge about the Holocaust, initiated and became the driving force behind the Task Force for International Cooperation on Holocaust Education, Remembrance and Research (ITF) in 1998. This organisation became an intergovernmental body with the purpose of placing political and social leaders' support behind the need for Holocaust education, remembrance and research both nationally and internationally.[39] Even though the organisation is not limited to Europe, a vast majority of today's 28 members are European countries and EU-member states. In 2000, Sweden extended its activities by organizing the Stockholm International forum on the Holocaust, where representatives from 46 states gathered with aims similar to the goals of the Task Force. The Stockholm Declaration adopted by this forum became the foundation of the ITF.

During this meeting, EU members initiated a boycott of the new coalition government of Austria, which included Heider's FPÖ, again with the most active participation of Göran Persson. Last but not least, Swedish EU-commissioner, Margot Wallström, while commemorating the sixtieth anniversary of the liberation of the ghetto in the Czech town of Terezín (Theresienstadt) in 2005, caused international controversy when she delivered a speech to journalists that linked opponents of the proposal for a new EU treaty with the Nazis saying:

> There are those today who want to scrap the supra-national idea. They want the EU to go back to the old purely intergovernmental way of doing things. I say those people should come to Terezín and see where that old road leads.[40]

An often-forgotten detail in this context is the significance of the definition of the Holocaust as the 'genocide of Jews, Roma and other groups'. This definition, which has in principle became the only one in the terminology of the EU, emphasises above all the similarities between the genocide of Jews, *Shoah*, and that of Roma, *Porrajmos*, at the expense of differences, while 'other groups' are often not even specified.[41] The genealogical perspective founded upon the fight against racism in the post-war era is evident. In Western societies and historical cultures this definition of the Holocaust has not stood out as especially problematic in relation to the Europeanisation process. However, in post-communist East and Central Europe, where the situation of the Roma is far more complicated, the question has been much more difficult to handle This is illustrated in the chapter entitled 'Pig farm as a Porrajmos remembrance site'.

The aspiration to utilise the Holocaust as the core of a historical primary narrative about the new Europe, in other words, an EU 'master narrative', is problematic from the perspective of the post-communist countries for two reasons.

Firstly, one is forced to accept this main narrative in a part of the world where the memory of the Holocaust was intentionally ignored and suppressed during basically the whole post-war era by the representatives of the governing ideology. This is further complicated by the fact that the narrative's West European main actors have little consideration for the traumatic legacy that this communist ideology, and the regimes the ideology supported, has left behind.

Secondly, a centralised initiative, governed from above, is being introduced at the same time as the post-communist countries, conversely, are attempting to rid themselves of earlier centralised thinking. As I will demonstrate, the significance of the EU's partial victories against nationalist forces in the Czech Republic and Slovakia can be seen as problematic when changes in political attitudes – made in connection with attempts to nationalise the Holocaust – are not followed by changes in the public's attitudes 'from below'. An important question is, naturally, for whom the EU initiative is mainly intended: is it for the central authorities or for 'ordinary people'? The fact that the Europeanisation of the Holocaust is primarily directed from above rather than developing more spontaneously from below gives the whole initiative a bureaucratic and formal character, as is also shown in the subsequent empirical chapters.

The Holocaust, historical cultures and research

As has already been established, this study has been written as an integral part of the Swedish project, 'The Holocaust and the European Historical Culture', the main aim of which was to study and analyse the Holocaust's position in the historical cultures of different European countries.[42] The study's theoretical framework is based upon research on historical consciousness. An important name in this context is the German historian, Jörn Rüsen, who has paved the way for understanding how historical consciousness functions and how it is expressed within a historical culture.[43] Moreover, Rüsen has pointed to a close connection between historical consciousness and a 'narrative competence', which expresses 'the ability of human consciousness to carry out procedures which make sense of the past, effecting a temporal orientation in present practical life by means of the recollection of past actuality', and has additionally drawn attention to the principles governing historical narratives.[44]

For research on questions regarding the Holocaust's place in different historical cultures, Peter Novick's study, *The Holocaust in American Life*, has been of pioneering significance.[45] This book does not cover the whole of American society, but deals primarily with American Jews. Its strength, however, lies in showing the processual and structural aspects of the American Jewish historical culture in relation to the Holocaust, while at the same time reflecting American and international aspects surrounding the memory and use of the genocide.

Another book I would like to mention is the British historian, Tony Kushner's, *The Holocaust and the Liberal Imagination*, which concerns the victorious democratic superpowers' reactions to the Holocaust during and after the Second World War.[46] Kushner has shown that not only totalitarian regimes have had problems dealing with the memory of the Holocaust but also pluralist societies whose historical cultures have been dominated by liberal values. Liberalism did not in any way mean that the British and American historical cultures automatically accepted and integrated Holocaust history. The Holocaust's true nature was seldom understood and the Jews often had to shoulder the blame for their own fate.[47] Concrete examples of how the memory of the Nazi past, including the Holocaust, developed in parallel in totalitarian and pluralistic societies after the Second World War and up to the fall of the Berlin Wall have been analysed by the American historian Jeffrey Herf.[48]

In relation to research on Czechoslovakia, the Czech Republic and Slovakia, this book attempts to at least partly fill a void that exists regarding historical-cultural research on the general role of history and the Holocaust's specific role in Czech and Slovak identity construction and societal development. As far as I am aware, no similar work has been published in either the Czech or Slovak context. It has been difficult for historical–cultural studies to gain recognition at all in these two countries.[49] There are, however, analyses lying close to certain aspects that I take up in my work.

The political scientist, Shari J. Cohen, analyses the leading Slovak elites' relation to history, which from the perspective of this study seems very relevant.[50] She focuses particularly on the period between 1989 and 1992 and sees Slovakia as a typical example of post-communist development in Central Europe. However, in her analysis of political culture, Cohen focuses mostly on the historical background of the elites and not their intentions and manner of using history. This explains what is, from my perspective, her very problematic sub-heading regarding an 'absence of history in postcommunist nationalism'. Because the leading post-communist elite consisted of people who for career reasons left the communist party and who for the same reason used nationalism, this means that their opportunism was not founded upon a clearly defined ideology and therefore not on a distinct history, either. After having shown how the elites were constructed, Cohen leaves the questions unanswered: what history they construct, and why?

The Czech-English anthropologist, Ladislav Holy, carries out a more general analysis of how the Czech national identity has been constructed in a society that is in the process of transformation after communism.[51] Despite analysing how history is perceived in Czech society – Slovak society is not examined – he sees his main task as being a cultural analyst of Czech politics. However, he does not draw attention to history's role in the Czech national identity as a process in which different historical narratives compete with each other and where the past is brought together with the present and with dreams about the future. Holy does not, therefore, discuss history's guiding role for the future and the concrete ways in which history is used for diverse purposes.

Both Cohen and Holy focus only on a part of the former Czechoslovakia, despite their having to relate the one national identity to the other. There is, in fact, only one study that, with the help of a comparative method, attempts to study history's place in both Czech and Slovak post-communist development. On the other hand, this work, by the Danish Slavistics scholar, Lone Sarauw, analyses the Czech and Slovak identities only in relation to the collapse of Czechoslovakia, and only takes up the historical events and conceptions that have had an impact upon the direct relations of both countries.[52]

There is no literature that demarcates and compares historical narratives in the Czech Republic and Slovakia after 1989. Neither does the study by Antohi et al (2007) published in English with the title *Narratives Unbound. Historical Studies in Post-Communist Eastern Europe* offer much help despite the inclusion of the word narrative in its title.[53] The sections on the Czech Republic and Slovakia deal primarily with their historiography and its thematisation. However, this does indicate, mainly in the Czech chapter, how little interest in the Holocaust there is among Czech historians.[54]

In both the Czech Republic and Slovakia, historical research still focuses on a historical development perspective. The newest book on 'the Czech question' presents how the Czech identity has been perceived by leading Czech historians and intellectuals at different stages in the development of Czech history. Two comprehensive volumes of the anthology, *Spor o smysl českých dějin* ('The dispute about Czech history's meaning'), describe different Czech views on Czech history, or rather its separate building stones. These authors, however, do not pose questions with a historical-cultural orientation about the circumstances and needs that stand behind this research, or about the factors that decide the legitimacy of a meaning; neither do they analyse the extent to which the historians' conceptions about the meaning of Czech history coincide with the needs and ideas of other societal groups. In this way the question as to whether one can really talk about *one* meaning as opposed to several is avoided.[55]

The same theoretical problems must be wrestled with regarding the recent Slovak study analysing 'Slovak historical myths', *Mýty naše slovenské* ('Our Slovak myths'). This group of Slovak historians admit, on the one hand, the great influence of myths on Slovak society, but assert, on the other hand, that these myths are false. Compared with historical facts, the myths are dismissed as direct lies. Thus, in theory, their influence upon Slovak society, including the authors themselves, has therefore no need of scrutiny.[56] Nevertheless, new interdisciplinary approaches to history are becoming more visible, especially in very recent years and among younger generations.[57]

In relation to the Holocaust itself, research on 'the final solution' in the Czech Republic and Slovakia is also dominated by a traditionalist view and conception of the historical development perspective as the only truly scientific one. A classic work in the Czech context is Miroslav Kárný's (1991) *Konečné řešení* ('The final solution') about the genocide of the Czech Jews as part of German-occupation politics.[58] This work, however, focuses primarily on German decision making in the occupied Czech territories of Bohemia and Moravia.

The Jewish minority's situation in Bohemia and Moravia at the end of the 1930s is examined in two books published by the Jewish Museum in Prague, *Židovská menšina v Československu ve 30. letech* ('The Jewish minority in Czechoslovakia during the 1930s'),[59] and *Židovská menšina za druhé republiky* ('The Jewish minority during the Second Republic').[60]

The Aryanisation process in occupied Bohemia and Moravia is studied in a work entitled *Arizace' a arizátoři* ('The Aryanisations and those Aryanised').[61] Czech anti-Semitism during the Second World War is primarily discussed in historical works directed towards analysing Czech extreme-right movements and their activities. Within this category belong Tomáš Pasák's study, *Český fašismus 1922-1945 a kolaborace 1939-1945* ('Czech fascism 1922–1945 and the cooperative politics 1939–1945');[62] Miroslav Gregorovič's book, *Kapitoly o českém fašismu* ('Chapters on Czech fascism');[63] and Jan Rataj's work, *O autoritativní národní stát. Ideologické proměny v druhé republice 1938-1939* ('On the authoritarian national state. Ideological changes in Czech politics during the Second Republic 1938–1939').[64] Recently a more comprehensive study in English on the genocide of Jews from Bohemia and Moravia was written by the historian, Livia Rothkirchen, who works in Israel.[65]

Among the most important books that reconstruct the chronology of the Slovak Holocaust are Ivan Kamenec's *Po stopách tragédie* ('The trail of tragedy'); Ladislav Lipscher's *Židia v slovenskom štáte* ('The Jews in the Slovak state'); and Eduard Nižňanský's *Nacismus, Holocaust, slovenský štát* ('Nazism, the Holocaust and Slovak state').[66] The lives of the Jewish minority in the Slovak state's initial period are studied in Eduard Nižňanský's book, *Židovská komunita na Slovensku medzi československou parlamentnou demokraciou a slovenským štátom v stredoeurópskom kontexte* ('The Jewish minority in Slovakia between the Czechoslovak parliamentarian democracy and the Slovak state in a Central European context').[67] Among the document collections dealing with the Holocaust in Slovakia are *Holokaust na Slovensku* ('The Holocaust in Slovakia') in seven volumes;[68] *Vatikán a Slovenská republika (1939-1945)* ('The Vatican and the Slovak Republic, about the relationship between the Vatican and Tiso's regime');[69] and part of a collection of Tiso's writings and speeches, *Jozef Tiso. Prejavy a články* ('Josef Tiso, speeches and articles').[70] A collection of survivors' memories from the Holocaust, *Prežili holocaust* ('They survived the Holocaust'), which marginally concerns even the post-war period, was based on Steven Spielberg's aforementioned witness initiative and its implementation in Slovakia. It has been published by ethnologist Peter Salner.[71] Salner is also the author of another relevant study on the Jewish minority in Slovakia, *Židia na Slovensku medzi tradíciou a asimiláciou* ('The Jews in Slovakia between tradition and assimilation').[72]

The Slovak Institute for the National Memory (*Ústav pamäti národa*), established in 2002 in Bratislava, was given the task by the Slovak parliament of studying the two totalitarian dictatorships that have left their imprint on the development of Slovakia and Czechoslovakia. Its aim is to 'spread ideas about democracy and the defence of freedom against regimes like the Nazi and communist ones', i.e., educating for democracy and not allowing dark history to be forgotten. The Institute focuses, above all, on making public the information that the Slovak and Czechoslovak secret services gathered on their citizens during the respective dictatorships. On its homepage, the Institute publishes facts about the repression of Slovak Jews during the Second World War and also offers video recordings of testimonies from those who survived the Holocaust.[73] However, as the institute has an ideological profile, its activities reflect all the problems connected with the effort to include the Holocaust into the dominant Slovak master narratives that will be presented later.[74]

The study of the Holocaust should also be among the tasks for the Czech Institute for the Study of Totalitarian Regimes (*Ústav pro studium totalitních režimů*), established at the beginning of 2008. The purpose of this Institute is to study both the Nazi and the communist periods, but even here the question is highly problematic. Emphasis has until now been almost exclusively placed upon the communist period.[75]

The first book to analyse the Holocaust in Bohemia, Moravia and to some extent also Slovakia from another, in this case sociological, perspective was published in 2006 in the USA. Its author, the Canadian sociologist, Alena Heitlinger, who herself has roots in the Czech Republic's Jewish minority, attempts to analyse the Czech-Jewish culture, including the memory of the Holocaust, during the communist era.[76] Rather than a historical-cultural study, the book is primarily a sociological examination of a selected Jewish group of about 200 members of whom roughly half fled from communism to live abroad. Questions regarding how the Jewish identity was formed in different generations during the post-war period are studied in relation to the communist power and ideology. This leads Heitlinger to the conclusion that the possibilities for Czech Jews to freely seek their identity have become much greater since the collapse of communism. She does not, however, confront the Czech-Jewish identification process with its diverse conceptions of the Czech national identity and different interpretations of Czech history, either before or after the fall of communism. Another book which should be mentioned in this context is Eleonóra Hamar's study, *Vyprávěná židovství* ('Narrated Jewishness'), which presents the author's empirical research into the narrative construction of Jewish identity among six Czech and Hungarian Jewish children of Holocaust survivors. Even though its focus is rather limited, this book is the first Czech study that deals in-depth with questions about the relationship between a specific historical narrative about the Holocaust and Jewish identity in post-war Czechoslovakia.[77]

Comprehensive materials that in different ways relate to the main questions of this book have been analysed. These comprise political and media debates; popular products, such as books, television programmes and films; and the scientific works written and published after 1989. At the centre stand those contributions that have been debated on a national level and have therefore been able to influence a large number of people. This does not mean that articles or other printed works published at local or regional levels or materials intended only for a limited group of readers, for instance the ethnic press, have been ignored. However, such materials are referred to only when they have had an impact outside their original limited sphere. The local debate from Svitavy, Oskar Schindler's hometown, is an example of this. Another is the debate surrounding the two labour camps of Lety and Hodonín, in Bohemia and Moravia, where imprisoned Roma awaited death during the war. In the analysis of the Slovak 'Múzeum SNP' in Banská Bystrica, all available original material, including the papers presented at various scientific conferences and publications published by the museum, has been used.

Notes

1. A detailed description of the project can be found in Klas-Göran Karlsson, *Folkmordet som spegel och symbolpolitik. Förintelsens plats i den europeiska historiekulturen*, Stockholm: Forum för levande historia, 2008.

2. Lubomí Lipták, *Storočie dlhšie ako sto rokov*, Bratislava: Kalligram, 1999, 153.

3. Vilém Prečan, 'Zuviel Vergangenheit: ein Bericht aus Prag', in Hans Süssmuth, Hg, *Transformationsprozesse in den Staaten Ostmitteleuropas 1989–1995*, Baden Baden: Nomos, 1998, 256–71.

4. Tony Judt, *Postwar: A History of Europe since 1945*, London: William Heinemann, 2005, 804.

5. Daniel Levy and Natan Sznaider, *The Holocaust and Memory in the Global Age*, Philadelphia: Temple University Press, 2005.

6. Lone Sarauw, *Together We Part: Collective Memory, Political Culture and Break-Up of Czechoslovakia*, Aarhus: University of Aarhus, 2004, 84–171.

7. Klas-Göran Karlsson, 'The Uses of History and the Third Wave of Europeanisation', in Bo Stråth and Malgorzata Pakier, eds, *A European Memory? Contested Histories and Politics of Remembrance*, New York: Berghahn Books, 2010, 38–55.

8. In 1992 the Maastrich Treaty gave European cooperation a new quality by changing the earlier European Economic Community (EEC) to the European Union (EU), namely therefore a union. In Article B it is stated that the EU in its security policy must act towards internationally strengthening the 'European identity'.

9. *Proceedings of the Stockholm International Forum on the Holocaust*, Stockholm: Svensk Information, 2000, 34.

10. Miroslav Kárný, 'Československé oběti německé okupace 1938–1945', in Ivona Řezanková, ed., *Cesta do katastrofy. Československo-německé vztahy 1938–1947*, Vrůtky, 1993, 113–19; and Pavel Škorpil, 'Problémy vyčíslení životních ztrát u československých obětí nacionálně socialistického Německa v letech 1938–1945', in Ivona Řezanková, ed., *Cesta do katastrofy. Československo-německé vztahy 1938–1947*, Vrůtky, 1993, 121–23.

11. For more about the specific situation of the Jews in the Sudetenland, see: Jorg Osterloh, *Nacionálněsocialistické pronásledování Židů v říšské župě Sudety 1938–1945*, Praha: Argo, 2010.

12. All these regions except Ruthenia were returned to Czechoslovakia after the Second World War. Ruthenia, however, became part of Ukraine and the Soviet Union.

13. I use the term *gypsies* in relation to the contemporaneous context during the Second World War. The term *Roma* is, however, used in its 1990s context.

14. Jan Rychlík, 'The Slovak Question and the Resistance Movement during the Second World War', in Mikuláš Teich, Dušan Kováč and Martin D. Brown, eds, *Slovakia in History*, Cambridge: Cambridge University Press, 2011, 193–200.

15. See Bradley Adams, 'The Politics of Retribution: The Trial of Jozef Tiso in the Czechoslovak Environment', in István Deák, Jan Gross and Tony Judt, eds, *The Politics of Retribution in Europe*, Princeton: Princeton University Press, 2000, 252–89. See also Ivan Kamenec, *Jozef Tiso 1887–1947. Tragédia politika, kňaza a človeka*, Bratislava: Archa, 1998, 127–44.

16. The question of the trial's judicial circumstances is discussed in the book *Proces s dr. Jozefom Tisom*, which was jointly written by Tiso's prosecutor, Anton Rašla and his lawyer, Ernast Žabkay, who were both Slovaks. Czechoslovak political circumstances are summarised by the Czech historian, Karel Kaplan in *Dva retribuční procesy. Komentované dokumenty (1946–1947)*, Prague: Ústav pro soudobé dějiny, 1992. See also: Anton Rašla and Ernest Žabkay, *Proces s dr. Jozefom Tisom*, Bratislava: Tatrapress, 1990. The literature on this subject is, however, very sparse.

17. Karl-Ernst Jeismann, 'Geschichtsbewusstsein', in Klaus Bergmann and Werner Bolt, eds, *Handbuch der Geschichtsdidaktik, Band 1*, Düsseldorf: Pädagogischer Verlag Schwann, 1979, 42.

18. Miroslav Hroch, 'Literární zdroje českého historického povědomí v 19. století', in *Polska, czeska i slowacka świadomość historyczna XIX wieku*, Warsaw: Zakład Narodowy im. Ossolińskich, 1979. See also Miroslav Hroch, 'Historické vědomí a potíže s jeho výzkumem dříve a nyní', in

Jiří Šubrt, ed., *Historické vědomí jako předmět badatelského zájmu: teorie a výzkum*, Kolín: ARC, 2011, 31–46.

19. See Zdeněk Beneš, *Historický text a historická kultura*, Prague: Karolinum, 1995, 167–80.

20. Jiří Šubrt and Štěpánka Pfeiferová, 'Nástin teoreticko-sociologického přístupu k otázce historického vědomí', in Jiří Šubrt, ed., *Historické vědomí jako předmět badatelského zájmu: teorie a výzkum*, Kolín: ARC, 2011, 21–30. See also Jiří Šubrt and Jiří Vinopal, *Historické vědomí obyvatel České republiky perspektivou sociologického výzkumu*, Praha: Karolinum, 2013.

21. Jörn Rüsen, *Berättande och förnuft*, Göteborg: Daidalos, 2004, 149–94.

22. Paul Ricoeur, *Time and Narrative: Volume 1*, Chicago and London: Chicago University Press, 1984, 11–19 and 193–217. Also Paul Ricoeur, *Time and Narrative: Volume 3*, Chicago and London: Chicago University Press, 1988, 99–123.

23. Hans-Georg Gadamer, *Sanning och metod – i urval*, Göteborg: Daidalos, 1997, 137–55.

24. Klas-Göran Karlsson, 'Historiedidaktik: begrepp, teori och analys', in Klas-Göran Karlsson and Ulf Zander, eds, *Historien är nu*, Lund: Studentlitteratur, 2004, 52–66; Klas-Göran Karlsson and Ulf Zander, eds, *Echoes of the Holocaust*, Lund: Nordic Academic Press, 2003, 38–43; and Klas-Göran Karlsson, *Historia som vapen*, Stockholm: Natur och kultur, 1999, 57–61.

25. Friedrich Nietzsche, *On the Use and Abuse of History for Life*, Sioux Falls, SD: EZreads Publications, 2010.

26. Karlsson and Zander, *Historien är nu*, 60–61.

27. See for example: Hilene Flanzbaum, ed., *The Americanisation of the Holocaust*, Baltimore, MD: The John Hopkins University Press, 1999.

28. Alvin Rosenfeld, 'Americanisation of the Holocaust', in Arvin Roselfeld, ed., *Thinking about the Holocaust after a Half Century*, Bloomington: Indiana University Press, 1997, 123.

29. Peter Novick, *The Holocaust and Collective Memory*, London: Bloomsbury, 2001, 133–34.

30. Edward T. Linenthal, *Preserving Memory: The Struggle to Create America's Holocaust Museum*, New York: Columbia University Press, 2001, 12.

31. See, for example: Pavel Barša, *Paměť a genocida. Úvahy o politice holocaustu*, Prague: Argo, 2011, 168–83.

32. For more on this subject, see Kristian Gerner, 'Hungary, Romania, The Holocaust and Historical Culture', in Klas-Göran Karlsson and Ulf Zander, eds., *The Holocaust on Post-War Battlefields*, Malmö: Sekel Bokförlag, 2004, 238–42.

33. See, for example, Ivan Kamenec, 'Reflections on the Holocaust in Slovak Society and Literature', in Klas-Göran Karlsson and Ulf Zander, eds., *Holocaust Heritage: Inquiries into European Historical Cultures*, Malmö: Sekel Bokförlag, 2004, 157–68.

34. For more on this subject, see Karlsson, 'The Uses of History'.

35. See Lothar Probst, 'Founding Myths in Europe and the Role of the Holocaust', *New German Critique*, No. 90, Autumn 2003, 45–58.

36. European Monitoring Centre on Racism and Xenophobia: 'Education on the Holocaust and on anti-Semitism', OSCE Conference on Anti-Semitism and other Forms of Intolerance, Cordoba, June 2005. See: http://eumc.europa.eu/eumc/material/pub/general/DIR-Pres-Cordoba-08Jun05.pdf

37. For more on this, see Fredrik Lindström, 'The First Victim? Austrian Historical Culture and the Memory of the Holocaust', in Karlsson and Zander, *Post-War Battlefields*.

38. See http//www.austria.org/book/presidency_4.html

39. See http://www.holocausttaskforce.org/about-the-itf.html

40. For more about this case, see, for example: *The Financial Times*, 12 May 2005. http://www.ft.com/cms/s/0/62129ae4-c309-11d9-abf1-00000e2511c8.html#axzz1hd8dmv00

41. See, for example: *The Holocaust, anti-Semitism and Racism*. European Parliament resolution on remembrance of the Holocaust, anti-Semitism and racism. www.europarl.europa.eu/sides/getDoc.do?pubRef=-//EP//NONSGML+TA+P6+TA-2005-0018+0+DOC+PDF+V0//EN.

42. Two other theses were written within the project, one about Israel and the other on Ukraine: Mikael Tossavainen, *Heroes and Victims: The Holocaust in Israeli Historical Consciousness*,

Lund: Lund University, 2006; and Johan Dietsch, *Making Sense of Suffering: Holocaust and Holodomor in Ukrainian Historical Culture*, Lund: Lund University, 2006. The project's analyses have also been published in the two volumes by Karlsson and Zander, *Echoes of the Holocaust* and *Post-War Battlefields*, and contributions from an international project conference are also summarised in *The Holocaust Heritage*. All these works, as with the latest book originating from the project by Kristian Gerner and Klas-Göran Karlsson, *Folkmordens historia*, Stockholm: Atlantis 2005, lie close to each other as they proceed from the same theoretical framework.

43. Rüsen, *Berättande och förnuft*; and Jörn Rüsen, 'Interpreting the Holocaust: Some Theoretical Issues', in Karlsson and Zander, *Holocaust Heritage*, 35–62.

44. Jörn Rüsen, *History: Narration–Interpretation–Orientation*, New York and Oxford: Berghahn Books, 2005, 26. See also Jörn Rüsen, 'Functions of Historical Narration – Proposals for a Strategy of Legitimating History in School', in *Historiedidaktik i Norden 3*, Malmö: Lärarhögskolan i Malmö, 1987, 28.

45. Peter Novick, *The Holocaust in American Life*, New York: Houghton Mifflin, 1999.

46. Tony Kushner, *The Holocaust and the Liberal Imagination: A Social and Cultural History*, Oxford: Blackwell, 1994.

47. Ibid., 273.

48. Jeffrey Herf, *Divided Memory: The Nazi Past in Two Germanys*, Cambridge and London: Harvard University Press, 1997.

49. Cf. Petr Kolář and Michal Kopeček, 'A Difficult Quest for New Paradigms: Czech Historiography after 1989', and Zora Hlavičková, 'Wedged Between National and Trans-National History: Slovak Historiography in the 1990s', both in Sorin Antohi, Balász Trencsényi and Péter Apor, eds, *Narratives Unbound: Historical Studies in Post-Communist Eastern Europe*, Budapest: Central European University Press, 2007, 173–248 and 249–310.

50. Shari J. Cohen, *Politics Without a Past: The Absence of History in Postcommunist Nationalism*, Durham, NC and London: Duke University Press, 1999.

51. Ladislav Holy, *The Little Czech and The Great Czech Nation*, Cambridge and New York: Cambridge University Press, 1996.

52. Sarauw, *Together We Part*.

53. Antohi, Trencsényi and Apor, *Narratives Unbound*.

54. Kolář and Kopeček, 'A Difficult Quest for New Paradigms', 206–10.

55. Miloš Havelka, ed., *Spor o smysl českých dějin 1895–1938*, Prague: Torst, 1995; and Miloš Havelka, ed., *Spor o smysl českých dějin 1938–1989*, Prague: Torst, 2006. See also Miloš Havelka, *Dějiny a smysl*, Praha: Nakladatelství Lidové noviny, 2001.

56. Eduard Krekovič, Elena Mannová and Eva Krekovičová, eds, *Mýty naše slovenské*, Bratislava: Academic Electronic Press, 2005.

57. See, for example, László Szigeti, ed., *Slovenská otázka dnes*, Bratislava: Kalligram, 2007; Adéla Gjuričová and Michal Kopeček, eds, *Kapitoly z dějin české demokracie po roce 1989*, Prague and Litomyšl: Paseka, 2008; Miloš Havelka, *Ideje, dějiny, společnost*, Prague: Centrum pro stadium demokracie a kultury, 2010; and Adéla Gjuričová, Michal Kopeček, Petr Roubal, Jiří Suk and Tomáš Zahradníček, *Rozděleni minulostí*, Prague: Václav Havel Library, 2011.

58. Miroslav Kárný, *'Konečné řešení'. Genocida českých židů v německé protektorátní politice*, Prague: Academia, 1991.

59. Miloš Pojar, Blanka Soukupová and Marie Zahradníková, *Židovská menšina v Československu ve 30. letech*, Prague: Židovské muzeum v Praze, 2004.

60. Miloš Pojar, Blanka Soukupová and Marie Zahradníková, *Židovská menšina za druhé republiky*, Praha: Židovské muzeum v Praze, 2007.

61. Drahomír Jančík and Aduard Kubů, *'Arizace' a arizátoři*, Prague: Karolinum, 2005.

62. Tomáš Pasák, *Český fašismus 1922–1945 a kolaborace 1939–1945*, Prague: Práh, 1999.

63. Miroslav Gregorovič, *Kapitoly o českém fašismu*, Prague: Nakladatelství Lidové noviny, 1995.

64. Jan Rataj, *O autoritativní národní stát. Ideologické proměny české politiky v druhé republice 1938–1939*, Prague: Karolinum, 1997.

65. Livia Rothkirchen, *The Jews of Bohemia & Moravia: Facing the Holocaust*, Lincoln and Jerusalem: University of Nebraska Press and Yad Vashem, 2005.

66. Ivan Kamenec, *Po stopách tragédie*, Bratislava: Archa, 1991; Ladislav Lipscher, *Židia v slovenskom štáte*, Bratislava: Print-servis, 1992; Eduard Nižňanský, *Nacizmus, Holocaust, slovenský štát*, Bratislava: Kalligram, 2010.

67. Eduard Nižňanský, *Židovská komunita na Slovensku medzi československou parlamentnou demokraciou a slovenským štátom v stredoeurópskom kontexte*, Prešov: Universum, 1999.

68. Eduard Nižňanský a kol., *Holokaust na Slovensku 1–7*, Bratislava: Nadácia Milana Šimečku, Židovská náboženská obec, Vojenský historický ústav, 2001–2005.

69. Ivan Kamenec, Vilém Prečan and Stanislav Škorvánek, *Vatikán a Slovenská republika (1939–1945). Dokumenty*, Bratislava: Slovak Academic Press, 1992.

70. Miroslav Fabricius and Katarína Hradská, *Jozef Tiso. Prejavy a články, zv. II, (1938–1944)*, Bratislava: AEPress, 2007.

71. Peter Salner, *Prežili holocaust*, Bratislava: Veda, 1997.

72. Peter Salner, *Židia na Slovensku medzi tradíciou a asimiláciou*, Bratislava: Zing-Print, 2000.

73. See http://www.upn.gov.sk

74. For more about ideological use of history by the Slovak Institute for the National Memory (Ústav pamäti národa, ÚPN) in Bratislava as well as by the similar institute, the Institute for the Study of Totalitarian Regimes (Ústav pro studium totalitních režimů, ÚSTR) in Prague, see Tomas Sniegon, 'Implementing Post-Communist National Memory in the Czech Republic and Slovakia: Institutes of "National Memory" in Bratislava and Prague', in Conny Mithander, John Sundholm and Adrian Velicu, eds, *European Cultural Memory Post-89*, Amsterdam and New York: Rodopi, 2013, 97–124. See also Peter Dinuš, *Vyrovnávanie sa s minulosťou?* Bratislava: Veda, 2010.

75. See http://ustrcr.cz/index-2html

76. Alena Heitlinger, *In the Shadow of the Holocaust and Communism*, New Brunswick and London: Transaction Publishers, 2006.

77. Eleonóra Hamar, *Vyprávěná židovství. O narativní konstrukci druhogeneračních židovských identit*, Praha: Sociologické nakladatelství SLON, 2008.

CHAPTER 1

Czech and Slovak historical narratives

In order to analyse historical cultures in the Czech Republic and Slovakia during the 1990s, I have demarcated four dominating historical narratives. These narratives have both influenced and been influenced by people's historical consciousness. It must be emphasised that they are not narratives that can automatically be found in their entirety or in a word-for-word form among specific individuals during a given time. Rather, they have been identified by extracting and determining the fundamental lines of development and ideal typical themes from many such narratives. They can be found in historical-cultural products, such as scientific works, history textbooks, museum exhibitions, films and political rituals. All of these ideal narratives were developed by leading political and intellectual actors and actor-collectives in order to give Czech and Slovak history a 'national' meaning, and at the same time to legitimise different interests and power positions in Czech and Slovak societies.

A methodology of this kind cannot, by its very nature, be substantiated in detail, because it is derived from extensive reading within the subject area rather than analyses of single works. The starting point is thorough understanding, which can only be obtained through a close proximity to the narratives, as well as a certain distance from them.

The threads of what takes place in the separate narratives will be referred to here as *plots*. The plots comprise the main themes or overall characteristics that lie beneath the narratives and decide their content.

The four historical narratives selected here are the Czech national-liberal narrative, the Slovak national-Catholic narrative, the Czechoslovak communist narrative and the Slovak national-European narrative. Chronologically, these narratives span the whole period from Czechoslovakia's formation in 1918 to the post-communist development and progress towards EU membership, via the Second World War, the communist period and the country's 'Velvet Divorce' at the end of 1992. However, each narrative places itself in relation to a certain period of Czechoslovakia's development, and it is presupposed that this particular period is especially worth remembering and functions as a signpost towards future development.

The first narrative relates to the period of 1918–1938, the second to the years 1939-1945, the third to the years 1948–1989, and the fourth and last to the post-1990 era. They reflect four different epochs: the interwar parliamentary democracy, the Second World War and Nazi dictatorship, the communist dictatorship, and the post-communist transformation and democratisation. Moreover, each period has its own particular focus. In all four narratives the Second World War plays a very important role. However, each narrative gives the war, and with it the whole historical development in the Czech Republic and/or Slovakia, a specific historical interpretation and meaning. Different starting points give different interpretative perspectives on history, as well as diverse future scenarios.

The Czech national-liberal narrative pays particular attention to the period between 1918 and 1938, the so-called first Czechoslovak Republic. The Slovak national-Catholic narrative allows history to culminate during the Second World War in the form of the very first Slovak nation state, in existence from 1939 to 1945. The Czechoslovak communist narrative sees the meaning of history in the communist system and therefore prioritises the post-war period up to 1989. Finally, the Slovak national-European narrative focuses on the independent post-communist and democratic Slovakia's entry into the EU and other Western political and economic structures.

All of these narratives were created during their respective periods in order to give legitimacy to that period's governing power. However, when each of the first three narratives lost their dominant positions after a regime change, they did not just disappear. They were preserved and further developed by both old and new supporters, who stood in opposition to the new authority. This often led to an idealisation of the earlier epoch and caused the contrasts between epochs to be accentuated in such a way as to demonstrate the deficiencies of the new dominant ideology and the new state-supporting historical narrative.

To this it should be added that the narratives do not just unite the historical events in the narrators' specific eras. They stretch into the future as well: towards those expectations, but also fears, that the narrators – with the help of the narratives – put forward as a prospects.[1]

In the case of the Czechs and Slovaks, this means that those who advocated these narratives during the 1990s wanted to organise the new situation in accordance with the main norms and values that they most appreciated in their favoured period. Supporters of the Czech national-liberal narrative strove for a parliamentary democratic system built according to the 'Czech liberal tradition', while supporters of the Slovak national-Catholic narrative wished for the disintegration of the common Czechoslovak state and fought for an independent Slovakia, with an emphasis on the national as well as the religious perspective. Those who defended the communist narrative wanted to let the communist ideology, with its historical-materialist class perspective, continue to dominate. The actors behind the Slovak national-European narrative wished to construct a historical narrative about Slovakia as a democratic part of Europe. To a certain extent, this narrative is an exception, because it is still in the process of fulfilling its state-supporting function in Slovakia. Taking into account its special character, I will therefore discuss it in greater depth in the fourth and last empirical chapter, which concerns its representation in the 'Slovak Museum of National Uprising' in Banská Bystrica.

All the different narratives are dependent on and have influenced each other, often as mirror images. However, in their fundamental interpretations of what is good and bad in history, they are mutually exclusive. During the periods when the Slovak national-Catholic narrative and that of Czechoslovak communism dictated the official versions of history, it was declared that all other historical narratives were illegal.

The competing narratives survived, however, because of certain non-official organisations and structures. In this respect, the relationship between the two narratives – both attached to totalitarian regimes – is interesting. When the Slovak national-Catholic narrative became illegal during the supremacy of the Czechoslovak communist narrative from 1948 to 1989, the communists fought openly and intensively against Slovak nationalism and its main symbol, Jozef Tiso, particularly in the early 1950s. Later, especially during the 1970s and 1980s, the Tiso regime was almost 'forgotten', i.e., it became a part of the communist ideological non-use of history. The national-Catholic narrative was no longer publicly attacked in order that it should be forgotten. It survived mostly due to the fact that it was maintained and developed outside Czechoslovakia's borders, within the Slovak-Catholic-orientated diaspora in the West.[2] The great influence from the diaspora made the Slovak situation during the first years after the fall of communism rather unique in the East European context – similar situations could be observed in a few other countries, i.e., Ukraine and Croatia. As will be demonstrated, the Slovak diaspora's representatives played an important role both in the division of Czechoslovakia and the development that followed in Slovakia, particularly between 1993 and 1998.

I am conscious of the fact that demarcating these four narratives poses certain problems. The Czech case, especially, can be perceived as simplified. During the interwar period, several different views on the 'Czech question' were in fact discussed within Czech historiography.[3] However, the Czech historian, Jan Křen, has summarised the interpretations from the interwar period into two main tendencies reflecting a splintered religious perspective. On the one side, according to Křen, is a conservative-Catholic interpretation; on the other side is an interpretation that can be described as national-Protestant, national-democratic and national-socialist.[4]

It must also be pointed out that it is not possible to use the interwar period's narratives in an analysis of the 1990s, for several reasons. All the narratives from that time had been formulated in academic debates ever since their plots had been decided in connection with the creation of Czechoslovakia. They were decided by the historical context of the time and could not encompass later traumatic events that formed the Czechs' historical consciousness. The 1938 Munich Agreement should be seen as the first main turning point, above all in the attitudes towards Czechoslovakia's relations with the West.[5] Domestically, the same event became essential for a later understanding of Czech-Slovak relationships.

The major historical changes, which at the level of foreign politics were influenced by the Second World War and the Cold War, and which in domestic politics were decided by two totalitarian regimes, led to the pluralistic debate on the disappearance of historical questions and a change of criteria. For example, two foreign invasions of Czechoslovakia brought out moral and national questions in a way that had not previously been seen as important. While the moral attitude towards the communist normalisation during the 1970s and 1980s still played an important role in the 1990s, the role of religious affiliation was of significantly less importance than it had been in the interwar period. There are most probably different opinions about these questions among the national-liberal narrative's main actors, but because the narrative first served to conquer the communist power and then to secure the new authority, the religious aspects in the interpretation of Czech history were not emphasised to an extent that could cause a break-up among sympathisers.

The impossibility of using narratives from the interwar period when analysing post-war Czechoslovakia is also emphasised by the historian Miloš Havelka, who after 1989 edited a comprehensive anthology of opinions on the 'Czech question' from the twentieth century.[6] When I demarcate the Czech national-liberal narrative, I therefore take as my starting point the analysis of the 1970s and 1980s by the previously mentioned anthropologist, Ladislav Holý, and his determination that the perception of Czech society during this period was decided by the communist regime on the one hand and leading oppositional activists on the other. Simultaneously, a large proportion of society, which the sociologist, Jiřina Šiklová, has called 'the grey zone',[7] existed in a problematically defined position between the two poles.[8]

This view is also shared by the historian, Milan Otáhal, in his book on the political philosophy of the anti-communist opposition.[9] The Czech national-liberal narrative is considered to be primarily constructed in opposition to the communist narrative, and not as one which first and foremost wants to be attached to any of the interwar era's main narratives. This does not exclude it from exhibiting certain tendencies that could be seen as early as the interwar period. My own view of continuity and discontinuity between historical discourses before and after the Second World War differs from that of Holý, who, in his section on 'national traditions and the imagining of the nation', emphasises the Czech Protestant-Catholic split as a long-term continuity, while simultaneously substantiating his argumentation with historical examples from different periods prior to the Second World War.[10]

As has been indicated, both moral questions and the emphasis on the Czech affiliation to either East or West can be seen as signs of immediate postwar needs and not as proof of continuity with the interwar era. It was precisely the emphasis on Czech affiliation to the West that made it possible for the national-liberal narrative to stand out as relatively stable during practically the whole of the 1990s, especially in comparison to the two Slovak narratives. As the Danish historian, Peter Bugge, has shown, this emphasis replaced the earlier intellectual debate over Central Europe during the 1990s, the goal of which was primarily to demarcate Czechoslovakia's position in relation to the East during the Cold War's final phase.[11]

Tendencies towards a polarisation were manifested in the Czech Republic first in connection with the country's entry into the EU in the early twenty-first century. Questions regarding the country's relationship with the EU and its centralised government brought more attention than earlier to a political right-left (non-communist) perspective.

This relative sense of agreement can be explained by the fact that all non-communist political parties in Czechoslovakia during the 1990s had similar foreign political priorities and a similar view on the economic transition from planned to market economy. It should also be observed that the two leading parties which controlled the Czech political scene after Czechoslovakia's division – the right-orientated ODS and the social democratic party – seemed much less interested in using history than their forerunner, Občanské fórum, the movement that after 1989 took power and profiled itself as solely against communism.

Soon after the fall of communism, Občanské fórum, with Václav Havel at its head, stressed the new politics' historical connection to the first Czechoslovak Republic. By contrast, the ODS, as I will show, made relatively infrequent use of history when focusing on economic questions and future prosperity. Nor did social democracy appear to have much to win by underlining its own historical course and creating a particular historical narrative. It was not in the post-communist social democratic interest to emphasise continuity with the old social democratic party that existed in Czechoslovakia before communism's victory in 1948, because it was exactly this party that helped the communists to power. The old social democratic party was not totalitarian, but shared, along with many Czech intellectuals, a conception of the Second World War as the capitalist system's final decline and the need for a new world inhabited by new human beings. This widespread view contributed to communism's relatively easy triumph in Czechoslovakia, despite the fact that the country had not yet been occupied by the Soviet army. As the historian, Bradley Adams, has shown, the communist takeover in February 1948 represented in many respects 'only a break in the continuity of modern Czech history, not the break itself'. The real break came, according to Adams, as early as after the 1938 Munich Agreement and during the Second World War, but did not show itself plainly until 1945.[12] Seeking direct roots in the time before communism was therefore too sensitive for social democracy, as well as for all the other political parties in the Czech Republic of the 1990s.

A manifest polarisation began to be visible first in connection with the parliamentary election of 2002 and the presidential election of 2003, when Václav Havel was replaced by Václav Klaus and when the EU began to be discussed from a right-left perspective. At that time, a new Czech historical narrative that could be described as Czech national-conservative was becoming more and more visible.[13] This development exceeds the time frame of the present work, but I would like to emphasise that I have not found any signs that the perception of the Holocaust has changed markedly since 2002, even though the number of occasions when the Holocaust has been mentioned or discussed has been higher than during the 1990s.

In Slovakia the post-communist polarisation occurred more rapidly because the antagonisms in society were easier to extinguish. The national-Catholic narrative was isolationist and inwardly directed. Its opponents had an outward orientation. While the outwardly orientated 'Czechoslovakism', which saw a democratic Slovakia as an organic part of Czechoslovakia, was substantially weakened and ultimately defeated as early as the beginning of the 1990s, it was later replaced by a similarly orientated 'Europeanism', which saw a democratic Slovakia as an organic component of a united Europe. The attitude towards Tiso's regime and, generally, to national and religious values created a clear dividing line between the national-Catholic and national-European narratives.[14]

Finally, I wish to point out that the use of these four historical narratives as ideal narratives does not mean that the boundaries between them are completely clear and that there have been no other narratives about the past. The chosen narratives can, however, in the context of the 1990s be described as hegemonic narratives, i.e., the narratives that decide how other narratives are to be formulated and which are, therefore, more important than others. One can confirm, modify or reject a hegemonic narrative, but one cannot ignore it.[15]

As an example, another Czechoslovak narrative was one that could be called 'national-reform-communist' or even 'marxist-revisionist'. After the fall of the communist system in Czechoslovakia, this narrative can be most simply described as a combination of the national-liberal and the communist narratives, because the post-communist debate on the events of 1968, which also applied to discussions among historians, above all concentrated on the question of the extent to which the Prague Spring was still about 'communism' or whether it could already be interpreted as 'democracy'.[16] The basis of this narrative was established during the period of the late 1950s and 1960s with important contributions from some Czechoslovak historians who belonged to the Communist Party but who had lost their initially radical Stalinist ideas.[17] In its focus was what the Czech political scientist, Michal Kopeček, described as 'searching for the lost meaning of the [Communist] revolution'.[18] The reform-communist narrative was most evident at the beginning of the 1990s but has since been pushed back, especially after the death of its main actor, Alexander Dubček, in 1992 and Czechoslovakia's division by the end of the same year.

The Jewish narrative and Theresienstadt

A logical question that arises in relation to the four main narratives is which of them lies closest to the Czech and Slovak Jews. Is there any narrative at all that can universally be described as Czech-Jewish or Slovak-Jewish? The selection of main narratives indicates that there is no such fundamental Jewish narrative that could influence the Czech and/or Slovak historical culture during the period of this study.

The Jewish complex of problems in the Czech Republic and Slovakia, and the questions surrounding the Czech and Slovak Jews' historical consciousness after the creation of Czechoslovakia, during the Holocaust and in the post-war era are so complicated that they deserve a separate study. Alena Heitlinger's analysis of questions about the Jews' identity during the communist regime and Eleonóra Hamar's study about the narrative construction of the Jewish identity among children of the Czech Holocaust survivors are, as noted, a first step in this direction. Yet a more complex historical-cultural study, including ethnic, religious, ideological and social aspects which concerns both Czech and Slovak Jews during the entire Czechoslovak period, is still lacking. Taking into consideration the Jewish historical culture's limited importance for the Czech and Slovak transformational process in the 1990s, as well as its complicated nature and this work's limited scope, I have chosen not to include an analysis of the Jewish historical culture here.

The Jews' position in Czech and Slovak society was complicated during almost the entire Czechoslovak period. The Jews had lived for many hundred years in the area that after 1918 had become Czechoslovakia. Before the Holocaust they comprised a group squeezed especially between Czechs and Slovaks on the one side and Germans and Hungarians – their ethnic main opponents – on the other.

The Jewish emancipation process took place during the nineteenth century at the same time as Slovaks and Czechs went through their 'national awakening'. The tension was manifestly apparent since the Habsburg monarchy had become a twin monarchy in 1867, a personal union between Austria and Hungary. Although the Jews never comprised a homogenous group, a significant number of them were identified with what was perceived as a 'higher culture' – which in Bohemia and Moravia meant German culture – or with the power that improved their societal position, which in the Slovak case was Hungarian culture. The Jews had difficulties being accepted as 'real Germans' among Germans in Bohemia and Moravia, but were, even so, perceived by the Czech nationalists as belonging to the 'other side'. Consequently, Czech anti-Semitism was coupled with the Czechs' anti-German sentiments.[19] At the close of the nineteenth and beginning of the twentieth centuries, when both nationalism and anti-Semitism grew in strength, the Jews became 'double strangers'. Some of them, especially some Jews from Prague, went so far as to describe their own situation in society as a 'threefold ghetto', which expressed their isolation as a race, a nation and a social group.[20]

It must be added that the 'anti-German sentiments' were not the only form of the Czech anti-Semitism before the Second World War. As the historian, Michal Frankl, shows in his recent study, Czech anti-Semitism of the late nineteenth century contained other aspects (i.e., ideological, cultural, economic) that made it less specifically Czech and more similar to anti-Semitic developments in other Central European countries.[21]

Slovak anti-Semitism had a stronger link to religious questions.[22] It was still the case, however, that anti-Semitism in Czechoslovakia, and particularly in Bohemia and Moravia, during the interwar era never reached the same level as in neighbouring Germany, Austria or Poland. Owing to Czechoslovakia's formation, Czech and partly even Slovak national demands had been satisfied, though a number of problems between the majority of society and the Jewish minority still existed. The Jews could choose to keep their German/Hungarian cultural orientation, to sympathise with Zionism, or lean towards the Czech or Slovak culture. After Hitler's takeover of power in Germany, Czechoslovakia often became seen as a protective zone for some German Jewish refugees. However, the country was not immune to increasing anti-Semitism by the end of the 1930s.[23] Moreover, as recent research shows, the perception of Czechoslovakia as a safe haven for Jewish refugees before the Second World War focused mainly on immigrant elites but ignored a number of restrictive aspects to the immigration policy of the interwar Czechoslovak state.[24]

After the Holocaust only a very small portion of the original Jewish population remained in the reunited Czechoslovakia. During the first three post-war years some were forced to leave Czechoslovakia together with Germans, while some became politically and ethnically 'invisible' and others were impressed by the communist ideology that was presented as consistently anti-fascist and promising a 'fair future' for all. The enthusiasm for communism decreased relatively quickly at the start of the 1950s, however, due to the Stalinist anti-Semitic wave that will be discussed later in this book. The Jewish culture, together with the memory of the Holocaust, was erased from the Czechoslovak historical culture. For example, during the communist epoch 85 Czech synagogues were closed.[25]

An exception can be found in the relatively short period of political de-Stalinisation and liberalisation in the 1960s, when Antonín Novotný, who had himself been imprisoned in the Mauthausen concentration camp during the Second World War, was both the highest leader of the Czechoslovak communist party and the country's president.[26] Because of the decreased political pressure, small Jewish communities became more active, at least temporarily. This was primarily evident in Prague. At the end of the 1950s, as the result of a Jewish initiative, a monument to the Holocaust's Czech-Jewish victims was created in the so-called Pinkas Synagogue in central Prague. It was completed in 1959 and opened in 1960 with approval from the communist authorities. The synagogue remained open only during the de-Stalinisation period. In 1966, it was closed to the general public; only a few actions were allowed there after this date. After 1968, it was not in active use. The Pinkas Synagogue was not reopened until 1992.[27]

The increasing interest in Jewish culture came not only from the Jews themselves, as can be illustrated by the fact that in 1963 the official Czechoslovak Authors' Union organised a conference on Franz Kafka's life and death, despite this author's view of the world being far from the obligatory optimism of official 'socialistic realism'. This conference became one of the first milestones among the Czech intellectuals who started the reform process subsequently halted by the invasion of the Soviet Union in 1968. Kafka's theme of alienation, in particular, attracted much attention and gained new relevance during this period of 'thaw'.[28]

After the failure of the 'Prague Spring', the situation of the Jews worsened substantially during the whole of the 1970s and 1980s. As Heitlinger points out, the Jewish minority in Czechoslovakia was neither strong nor homogeneous when communist supreme power came to an end.[29]

A Jewish historical narrative has, in other words, almost always been absent from the main narratives in both the Czech and Slovak historical cultures. However, some Jewish voices are mentioned in relation to the Holocaust discussions of the 1990s. These are not primarily orientated towards the discursive main narratives but towards the actor perspective current at that time.

The Czechoslovak territory's most important symbol of the Holocaust is located in Terezín, site of the internationally known former ghetto and concentration camp, Theresienstadt, about sixty kilometres from Prague in today's Czech Republic. Theresienstadt served a special function in the Nazi propaganda when, in 1944, the Nazis allowed the International Red Cross to visit the site in order to see that there was no violent oppression of the Jews, but rather a relatively 'happy living' Jewish society. The Red Cross' three representatives – one from Switzerland and two from Denmark – were completely misled and never got to see the camp's real character. The Nazis forced the German-Jewish actor and director Kurt Gerron, himself a prisoner there, to make a propaganda film showing the 'happiness' of Theresienstadt to the world, and particularly to the Western general public. However, the film, *Der Führer schenkt den Juden eine Stadt* ('The Fuhrer gives the Jews a town'), was never distributed. Apart from approximately twenty minutes of footage, the film was destroyed at the end of the war when Gerron was murdered in Auschwitz-Birkenau. About 140,000 people who were classified as Jews according to the Nuremberg laws were taken to Theresienstadt during the Second World War. Almost 35,000 of them died there upon arrival. Because Theresienstadt was not an extermination camp with its own gas chambers, a total of 63 transports comprising 87,000 people were dispatched onwards to the East. Only 3,500 or so would later be able to return home.

Immediately after the Second World War, the camp served as an evacuation point for the former prisoners who were repatriated and sent home. During the first post-war years, it served as a prison for people who were sent to Germany as part of the massive transfer of the 'Sudeten Germans' from Czechoslovakia.[30]

In 1947 Terezín/Theresienstadt was declared a 'monument of the national suffering'. However, it did not mean that the suffering of all its prisoners was to be remembered. From an ethnic perspective, the suffering of Czech prisoners received most attention, despite the fact that Theresienstadt had, above all, been seen as part of the 'final solution of the Jewish question'. When the Theresienstadt ghetto was established by the Nazis, the town of Terezín itself was emptied of its civil population. However, the so-called 'Little Fortress' was used to incarcerate not only Jews but also political prisoners, which made it easier for the Czechoslovak authorities to later 'de-Jew' Terezín's history. In the 'Little Fortress' a museum was eventually opened, one in which even the Jewish prisoners were presented as 'victims of fascism', but without their Jewish ethnicity being specified.[31]

Nevertheless, sometimes it seemed that the memory of Jewish suffering was not completely ignored. In April 1950, for example, the Czechoslovak communist government decided to establish a memorial dedicated to Jewish suffering during the period of imprisonment in Terezín. An exhibition on this subject was prepared by the State Jewish Museum in Prague, which was just undergoing a transfer to state ownership, and approved by the government officials later that year. However, the memorial was never realised due to the development of the Stalinist policies in Czechoslovakia.[32]

The museum reflected the political liberalisation that began in the 1960s with the opening in 1961 of a small but, up to then, very unusual exhibition about the ghetto's organisation during the Nazi period. Two years later a similar exhibition followed about the uprising of the Warsaw ghetto in 1943. After 1968, however, a radical change took place. Before the collapse of the 'Prague Spring 'movement the opening of a permanent museum about the ghetto in Theresienstadt was planned in a building where young Jewish boys were imprisoned during the war. During the 1970s, a completely different museum was created in the building in question; one concerning the heroic struggle of the workers' movement and the history of the Czech police in northern Czechoslovakia after 1948. The originally planned museum about the Theresienstadt ghetto did not open until 1991.

Jan Munk, the director of the Terezín Memorial, admitted that the opening of the Ghetto Museum in 1991 was motivated more by the activity of the organisation of former prisoners, *Terezínská iniciativa*, and the visit of Israeli President, Chaim Herzog – the first official visit to post-communist Czechoslovakia – than by the domestic political elites' interests and needs.[33] At the same time, the new Czechoslovak president, Václav Havel, personally played an important role when the building of the former police museum was given to the Ghetto Museum.[34]

Since then, the former concentration camp in the Ghetto Theresienstadt has been included in the Czech-Jewish historical culture but its role in the Czech historical culture has been much more problematic. As Heitlinger reminds us, Theresienstadt has become an important part of global Jewish historical culture, which also includes the Pinkas Synagogue and Jewish Museum in Prague. The latter has through foreign interest actually become the most visited museum in the whole Czech Republic.[35] While there is no doubt that the memory of the Holocaust in general has 'returned' to Terezín since the early 1990s and that the place has played an important role in Jewish historical culture, most of the memorial's own activities have focused on the local history of the place without attempts to raise new questions and create a new meaning for the Holocaust within Czechoslovak and Czech historical culture. The exhibitions there have focused mainly on the various cultural activities of the former prisoners.[36] In other words, the Jews were made visible as victims of the Nazi perpetrators in Terezín after 1989 and they started to share the role of victims with the Czech prisoners of the camp. However, new questions about the relationships between the two victim groups were not raised during the 'long 1990s', leaving the Czechs and the Jews separated.

Commercialised tourism is primarily linked to foreign visitors, and Terezín has been visited mainly by Western tourists.[37] The situation is very similar in the case of the Jewish town in the centre of Prague, but the income from the Jewish sites in Prague enables the Jewish community in the Czech Republic to finance its activities, such as the reconstruction of synagogues and cemeteries which had been devastated and which were returned to the Jewish community after 1989, thus spreading information about the Holocaust.[38] The Jewish Museum in Prague was given back to the Jewish community in 1994 having been owned by the Czechoslovak and Czech state since 1950. The Czech Jewish community took it as a challenge and a chance to show its own ability to take care of the precious Jewish heritage in the Czech capital, as well as to prove its new consolidation both within the Czech society and internationally.[39]

The separation between Czech and Jewish historical cultures is among the main reasons why there is not a special chapter in this book dedicated to the development of the Terezín Memorial after 1989. This might be especially surprising due to the fact that the book contains a chapter about another museum, the Museum of the Slovak National Uprising in Banská Bystrica, Slovakia. When writing the manuscript I considered including a separate chapter about Terezín, but in the end, and after much thought, decided against this.

The character of the places with the official names 'The Terezín Memorial' and 'The Museum of the Slovak National Uprising' is very different. The main difference is that, as a former concentration camp and ghetto, Terezín is a place with a direct connection to the Holocaust, whereas Banská Bystrica is not. Despite this, or perhaps because of it, Terezín has focused primarily on the reconstruction of 'authentic memory', i.e., on documenting German atrocities during the Second World War and paying tribute to the prisoners who were murdered there. The aspect of making sense of Czech history related to the Holocaust is, as already mentioned, missing. On the contrary, Banská Bystrica has tried to present the Holocaust within the context of both Slovak wartime and post-war history, creating a completely new view of the Holocaust while constructing the Slovak national-European historical narrative. After the division of Czechoslovakia, the museum in Banská Bystrica officially declared far more ambitious plans than those of the museum in Terezín. While historians in Terezín focused almost exclusively on the history of this site during the Second World War, their colleagues in Banská Bystrica wanted to turn the museum into an institute of contemporary history.

The Terezín Memorial consists of no less than three different places: the former ghetto, the centre of Jewish memory; the Little Fortress, the centre of Czech memory; and a former concentration camp in Litoměřice near Terezín, which is not directly connected with the town of Terezín itself. To analyse all aspects of the memory of the Second World War and the Holocaust in the entire complex of the Terezín Memorial would require a separate study; one exceeding the framework of this book. Another reason for excluding a chapter on Terezín is that some already published studies have concluded that the memory of the Holocaust and that of the Czech suffering in Terezín were indeed kept apart during the long 1990s and that Terezín was ignored both in Czech textbooks and in Czech historiography during the first post-communist decade.[40]

Nevertheless, I would like to mention two specific activities in connection with the Terezín Memorial, even though they have not yet visibly challenged the existing Czech master narratives. Both can be seen as a part of the process of

Europeanisation which I have described earlier. The first one is the programme of education for Czech teachers about the Holocaust which has been included into the Task Force for International Cooperation on Holocaust Education, Remembrance and Research, initiated by the government of Sweden. The second one is a scientific conference, *Fenomén Holocaustu* ('The Holocaust phenomenon'), which was organised by the Czech president, Václav Havel, and the Terezín Memorial in October 1999. This conference was the result of a political initiative involving the President. It can be seen as a reaction to the requirements of European institutions, as well as to international criticism over the Czech treatment of the memory of the *Porrajmos*, the Holocaust of the Roma, which is described in the chapter 'Pig Farm as a Porrajmos remembrance site'. It was certainly not a coincidence that the lectures about the Porrajmos occupied one third of the conference programme. This conference also became a part of the Czech activities connected to the Task Force.[41]

The main plots of the primary narratives

The Czech national-liberal narrative perceives the meaning of Czech history as being the creation of the first Czechoslovak Republic after the First World War.[42] The Republic is seen as the result of the Czech – and even Slovak – nation's logical and natural historical right to exist independently in its own state. This new state included Bohemia and Moravia, which were within the historical boundaries of the old Czech kingdom. The fact that Czechoslovakia survived the interwar period as the only Central European parliamentary democracy, without totalitarian or at least autocratic rule, is explained by a long democratic tradition, which made the Czechs feel superior not only to all other ethnic groups in Czechoslovakia, but also to Germans, Russians, Poles, Hungarians, Romanians and other nationalities in the country's vicinity. The image of a superior Czechoslovakia was strengthened by the country's high economic and cultural status.[43]

The Second World War was a fatal blow to the Czechoslovak idyll. The narrative tells us that the state was abandoned in Munich in 1938 and then betrayed by the Slovak nationalists as well. During the war, Bohemia and Moravia became an occupied protectorate, where the German occupiers were fully responsible for all the ills occurring in, for example, Lidice and Theresienstadt.

According to this narrative, the post-war communist development completed the decay in a much more dramatic manner – communism was a foreign element. After the fall of communism, it was time to recreate the interwar era's prosperity and democracy. It is possible to explain the fact that Czechoslovakia neither defended itself against Hitler's Germany nor against Stalin's (and later Brezhnev's) Soviet Union due to the Czech cultural sense of superiority and non-violent tradition, or, as a Czech historian expressed it, by a Czech 'non-heroic sobriety', which actually led to the country's even greater spiritual, social and economic development.[44] The same narrative has given the name to the 'Velvet Revolution' and is seen, finally, as having led to a 'Velvet Divorce' of Czechs and Slovaks when Czechoslovakia in the end dissolved.

The narrative's foremost figure is the first Czechoslovak President Tomáš Garrigue Masaryk, a politician but also a philosopher, professor, scientist and journalist. He personifies Czech high culture. During the Czechoslovak period he fit perfectly into the Czech-Slovak pattern, as he was the son of a Czech mother and a Slovak father. During the First World War he led the movement for an independent Czechoslovakia and had good relations with important Western statesmen, among them the American President, Woodrow Wilson. This, together with the fact that Masaryk's wife was American and the fact that the first documents between exiled Czechs and Slovaks, which de facto established Czechoslovakia, were signed in the USA after Masaryk's activities in France and Great Britain, strengthens the symbolic link between Czechoslovakia and the West. No less symbolic is Masaryk's death in September 1937 – one year before the Munich Agreement destroyed 'his' state. Masaryk's death has thus a sad parallel in the interwar period's Czechoslovak democracy and its tragic demise.

It is important to explain why the narrative is perceived as especially Czech when, in fact, it concerns the whole of Czechoslovakia. The reason is that it was built upon the conception of a united Czechoslovak nation that was temporarily created by Czechoslovakia's founders in order to get it recognised as a nation state at all. This ideological construction emphasised the cultural proximity between Czechs and Slovaks and included only these particular groups. The Czechoslovak nation, however, had two different languages, and the Czech-speaking part was about three times larger than the Slovak-speaking part. All other groups and minorities living in Czechoslovakia's territory were excluded.[45]

Without the newly constructed nation, neither Czechs nor Slovaks could reach a clear majority in the state, which also included Germans, Hungarians and other ethnic minorities.[46] The Czechoslovak nation existed formally until 1938, but it was clearly Czech-dominated and corresponded to, above all, Czech national conceptions.[47] The anthropologist Ladislav Holý therefore describes the Czech stance within the Czechoslovak ideology as an expression of 'the nationalism of a dominant nation'.[48] In combination with other problems of the time, this fuelled Slovak demands for Slovak autonomy within Czechoslovakia as early as during the interwar period.[49] As the political scientist Elisabeth Bakke has shown, it was precisely Czechoslovakism and the opposition to the Czech dominance which completed the process of constructing a Slovak national consciousness. The conception of 'Slovak-ness' which developed during the interwar era gradually assumed a much more distinct form than that which pertained when Czechoslovakia was created.[50]

The Slovak national-Catholic narrative is directly linked to these autonomist and nationalistic demands from the interwar period, but developed first
during the Second World War when Germany forced Slovakia to separate itself
from Bohemia and Moravia. The Slovak state that existed between 1939 and
1945 is portrayed as the result of 'the Slovak nation's thousand-year struggle'.[51]
The narrative maintains that the Slovaks had been forced to fight a hard battle
against the Hungarians, who had oppressed them until 1918, and then against
the Czechs, who had initially promised that the Slovak nation would be regarded
as equal in the new common state, but who had then broken their promises
and replaced the Hungarians as the Slovaks' oppressors. The first Slovak state in
history is perceived as having been greeted with enthusiasm by all 'real Slovaks',
who comprised most of the country's inhabitants. According to the narrative, it
was necessary to make concessions to Germany throughout the whole war, but
the concessions were logical considering the difficult times and complicated
circumstances. In order to survive and preserve the nation's existence, it was
absolutely necessary to compromise – and this is the moral of the narrative – in
order to avoid the same fate as Bohemia and Moravia, or worse. The narrative
suggests that Hitler might otherwise have allowed Hungary to occupy Slovakia
again, which would certainly have led to the end of the nation.[52]

Despite many problems, the first Slovak Republic managed surprisingly
well during almost the entire war, both militarily, as great losses of human life
were avoided, and financially, as its industry remained active. There was more
than enough of what was needed, particularly when comparing the Slovak situation with that of neighbouring countries. The advocates of the narrative admit
that weapons were manufactured for the Third Reich and that the country had
an agreement with Germany that subordinated Slovak politics to Berlin. Yet
they maintain that this did not mean Tiso's Slovakia was a completely subordinate satellite state of Germany, as Slovakia was recognised both de facto and de
jure by a large number of countries.

The quiet life of the first Slovak state ended in August 1944, when, according to the narrative, a number of traitors – who felt that the war was too close
and that they must save their own skins – organised a revolt against the state that
was put down by occupying German troops. Though the Soviet Union subsequently marched closer, its advance towards Berlin was not seen as Slovakia's
liberation.[53]

The narrative points out that the Czechs, with President Edvard Beneš at
the forefront, were successful in their revenge and managed to accomplish the
restoration of Czechoslovakia. Working together with Stalin's Soviet Union,
the government in Prague then managed to terminate the bright Slovak period
entirely by importing communism to Slovakia and forcing the free Slovak
nation to accept it. The first post-war parliamentary election in 1946 clearly
demonstrated that communism and the Soviet Union were much more popular
among Czechs than Slovaks.[54] After the fall of communism, the narrative

suggests, it was time to reintroduce and develop an independent Slovakia in which the Slovaks could once again govern themselves.

Apart from resistance against Hungary and the Czechs, the Slovak language and Christian Catholic values are, according to the narrative, the Slovak national identity's most important building blocks.[55] The main bearer of Slovak-ness during the Second World War was therefore the Slovak Catholic Church and its political ally Hlinka's Slovak People's Party (*Hlinkova slovenská ludová strana*), which was founded already before 1918. This was a protest movement against Hungary which since 1925 had borne the name of its founder, the Catholic priest, Andrej Hlinka, who died in 1938. Ever since 1919 this party had fought for Slovakia's autonomy within Czechoslovakia. After Hlinka's death, the party was led by another Catholic priest, Jozef Tiso, who in 1939 became the first-ever Slovak president. The Slovak unity during the war, and the narrative's principle message, is expressed by the party's main slogan: 'One God, one nation, one organisation'.

It is clearly evident that this narrative's main hero is Jozef Tiso, a man whose devotion to his own nation cannot be questioned. It is claimed that he would have done anything for the good of the country, even if on a few occasions he was forced to compromise with Germany, for example by accepting Germany's help against the rebels at the end of the war and conferring distinctions upon German soldiers for their contribution in defeating the Slovak traitors. The narrative further explains that had he not done so, a massive bloodbath would have followed in which far more Slovak blood would have been spilled. Tiso's death in 1947 turned him into the narrative's martyr – he was executed after the Czech- and communist-dominated tribunal had sentenced him to death and the Czechoslovak President, Edvard Beneš, had refused to pardon him.

The third main narrative, the Czechoslovak communist narrative, is based on the theory of class struggle, but it is not devoid of ethnic aspects. The narrative's foundations were established in the 1920s in Masaryk's Czechoslovakia by the Czechoslovak Communist Party, founded in 1921 and inspired by the October Revolution in Russia. However, as a coherent narrative it was formed subsequent to a majority of the Czechoslovak territory being liberated by the Soviet Red Army. Its task then was to legitimise strong ties between Czechoslovakia and the Soviet Union, and also other Eastern European countries with a communist regime, and to show the country's distance to the imperialist and reactionary politics of the West. The Soviet Union was praised as the communist movement's unquestioned leader, it being the largest Slavic sister nation and the country whose experiences were decisive for Czechoslovakia's future.

The narrative's normative future aspect is based on the historical materialist idea that the working class represents progress, and that it therefore not only writes the correct history but also will control the future. After the collapse of communism, the emphasis on Czechoslovak-Soviet relations and relations to other communist countries and their working class disappeared from the narrative, because other countries chose alternatives to communist development and the Soviet Union disintegrated in 1991. However, opposition to the West and capitalism remained among the narrative's characteristics.

The Czechoslovak communist narrative has its historical starting point in the Munich Agreement between Germany, Great Britain, France and Italy in September 1938. It makes this event and its immediate continuation – the splitting up of Czechoslovakia and the German occupation of Bohemia and Moravia – the greatest trauma in Czechoslovakia's modern history. The Agreement proved, according to the narrative, the degeneration of bourgeois Czechoslovakia and the Western powers.[56] The politics of the governing non-socialist parties and their trust in the traitorous great powers of France and Britain are viewed by the narrative as a complete failure, because none of these great powers actually wanted to help stop Hitler in time.[57] With the Cold War's development, the USA was also included among these passive states. In strong contrast to all this was the Soviet Union, which the narrative portrays as the Czechoslovak people's only faithful ally, on call and prepared to help.

Strong support for the Soviet Union among the masses led, quite logically, to the victory of the Communist Party of Czechoslovakia in the first post-war election in Czechoslovakia in 1946, despite the fact that there existed, in Slovakia particularly, remnants of fascism. These remnants were successfully eliminated when the Communist Party took power. The narrative admits that certain wrongs occurred during Stalin's time in power, which lasted until his death in 1953. However, it claims that they were not due to any deficiencies in the system, but rather were caused by Stalin's poor personal qualities and his abuse of power. The Soviet Communist Party and its Czechoslovak counterpart were, according to the narrative, strong enough to correct all the mistakes, condemning the cult of Stalin as a phenomenon 'which was alien to Marxism-Leninism'.[58]

In the narrative's view, counter-revolutionary powers – in cooperation with the West – never stopped exploiting possible opportunities to destabilise the socialist bloc. They were partly successful in Hungary in 1956 and also during the 1968 'Prague Spring', when they even managed to infiltrate the highest leadership of the Communist Party of Czechoslovakia. It was the domestic 'healthy forces' and brotherly military assistance from the Soviet Union and four other Warsaw Pact countries which, according to the narrative, rendered it possible to save socialism in Czechoslovakia and normalise the situation. All counter-revolutionaries and revisionists were expelled from the Party, which had learned the lesson summarised in a document entitled *Poučení z krizového vývoje ve straně a společnosti po XIII. sjezdu KSČ*, 'Lessons from the crisis development'.[59] From an ideological viewpoint, *Poučení* became the most important signpost during the 1970s and 1980s. At the end of the latter decade, the imperialism represented by the USA and the rest of the Western world was successful in conquering the Soviet Union and its allies in Europe; yet as, the narrative tells us, the future will show that truth and historic justice are on the side of communism.

In regard to the last narrative, the Slovak national-European narrative, which is the newest among the four, I will here only mention that its main goal stands in opposition to both the communist and the national-Catholic narrative. This narrative's starting point is the Slovak national uprising against the Tiso regime in August 1944, which it uses as the basis of a new Slovak effort to establish democracy and affiliation with a democratic Europe. The new narrative is not as well developed as the others; it is not consistently anti-Czech, but the narrators have difficulties giving a clear explanation for why Czechoslovakia ceased to exist in 1992. The Slovak national uprising is, in fact, the only event given a distinct position in the narrative, where it functions as a main symbol of Slovakia's struggle against dictatorship and support for European democracy. It can be described as a positive alternative to a preoccupation with Tiso and his pro-Nazi regime of obedience.

Narrators – bearers of historical culture

The main actors who stood behind the first of the primary historical narratives during the early post-communist development in first Czechoslovakia and then the Czech Republic and Slovakia were representatives of the Czech national-liberal narrative. They were the opposition groups who had stood against the previous political regime and its version of the communist narrative, which had developed in Czechoslovakia during the so-called normalisation period of 1968–1989. In the Czech lands, the main actors were particularly found within the human rights movement, *Charta* 77. They had been supported by radio stations during the Cold War, which were situated in the West and had transmitted their programmes to Czechoslovakia in the Czech and Slovak languages: the BBC, Radio Free Europe, Voice of America and Deutsche Welle. Because the foreign radio stations either completely terminated their transmissions in the Czech language or substantially scaled back their activities when the Czech domestic mass media became free, I will primarily focus on those actors who were in the Czech part of Czechoslovakia and who after 1989 took over political power in the country.

The group's most important representatives were post-communist Czechoslovakia's and the new Czech Republic's first President, Václav Havel; the Czech Prime Minister, Petr Pithart; Foreign Minister, Jiří Dienstbier and several other politicians and non-politicians, the latter mainly historians and intellectuals. During the communist era they had been able to spread their thoughts only to a limited extent via illegally disseminated documents often in primitive typewritten form – so-called *samizdat* – and through the foreign radio transmissions already mentioned. To a limited degree it had also been possible to read the works of prohibited authors in a proper book format in foreign editions smuggled into Czechoslovakia, and starting in early 1988, *Charta 77* had illegally distributed a journal named *Lidové noviny*. All of these forbidden texts could first be published officially only in the beginning of 1990.

Havel, who was often compared to Tomáš Masaryk as 'an intellectual who was first seen as marginal by society but who during the revolution will come to personify the nation',[60] expressed admiration for his idol as 'a true democrat and great humanist', and for the whole of Masaryk's Czechoslovak Republic. He claimed that the first republic had strongly identified itself with Masaryk's high ethics. As early as in his first New Year's speech as Czechoslovakia's president in 1990, Havel encouraged his countrymen to renew the first republic's political concept.[61] Even before the presidential election, also in a televised speech, Havel coupled Masaryk with 'our best traditions connected to the peace ideal'.[62]

Others revered Masaryk as well. Petr Pithart emphasised Masaryk as a man who 'founded both the state and the nation's modern thinking'.[63] At an academic conference, dedicated to the anniversary of the former president's birth, the philosopher, Milan Machovec, described Masaryk as 'the first modern Czech person and thinker' and also as 'the perhaps first idealist in history who successfully carried out most of his plans'.[64] The art historian, Josef Kroutvor, wrote thus about Czechoslovakia in the interwar period:

> The first republic's hallmark was above all decency: human tolerance, the democratic principles' strong and weak sides. The new republic was not only a change of regime, a more modern shaping of domestic conditions. For the first republic it was about more than simply political change, the new form of government was an attempt to realise a new moral orientation for the nation.[65]

The idea of the Czech nation's superiority, particularly in comparison to other nations in Eastern and Central Europe, can be illustrated by two examples. The first is found in a book by the historian, Jan Křen, which refers to 'white patches' in Czech history; times when the first republic in 'both a socially and politically unnatural way' became mixed up with a group of 'European developing countries situated far below [the Czech] level of civilisation'.[66] The second is found in the statements of the Czech author, Ludvík Vaculík, who provoked much anger in Slovakia by explaining 'the historical difference' between the Czech and Slovak nations in terms of the Slovaks' 'democratic immaturity', a result of them having 'never dealt with their fascist past'. According to Vaculík, the Slovaks were 'not ready enough for a free and equal relationship with other nations'.[67] His view was not wholly unique within *Charta 77*, which never gained massive support in Slovakia.[68]

Even those who did not grasp the political discourse could hardly miss the clear manifestations of the Czech national-liberal narrative in the public arena. Its expressions were particularly noticeable just after 1989, when most Czech cities and villages changed the names of their streets and squares. There was often a return to the names they had borne during the era of the first republic. Lenin Street or Lenin Square, Marx Street or Engels Square were changed to Masaryk Street or to names reflecting those of other political leaders of the interwar period. Václav Havel himself, who lived during communism on Engels Quay in Prague, took the initiative of changing the quay's name to Rašín Quay, after the interwar period's Czechoslovak Finance Minister, Alois Rašín, who actively contributed to Czechoslovakia's founding in 1918 and who only five years later was murdered by a communist sympathiser.

Although the Czech national-liberal narrative included visible nationalist elements, it could not be perceived as exceptionally radical. No ethnic group was ascribed collective guilt for the oppression of the Czechs, and the narrative's supporters used no historical arguments for their possible demands for revenge. No dictatorship was advocated and the importance of Czech history was seen as national-democratic: that is to say, ethnically accentuated, but pluralistic. *Charta 77* was established in 1977 as a direct consequence of the conference on Europe's security and cooperation that took place in Helsinki in 1975, and it used the first republic as the antithesis to the communist dictatorship and linked it to their demands for respect for human rights. As I will discuss later, *Charta 77* was not quite homogeneous and the narrative got its fully pro-Western character only after 1989. I will also show that the main actors behind the Czech national-liberal narrative aired Czech-critical points of view as well, particularly in relation to the Czechs' actions against the so-called Sudeten Germans in 1945 and 1946. However, the first republic, its greatness and its exclusively democratic character, was never questioned.

It was therefore never debated whether the interwar period's democracy was really the result of the Czech democratic-liberal tradition, an elevated cultural level and the humanism of the republics highest leaders, or whether there simply was no obvious alternative in ethnically divided Czechoslovakia because of the absence of a clearly dominant group that could seize enough power to effectively suppress the others in the same way as in neighbouring countries with a more dominant ethnic majority. Nor was there debate as to what motivation the other major ethnic groups – the Germans and Hungarians – had for not fighting for 'their' nation states, which were just beyond the border, when their political power was limited by the Czechoslovak majority ideology. The Czech nation as 'a single organism with a single mentality' was never questioned.[69]

The diaspora and the communists

At the end of the 1980s, the Slovak national-Catholic narrative's foremost advocates and developers were certain anti-communist and anti-Czech groups within two organisations, one situated within and the other outside Slovakia. These were the so-called *Svetový kongres Slovákov*, the 'Slovak World Congress' (SWC), which had its centre in Canada, and the Catholic Church in Slovakia, i.e., the part of the church unwilling to cooperate with the communist regime.[70] After the collapse of communism, exiled Slovaks were able to spread their narrative directly into Slovakia. They were assisted by members and supporters of several ultra-nationalist political parties established in Slovakia soon after the 'Velvet Revolution', and by the political-cultural organisation, *Matica slovenská*, whose task since 1863 had been to preserve the Slovak language and develop Slovak culture. Assistance was also provided by certain new Christian-democrat parties, which could not be perceived as overtly extremist. The most important of these parties was *Kresťanskodemokratické hnutie*, 'The Christian-democratic movement' (KDH), whose chairman, Ján Čarnogurský, was the Slovak Prime Minister between 1991 and 1992.[71]

The ecclesiastical subculture within historical culture in post-war Slovakia is still almost completely uninvestigated. The Catholic Church was persecuted by the communist regime but retained a relatively extensive influence in Slovakia. Some reports indicate that up to 3.5 million of 5 million Slovaks professed to being of the Catholic faith. The group leading the resistance against communism within ecclesiastical circles was called the Secret Church.

How much the Secret Church's resistance to communism was due to sympathies for Tiso and his state, and to what extent it was based on a fight for democracy and human rights as a counterweight to the communist dictatorship, we still do not know. However, it is clear that the memory of Tiso was important for the church's representatives. Bishop Ján Chryzostom Korec, who had been illegally active as a bishop since 1951 and was the Secret Church's most known representative, honoured Jozef Tiso's memory in Slovakia at the very first public ceremony after the 'Velvet Revolution'. On 8 June 1990 he unveiled and inaugurated Tiso's memorial plaque in Bánovce nad Bebravou, where Tiso had been active from 1913 until the Second World War. That Korec linked his great prestige as a fighter of communism with his respect for Tiso had significant symbolic value and was much discussed in the media. The fact that the Catholic Church neither criticised Korec, nor distanced itself from Tiso also sent a clear signal to the public.

Further expressions of the church's attitude to Tiso were manifested during diverse ceremonies to his memory, as when a cross on Tiso's grave in Bratislava was sanctified in March 1991. Two years later, on a similar occasion at the grave, the Catholic priest, Ladislav Šimončík, explained that 'it was not Tiso who was the criminal but those who executed him and in this way insulted the Slovak nation and its right to an independent state'.[72]

The church's highest representatives made clear that they gave their support to the nationalists and their conception of the Slovak nation as a compact entity in which Catholicism would play a dominant role. In a pastoral address expressing the church's official attitude on the eve of the first free election in 1990, which was read in all Slovak churches, it was emphasised that all church members had a duty to vote for movements ensuring that people in Slovakia lived 'according to Christian rules which correspond to the will of God'. The demand was further elucidated by encouraging people to vote for those political parties which had a Christian political programme.[73] The following year, in March 1991, another public document that primarily addressed all Slovak believers was published, in which the leading Slovak bishops, including Archbishop Ján Sokol, Ján Chryzostom Korec and Dominik Hrušovský, who served as 'bishop for Slovaks living abroad', observed that 'our nation is mature enough today not to let itself be politically manipulated by others'.[74]

The Slovak World Congress, the most important organisation of exiled Slovaks during the last decades of the Cold War, had also played a very active role in defending Tiso and the wartime Slovak state. During the 1970s and 1980s, the organisation had attempted to unite all Slovak emigrants who saw both communism and coexistence with Czechs as part of the same state as 'the enemies of a free Slovakia'. For several decades the Slovak attitude to history corresponded almost exactly to the British sociologist Robin Cohen's definition of a 'typical diasporal behaviour', based on a common sentiment towards a distant and in fact unreachable home. Cohen has listed nine typical aspects of a diaspora, of which three are particularly important for analysis of a phenomenon I will refer to as a diasporal-historical culture. The first of these is 'collective memory and myth about the homeland, about its location, history and achievements'. The second is an 'idealisation of the putative ancestral home and collective commitment to its maintenance, restoration, safety and prosperity, even to its creation'. The third and last is a 'strong ethnic group consciousness sustained over a long time and based on a sense of distinctiveness, a common history and the belief of the common fate'.[75]

The SWC had been founded in 1970 after the collapse of the Prague Spring movement, when several smaller groups coalesced. It had become visible in connection with its protests against the Warsaw Pact's occupation of Czechoslovakia, but to a great degree represented the older generation of emigrants, i.e., those who had fled Czechoslovakia when Tiso lost power at the end of the Second World War, and who feared the revenge of the communist regime. The role given to Tiso in the diaspora's narrative was so dominant that no other Slovak politician was able to challenge it.

The diaspora had large resources for disseminating its narrative around the whole of Slovakia. At the same time, its organisations financed the domestic nationalist movement. According to some reports, those who wanted to separate Slovakia from the Czech lands received up to 3.7 million British Pounds Sterling during the first months after the Velvet Revolution alone.[76] The SWC expressed its support in another way as well; in May

1990 Cardinal Ján Chryzostom Korec was bestowed the SWC award, 'The National Prize'.

The offensive from dispersed Slovaks was made easier by the fact that it concerned people without roots in the communist regime, but who came from the West and therefore had an important psychological advantage. As I will show, however, the diaspora's ideology did have direct roots in the Slovak regime of the Second World War.

The most radical form of the Slovak national-Catholic narrative was expressed in a number of books in Tiso's defence, written by the diaspora's two most active and influential ideologues and history users, Milan Ďurica and František Vnuk.[77] These authors supplied Tiso's sympathisers with 'historical evidence' to use against the narrative's opponents.[78] Ďurica had a professor's title in church history from the ecclesiastical university in the Italian town of Padova. Vnuk's professor's title from Adelaide, Australia was in metallurgy rather than history, but he was still sometimes presented as a history professor. At the close of the 1980s and beginning of the 1990s, Vnuk was the Vice Chairman of the SWC. Vnuk's and Ďurica's significance as the diaspora's most important history users in Slovakia of the 1990s was indirectly acknowledged by their opponents as well – it was these two men who in relation to the national-Catholic narrative were criticised most frequently.

Vnuk's and Ďurica's first books to be published in Slovakia had been written earlier, some even well before 1989. In Vnuk's case the book, *Neuveriteľné sprísahanie* provoked much attention as he dismissed the Slovak national uprising against the Tiso regime as 'anti-national treason'.[79]

Ďurica had been the first to attempt to compile Tiso's biography 'in accordance with research based on new documents made public since the beginning of perestroika in the mid-1980s'. There had not been any similar book on the Czechoslovak market since Tiso's death in 1947, and Ďurica's Tiso biography was therefore especially important because it met with no competition.[80] It was first published in Italy in 1989, during Ďurica's time in exile, and was published in Slovakia in 1992, early on after communism's collapse, but this publication comprised only the first volume, dealing with Tiso's life until 1939.[81] The second volume, about the years 1939–1947, which was to have been published soon after, did not appear until 2006.[82] The first published volume demonstrated that the project was wholly focused on defending Tiso by emphasising his love for the nation and the religion. However, there was no analysis of Tiso's relation to the interwar period's anti-Semitism, which later played a significant role during the Holocaust. Ďurica ignored the anti-Semitic sentiments expressed by Tiso, both in his political texts and speeches and in the newspaper articles published in the mass media of the time.[83]

Ďurica and Vnuk received support from a Slovak historian, Anna Magdolenová, as well as some non-historians who were publishing texts in Tiso's defence. Members of the latter group, which included Gabriel Hoffmann,

Anton Porubský and Josef Kirschbaum, came from the diaspora as well as from
Slovakia. A group called *Priatelia prezidenta Tisu* ('Friends of President Tiso'),
was also involved in trying to persuade the Vatican to canonise Tiso.

Among the important questions that were never asked by the advocates
of the Slovak national-Catholic narrative was how legitimate Tiso's state had
been when it completely subordinated its politics to those of Nazi Germany.
Slovakia had participated in the attacks against Poland in 1939 and the Soviet
Union in 1941, and had declared war against the USA and Great Britain. Tiso
had prohibited all Slovak parties except the government party, Hlinka's Slovak
People's Party, which had never received support from a majority of the Slovaks.
Additionally, it had never been explained in his anti-communist texts and assertions why a system governed by violence by a single leader and a single party
was better than another; that is to say, why Tiso's dictatorship should have automatically been perceived as better than communism just because one was 'ours'
and the other 'theirs'. However, the most difficult problem for the advocates
of this narrative was the fact that 'the Christian Slovakia', which had not been
occupied by Germany, in 1942 had commenced deportations of tens of thousands of Slovak Jews – Slovakia's own citizens – to death camps, and had even
paid Germany to have it done.

The communist narrative had been produced and modified prior to 1989
within the highest political and ideological leadership of the Communist Party
of Czechoslovakia. It had been distributed, with varied intensity, by a large
number of official, state-owned and state-controlled channels, such as the mass
media, film companies and book publishers. It had further been emphasised
on important days of commemoration and, last but by no means least, had
been present in the school curriculum at different levels. During the 1970s
and 1980s, the clearest summary of this narrative had existed in the form of
the aforementioned document, *Poučení z krizového vývoje ve straně a společnosti
po XIII. Sjezdu KSČ*. This text had been intended as a directive on how the
Second World War and particularly the post-war years in Czechoslovakia were
to be understood and interpreted by all those who did not wish to come into
conflict with the communist regime.

Despite the Communist Party of Czechoslovakia having had about 1.7
million members before the Velvet Revolution, it was relatively difficult to
identify the communist narrative's actual bearers between the fall of communism and the mid-1990s. The narrative first needed to be adapted to the new
reality, in which Soviet communism could no longer be depicted as an entirely
progressive and successful project. The Soviet Union had collapsed from within
and no longer existed, and many eyewitnesses from the whole of the former
Eastern Bloc could, with the help of newly opened archives, provide evidence
of crime and brutality that had occurred under the leadership of the communists. It took time, therefore, to change and harmonise the interpretation of
history. There were also very few, apart from the old regime's most prominent

members, who wished to step forward and defend the communist narrative as a credible alternative for the 1990s. This did not, however, mean that the communist narrative as such suddenly disappeared: literally all Czechs and Slovaks of school age and older had been influenced by it over a long period of time and could not simply abandon it from one day to the next. It was not until the close of the 1990s that the link between the communist, ideological interpretation of history and actual communist politics, represented by the non-reformed communist party which was now called the 'Communist Party of Bohemia and Moravia' (KSČM), began to be examined more openly as an expression of dissatisfaction with post-communist developments, especially in the Czech Republic.

Slovakia's communist party transformed itself soon after the collapse of communism into a left-wing party with the name *Strana demokratickej levice* ('Democratic Left Party' [SDL]), and claimed that it did not have any direct relation to the totalitarian Communist Party of Czechoslovakia. However, traces of the communist narrative could be clearly observed in this party as well, as I will show in my final empirical chapter on the 'Slovak National Uprising Museum' in Banská Bystrica.

Questions relating to the Second World War, which the communist narrative's supporters never thoroughly discussed, were similar to those absent in the Slovak Catholic-nationalist context. Why did one totalitarian system become better than another? Why was the human worth of those belonging to the 'right class', i.e., the working class, automatically greater than that of everyone else?

Notes

1. See Martin Alm, 'Historiens ström och berättelsens fåra', in Karlsson and Zander, *Historien är nu*, 237–51.

2. See, for example, Ivan Kamenec, 'Rozdvojená historiografia', in Ivan Kamenec, ed., *Hladanie a bludenie v dejinách*, Bratislava: Kalligram, 2000, 294–99.

3. See Havelka, *Spor o smysl českých dějin I.*

4. Jan Křen, 'K diskusím o pojetí českých dějin', in Havelka, *Spor o smysl českých dějin 2*, 603–8.

5. Jan Křen, 'Historické proměny češství', in Havelka, *Spor o smysl českých dějin 2*, 587–88.

6. Miloš Havelka, '"Smysl" a "pojetí" a "kritiky dějin"; historická "identita" a historické "legitimizace" (1938–1989)', in Havelka, *Spor o smysl českých dějin 2*, 7.

7. Jiřina Šiklová, 'The "Grey Zone" and the Future of Dissent in Czechoslovakia', *Social Research* 57, 1990, No. 2.

8. Holy, *The Little Czech*, 27–33.

9. Milan Otáhal, *Opozice, moc, společnost 1969/1989. Příspěvek k dějinám 'normalizace'*, Prague: Maxdorf, 1994.

10. Ibid., 114–37.

11. Peter Bugge, 'The Use of the Middle: Mitteleuropa vs. Střední Evropa', *European Review of History* 6, 1999, 15–35. See also: Peter Bugge, 'Příběh, prostor, konec – středoevropská literatura

jako téma v české kulturní debatě osmdesátých let', in DanielVojtěch, ed., *Česká literatura na konci tisíciletí*, Prague: Ústav pro českou literaturu AV ČR, 2001, 401–12.

12. Bradley Adams, *The Struggle for the Soul of the Nation*, Lanham, MD: Rowman and Littlefield Publishers, 2004, 275.

13. An important part of this attempt was an effort to institutionalize Czech 'national memory'. See Tomas Sniegon, 'Implementing Post-Communist National Memory in the Czech Republic and Slovakia: Institutes of "National Memory" in Bratislava and Prague', in Mithander, Sundholm andVelicu, *European Cultural Memory*, 97–124.

14. See Pavol Lukáč, 'Historická a politická identita Slovenska na prahu jeho intergácie do EÚ', in Szigeti, *Slovenská otázka dnes*, 341.

15. Cf. Martin Alm, *Americanitis: Amerika som sjukdom eller läkemedel. Svenska berättelser om USA åren 1900–1939*, Lund: Lunds universitet, 2002, 25–26.

16. A big debate among Czech historians was published in the journal, *Soudobé dějiny*, emanating from the Czech Scientific Academy. See *Soudobé dějiny* 1/1993, 14–15; *Soudobé dějiny* 2–3/1994, 338–64; and *Soudobé dějiny* 4–5/1994, 598–622.

17. See Vítězslav Sommer, *Angažované dějepisectví. Stranická historiografie mezi stalinismem a reformním komunismem (1950–1970)*, Prague: FFUK and Nakladatelství Lidové noviny, 2011, 405–29.

18. Michal Kopeček, *Hledání ztraceného smyslu revoluce*, Prague: Argo, 2009.

19. Helena Krejčová, 'Židovská komunita v moderní české společnosti', in Václav Veber, ed., *Židé v novodobých dějinách*, Prague: Karolinum, 1997, 20.

20. Ibid., p. 20. For more complex discussion about the development of Jewish identity in the lands of Bohemia and Moravia, see Kateřina Čapková, *Czech, Germans, Jews? National Identity and the Jews of Bohemia*, New York and Oxford: Berghahn Books, 2012.

21. Michal Frankl, *Emancipace od židů. Český antisemitismus na konci 19. století*, Prague and Litomyšl: Paseka, 2007.

22. See Ezra Mendelsohn, *Jews of Central Europe Between the Wars*, Bloomington: Indiana University Press, 1983, 139–42. It must be added that the question of the anti-Semitism in Czechoslovakia presented here is very simplified. There was no singular approach in the whole country and there were significant differences between Prague, Bohemia, Moravia, Slovakia and Ruthenia.

23. See Jaroslav Bubeník and Jiří Křesťan, 'Zjišťování národnosti a židovská otázka', and Alexandra Blodigová, 'Státní příslušnost – úprava státního občanství v Československu do roku 1942', both articles in Helena Krejčová and Jana Svobodová, eds, *Postavení a osudy židovského obyvatelstva v Čechách a na Moravě v letech 1939–1945. Sborník studií*, Prague: Ústav pro soudobé dějiny, 1998, 11–49.

24. Kateřina Čapková and Michal Frankl, *Nejisté útočiště. Československo a uprchlíci před nacismem, 1933–1938*, Prague and Litomyšl: Paseka, 2008.

25. Ruth Ellen Gruber, *Virtually Jewish: Reinventing Jewish Culture in Europe*, Los Angeles: University of California Press, 2002, 78.

26. There is, however, no automatic connection between Novotný's wartime imprisonment and the mentioned openness of the 1960s. In fact, Novotný was not considered as a liberal politician, either during the 1950s or during the 1960s. The political liberalisation of Czechoslovakia known as the Prague Spring started first when Novotný was forced to step down both as the President of Czechoslovakia and the leader of the Czechoslovak Communist Party. Nevertheless, research about Novotný's relationship to the Holocaust and its memory is still missing.

27. Magda Veselská, *Archa paměti. Cesta pražského židovského muzea pohnutým 20. stoletím*, Prague: Academia and Židovské muzeum, 2012, 195 and 248.

28. Michal Kopeček, *Hledání ztraceného smyslu revoluce*, 322.

29. Heitlinger, *In the Shadows of the Holocaust*, 209–10.

30. See Marek Poloncarz, *Internační tábor pro německé obyvatelstvo. Malá pevnost Terezín 1945–1948*, Terezín: Památník Terezín, 1997.

31. Heitlinger, *In the Shadows of the Holocaust*, 53–58; and Vojtěch Blodig, 'Památník Terezín v minulosti a současnosti', in Christoph Cornelissen, Roman Holec and Jiří Pešek, *Diktatura – válka – vyhnání. Kultury vzpomínání v českém, slovenském a německém prostředí od roku 1945*, Ústí nad Labem: Albis International, 2007, 206.

32. Veselská, *Archa paměti*, 165–67.

33. See Jan Munk, 'The Terezín Memorial in the Year 2000', *UNESCO, Museum international*, LIII, 1, 2001, s. 17–20; http://unesdoc.unesco.org/images/0012/001227/122716e.pdf#122699; and Jan Munk, *60 let památníku Terezín / 60 years of the Terezín Memorial*, Terezín: Oswald Publishers, 2007, 25.

34. Blodig, 'Památník Terezín v minulosti a současnosti', 210.

35. Ibid., 54.

36. Munk, *60 years of the Terezín Memorial*, 30.

37. During 2004 and 2005, for example, as many as 80 per cent of visitors to Terezín were foreigners. See http://www.pamatnik-terezin.cz/showdoc.do?docid=325

38. See, for example, an interview with Leo Pavlát, the Jewish Museum's director, in the journal *Terezínská iniciativa*, No. 40/October 2007, 4–5.

39. See Leo Pavlát, 'V muzeu výjimečné historie i současnosti', in Veselská, *Archa paměti*, 248.

40. See Kolář and Kopeček, 'A Difficult Quest', 206–10. See also Michal Frankl, 'Holocaust Education in the Czech Republic, 1989–2002', in *Intercultural Education*, Vol. 14, No. 2, June 2003, 176–89.

41. For the complete content of the conference including the speech by Václav Havel, see Vojtěch Blodig, ed., *Fenomén Holocaust / The Holocaust Phenomenon. Sborník mezinárodní vědecké konference*, Terezín: Památník Terezín, 1999.

42. In my demarcation of the separate historic primary narratives, I started out especially with the following historical studies and works: *Dějiny KSČ v datech*, Prague: Svoboda, 1984; Havelka, *Spor o smysl českých dějin*; Stanislav J. Kirschbaum, *A History of Slovakia: The Struggle for Survival*, New York: Palgrave Macmillan, 1995; Milan Ďurica, *Dejiny Slovenska a Slovákov*, Bratislava: SPN, 1996; Holý, *The Little Czech*; Havelka, *Dějiny a smysl*; Krekovič, Mannová and Krekovičová, *Mýty naše slovenské*; Havelka, *Spor o smysl českých dějin*.

43. Cf. Eduard Kubů and Jaroslav Pátek, *Mýtus a realita hospodářské vyspělosti Československa mezi světovými válkami*, Prague: Karolinum, 2000, 5.

44. See František Šamalíks' introduction in Milan Hübl, *Češi, Slováci a jejich sousedé*, Prague: Naše vojsko, 1990, 16.

45. See, for example, Elisabeth Bakke, 'The Making of Czechoslovakism in the First Czechoslovak Republic', in Martin Schulze Wessel, ed., *Loyalitäten in der Tschechoslowakischen Republik 1918–1938. Politische, nationale und kulturelle Zugehörigkeiten*, Munich: R. Oldenbourg Verlag, 2004, 23–44.

46. According to the census of 1921 there was a total of 13.6 million inhabitants in Czechoslovakia. Among them were about 8 million 'Czechoslovaks', of whom 6 million (circa 44 per cent of the whole population) spoke Czech and 2 million (about 15 per cent) had Slovak as their native language. The Slovak-speaking (Slovak) group was, however, in itself smaller than that of Czechoslovak Germans (often called Sudeten Germans), who numbered 3.2 million. In fourth place were the 786,000 Czechoslovak Hungarians. All the other groups were smaller and thus less important in this context.

47. See Barbara Törnquist-Plewa, 'Contrasting Ethnic Nationalisms: Eastern Central Europe', in Stephen Barbour and Cathie Carmichael, eds, *Language and Nationalism in Europe*, Oxford: Oxford University Press, 2001, 183–220, but especially 206–15.

48. Holý, *The Little Czech*, 6–7.

49. For more about this, see, for example, Carol Skalnik Leff, *The Czech and Slovak Republics: Nation Versus State*, Oxford and Boulder, CO: Westview Press, 1997, 24–29; Jan Rychlík, 'Czech–Slovak Relations in Czechoslovakia 1918–1939', in Petr Kaleta, ed., *Národnostní otázka v Polsku a Československu v meziválečném období*, Prague: Masarykův ústav AV ČR, 2005, 108–22.

50. Elisabeth Bakke, *Doomed to Failure? The Czechoslovak Nation Project and the Slovak Autonomist Reaction 1918–1938*, Oslo: University of Oslo, 1999, 286–313.

51. See, for example, Anna Magdolenová, 'Vznik a vývoj idey Slovenskej štátnosti', in Gabriel Hoffmann, ed., *Zamlčená pravda o Slovensku*, Partizánske: Garmond, 1996, 90–95.

52. Cf. Ctibor Greguš, *Slovensko – dlhá cesta k suverenite*, Bratislava: Tatrapress, 1991, 100–28.

53. Štefan Glejdura, 'Dejinné metamorfózy Slovenska v rokoch 1945–1975', in Jozef Rydlo, ed., *Slovensko v retrospektíve dejín*, Lausanne: Liber, 1976, 158.

54. Ibid., 160.

55. See, for example, Jozef Kirschbaum, ed., *Slovak Culture through the Centuries*, Toronto: SWC, 1978, Introduction, by J. Kirschbaum, 5–7.

56. Cf. Jan Tesař, *Mnichovský komplex*, Prague: Prostor, 2000, 12–13.

57. During the 1970s the communist interpretation of Munich and the whole Second World War was expressed in three important films, which were part of the largest war project in Czechoslovak film history and all created by the same director, Otakar Vávra. The films comprised a trilogy starting in Munich in 1938. The trilogy's separate parts are entitled *Dny zrady* ('Days of treason'), *Sokolovo* (after a village in today's Ukraine) and *Osvobození Prahy* ('The liberation of Prague'). For more on the ideological significance of these films, see Milan Ducháček, 'Pražský květen 1945 očima Otakara Vávry', in Petr Kopal, ed., *Film a dějiny*, Prague: Nakladatelství Lidové noviny, 2005, 253–64.

58. *Ilustrovaný encyklopedický slovník*, del 3, Prague: Academia, 1982, 393.

59. *Poučení z krizového vývoje ve straně a společnosti po XIII. sjezdu KSČ* ('Lessons from the crisis development within the party and society after the XIII congress of the Communist Party of Czechoslovakia'), Prague: Svoboda, 1970.

60. Jacques Rupnik, *Jiná Evropa*, Prague: Prostor, 1992, 245.

61. Václav Havel on Czechoslovak television, 1 January 1990. He was elected as president only three days earlier, 29 December 1989.

62. Václav Havel on Czechoslovak television, 16 December 1989.

63. The Czechoslovak news agency ČTK, 7 March 1990.

64. *Lidové noviny*, 2 March 1990.

65. Josef Kroutvor, *Potíže s dějinami*, Prague: Prostor, 1990, 13.

66. Jan Křen, *Bílá místa v našich dějinách*, Prague: Lidové noviny, 1990, 36.

67. Ludvík Vaculík, 'Naše slovenská otázka', *Literární noviny* 5/1990. The article was published once more in Nr. 32/1992.

68. The Czech historian, Jan Rychlík, found less than twenty Slovak names among the circa 1,800 who signed the Charta during the whole period of 1977–1989. See Jan Rychlík, *Rozpad Československa. Česko-slovenské vztahy 1989–1992*, Bratislava: AEPress, 2002, 44. The Charta-centred Czech criticism of the Slovak anti-communist opposition is also analysed in Jaroslav Cuhra, 'Katolická církev a odpor vůči normalizačnímu režimu', in Petr Blažek, ed., *Opozice a odpor proti komunistickému režimu v Československu 1968–1989*, Prague: Dokořán, 2005, 67–78.

69. Cf. Chad Bryant, 'Whose Nation? Czech Dissidents and History Writing from a Post-1989 Perspective', *History & Memory* 12(1), Spring/Summer 2000, 30–64.

70. According to information on the whole of Czechoslovakia there were 8,230 churches and 4,500 priests in 1983. About 10 per cent of them participated in the movement, *Pacem in terries* ('Peace on earth'), which took its name from the Pope's 1963 encyclical but which actively cooperated with the otherwise atheist communist regime. The attitudes towards Tiso within the Catholic Church's Czech section are, however, completely unknown.

71. Among the extreme nationalist parties were, for example, *Slovenská národná strana* (the Slovak National Party); *Slovenská ľudová strana* (SLS, the Slovak People's Party); *Strana národného zjednotenia Slovákov* (the Party for the Slovaks' National Unity); and *Slovenský národný kongres* (SNK, the Slovak National Congress).

72. ČTK, 14 March 1992.

73. *Katolícke noviny*, 19/1990.

74. ČTK, 19 March 1991.

75. Robin Cohen, *Global Diaspora: An Introduction*, Seattle: University of Washington Press, 1997, 26.

76. *The Times*, 10 April 1990.

77. For more, see Zora Hlavičková, 'Wedged between National and Trans-National History: Slovak Historiography in the 1990s', in Antohi, Trencsényi and Apor, eds, *Narratives Unbound*, 258–64.

78. See, for example, Cohen, *Politics Without a Past*, 125.

79. František Vnuk, *Dedicstvo otcov*, Bratislava: Alfa Omega, 1991; and František Vnuk, *Neuveritelné sprísahanie*, Trenčín: Vydavatelstvo Ivana Štelcera, 1993.

80. There were two books within the Slovak diaspora during the Cold War which dealt with Tiso's life, one written by František Vnuk. These were Konstantin Čulen, *Po Svätoplukovi druhá naša hlava. Život Dr. Jozefa Tisu*, Middletown, PA: Slovak League of America, 1947; and František Vnuk, *Dr. Jozef Tiso: President of the Slovak Republic*, Sydney: Association of Australian Slovaks, 1967.

81. Milan Ďurica, *Jozef Tiso – slovenský kňaz a štátnik I, 1887–1939*, Martin: Matica slovenská, 1992.

82. The second attempt at writing a Tiso biography appeared in 1998 when the historian, Ivan Kamenec, published the book *Dr. Jozef Tiso 1887–1947*.

83. A collection of Tiso's speeches and texts from the time before he became president was published in 2002 by the Slovak Academy of Sciences' Historical Institute in Bratislava. Even here the period covered was only up to the beginning of the Second World War. Although this book is only a collection of Tiso's political thoughts, rather than a study, it makes evident that the list of subjects pursued by Tiso during the interwar era was significantly broader than that expressed in Ďurica's book. While Ďurica described Tiso's thoughts as focused on Slovak politics and attempts to achieve Slovak equality in relation to its neighbours, the collection includes even Tiso's thoughts about war and his relation to the Jewish minority in Slovakia. See Miroslav Fabricius and Ladislav Suško, *Jozef Tiso. Prejavy a články (1913–1938)*, Bratislava: AEP, 2002.

CHAPTER 2

The Holocaust in Czechoslovak historical culture before 1989

Between the Slánský trial and individualisation on the cinema screen

Within the field of Holocaust research, it is nowadays taken for granted that interest in what happened to European Jews during the Second World War was first awakened in Western societies in connection with the trial of Adolf Eichmann in Jerusalem at the beginning of the 1960s.[1] As Peter Novick has shown, the latest wave of Holocaust interest, which influenced Europe during the 1990s, started in the USA at the close of the 1970s, due very much to the American television series, *Holocaust*, which was broadcast all over the world.[2] Western European interest in the Holocaust has thus been triggered by two strong non-European impulses, one Israeli and one American, in combination with several other processes and events. The years between the end of the Second World War and the Eichmann trial are seen in such interpretations as the time 'without the Holocaust', in the sense that the Nazi genocide of the Jews did not play any leading role in political, cultural and scientific contexts.

The situation in Eastern Europe tends to be interpreted even more unequivocally: because the communists monopolised power and chose to one-sidedly highlight communist suffering and heroism during the war, few or no public expressions of the memory of the Holocaust existed during the communist era. However, the actual explanation is somewhat more complicated. The unwillingness to draw attention to Jewish suffering has sometimes been attributed to a widespread anti-Semitism or fear of promoting a Jewish identity, or to concerns that the Holocaust might be linked to a partly contemporaneous terror in Stalinist Eastern Europe.[3] Even so, the silence seems surprising when it concerns a region in which the Jewish inhabitants were struck hardest by the Holocaust. But was the communist silence equally effective in the whole of Central Europe and during all the development phases of communism in the post-war period?

I do not wish to question the general interpretation of the communist system's relation to the Holocaust in this chapter, as the existent research indicates that the communist countries, including those that in different ways were most affected by the Holocaust, were very effective in their non-use of the Holocaust.[4] However, I will try to add nuance to the solely black-and-white portrayal in the case of Czechoslovakia. Here the reality was more complex, particularly during the end of the 1950s and the early 1960s, where the development does not fit into the general historical-cultural pattern.

The period of bad conscience

The post-war era's introductory period between 1945 and the communist take-over of power in February 1948 brought with it great changes for the reunited Czechoslovakia. Our knowledge about the societal problems that Holocaust survivors had to struggle with when trying to re-adjust to daily life is still insufficient. The limited research on Czechoslovakia and the Jews during these years focuses above all on top-level politics: prior to 1948, Czechoslovakia expressed strong support for the new state of Israel and even sent military assistance to the Middle East. At the same time, anti-Semitic traits were strengthened in the Czechoslovak society[5] and the emigration of Czech and Slovak Jews to Palestine drew attention.[6]

Despite a focus on the development of top-level politics, some smaller studies show that the Jews' situation after returning home was very complicated in relation to 'ordinary Czechs' and 'ordinary Slovaks'. These studies demonstrate that not all the problems between the majority population and the Jewish minority could be blamed on 'German occupiers' or 'communists'. Many conflicts were reported during the first post-war years when a fragment of the original Jewish population returned from the concentration camps and requested the restitution of property that had been confiscated or hidden in the homes of their Czech neighbours during the war. Those Czechs who did not want to give anything back showed their negative attitude towards the Jews in a manner that the Czech historian, Helena Krejčová, has described as 'the anti-Semitism of the bad conscience'. According to Krejčová, this bad conscience did not function as an impetus for moral self-examination, but rather as a propelling force for aversion to the Jews.[7] The tension intensified when the Sudeten Germans were driven out of Czechoslovakia and their property became attractive to those who wanted to loot. These people did not care that some of the German property only came into German ownership during the Second World War, after having been confiscated from those deported and murdered. Nor did they show any compassion towards, or consideration for, the original Jewish owners. As Krejčová also points out, it was not unusual for the Jews, who had considered themselves German and been identified with the German nation before the war or who had a German partner, to be harassed as if they themselves were German perpetrators, even when they were able to show that they had just returned from the concentration camps.

The situation in Slovakia was even more complicated and culminated in some pogroms, especially in Prešov and Topolčany in 1945 and in Bratislava in 1946 and 1948.[8] Even so, anti-Semitism, as opposed to an anti-German stance, never became a dominating official ideology in the Czechoslovak state between 1945 and 1948.[9]

Among the historical-cultural objects that can be studied, memorial plaques and monuments to the war's victims are perhaps the most interesting, because they indicate the level of respect for different victim groups demonstrated immediately after the war. The memorials were not intended first and foremost for the victims of the Holocaust. While memorial plaques appeared on different houses in Prague soon after Germany's surrender, dedicated to those Czechs who had lost their lives in the Prague Uprising of 5–8 May 1945, there were no corresponding name plaques to mark places in Prague associated with the vanished Jewish inhabitants. If Jews were mentioned at all, it was done so in a very muddled way. For example, in 1947 a large monument to the memory of Second World War victims was built in the Moravian city of Vsetín, upon which the 23 non-Jewish victims from the city were all named in full. Although there were three times as many Jewish victims of the Holocaust, these people were not identified by name. Instead there is a line of additions with a concluding description '... and 69 victims of racial oppression'.[10]

The first written depiction of life in Auschwitz came as early as 1946 in the form of a book with the title, *Továrna na smrt* ('The death factory').[11] It attracted notice even abroad as its authors were two Jewish prisoners, Ota Kraus and Erich Kulka, who apart from having been inmates of Auschwitz-Birkenau had also been imprisoned during the war in Dachau, Sachsenhausen, Neuengamme and Buchenwald, yet in the end had managed to survive the Holocaust. Other survivors published their memories during this period as well, either as documentary descriptions or as novels. The novel, *Život s hvězdou* ('Life with a star'), by Jiří Weil,[12] has also gained international recognition.[13]

The first Czechoslovak historical-cultural expressions connected to the Holocaust were primarily related to an existential use of history. The authors wanted to publish their testimonies to draw attention to the suffering during the Holocaust and make certain that it would not be forgotten. Society would at the same time, by gaining more knowledge about the Jews' suffering, better understand the nature of the Holocaust and the great trauma of its survivors.

Strong existential and moral currents also lay behind the first Czechoslovak artistic film about the Holocaust, which appeared relatively soon after the war. This film, *Daleká cesta* ('The long journey'), was made by the Czech director, Alfred Radok. It had gone into production during the dramatic time when the communist party was seizing power, but it was first shown in 1949 when the takeover was complete. For Radok the film was not only dramatic on a political and creative level. His work of art depicted Theresienstadt (Terezín), where both his father and grandfather had been killed during the Holocaust just a few years earlier. During filming, Radok never entered the room in which his father had been murdered.[14] Moreover, he had himself been imprisoned for a few months at the end of the Second World War, though he had managed to escape from the Klettendorf camp near Wroclaw.

Radok's *Daleká cesta* concerns two doctors: one female, simply called Hana, and one male, Antonín Bureš, who are colleagues and close friends but not in a romantic relationship. Everything changes when Hana loses her job due to her Jewish roots. To save her from being deported, Antonín decides to marry her. Thanks to this mixed marriage – he is Czech – Hana is the only member of her whole family to be saved. Both she and her husband are subsequently imprisoned anyway, but they manage to survive the Holocaust.

Radok's film later drew attention in the West, primarily due to Radok's talent as a director. He refused to make a 'realistic' film about the Holocaust – only one person dies in the entire film – but used a number of symbols and allegorical scenes to underline the Holocaust's absurdity. In a sadly ironic context, he even used parts of the German film director, Leni Riefenstahl's 1934 propaganda film about the Nazi party, *Triumf des Willens* ('Triumph of the will').

Radok's portrayal in the film of the relations between Czechs and Jews can be interpreted in two different ways. Because Antonín is a Czech and decides to save his friend and colleague, Hana, he can be seen as a representative for the Czechs who helped their Jewish compatriots and attempted to save them. However, those who forced Hana to leave her work, who Aryanised the Jews' property and observed their fate without interfering, were Czechs as well, a fact which makes the film's message problematic. This latter interpretation predominated among the official authorities in communist Czechoslovakia, even before the film had been distributed. The director was forced to soften his indirect criticism, but even after this his film was marginalised. The film was not directly forbidden in 1949, but it was shown only a few times at smaller cinemas in Prague suburbs for a very limited number of people. The official premiere did not take place, even though it had been planned. The film simply received no further distribution, though it was not officially banned until 1968 when Alfred Radok emigrated to Sweden, where he lived until his death in 1976.[15]

The repressive measures taken against the film, *Daleká cesta*, clearly illustrate the view of the Holocaust on the part of the new Czechoslovak regime. It was not among the building blocks of the Czechoslovak communist narrative between 1948 and 1989. The Jews were never acknowledged as the largest ethnic group to suffer from the Nazi genocide. Instead, the aim of official propaganda was to show the communists as both the main victims of the Nazi regime and as the uncontested leaders of the resistance movement against Hitler.

Stalinist communism, anti-Semitism and the Holocaust

The communist ideology, which used the successes of the Soviet Union in the war against Nazism for its own legitimisation, demonstrated clear anti-Semitic tendencies after the Holocaust as early as the end of the 1940s. Communist anti-Semitism was structured differently to that of the Nazis. Its major eruption during Stalin's time in power, just a few years after the Red Army had witnessed the terrible results of the Holocaust when liberating Auschwitz-Birkenau and several other camps, came relatively quickly.

In 1942, Stalin allowed the formation of the Jewish Anti-Fascist Committee (JAC), which became very active in documenting Nazi German crimes against Jews. Two of the Soviet writers, Ilya Ehrenburg and Vasily Grossman, became the main authors behind *The Black Book*, one of the very first publications accusing the Third Reich of genocide.[16] However, handed over to the JAC, this text was banned from official publication in the Soviet Union since it conflicted with the propaganda goals of the Soviet ideology at the end of the war. Already in 1946, Stalin had given an order to accelerate removal of the 'cosmopolitan' cadres, primarily ethnic Jews, from Soviet bureaucratic structures. As historian, Vladislav M. Zubok, wrote, 'Soviet Jews had served the Soviet regime, filling the ranks of the professional and cultural elite for two decades. Now it was time to purge them'. As late as 1948, however, Stalin authorised massive military assistance to Israel through Czechoslovakia and the Soviet Union recognised the state of Israel de jure, before the USA did the same.[17] Soon after this, the situation became much worse for the Jews, not only in the Soviet Union but also within the entire Soviet bloc.

According to the French political scientist, Laurent Rucker, for example, the targeting of Jews for oppression during Stalin's final years in power can be explained by the coinciding of certain factors at this specific time. One of the most important was the international situation, characterised by increased tension at the beginning of the Cold War and Israel's decision to seek its allies in the West and not the East, as well as anti-Semitism in Soviet society. Another, according to Rucker, was a power struggle between diverse groups within the highest communist leadership. In Rucker's view, the 'Jewish card' could be played against any opponent that was to be weakened or eliminated.[18]

That it was in fact the Red Army which liberated Auschwitz-Birkenau and Majdanek (other extermination camps, Belzec, Sobibór, Treblinka and Chelmo, were razed to the ground before the war's end) and had therefore directly witnessed the Holocaust's immediate effects did not matter in this context, because the Holocaust never had an important role either at the ideological level or in the Soviet-communist/Russian national historical cultures.[19]

The Czechoslovak communists initially attempted to maintain good relations with the new Jewish state of Israel. The sudden change came in 1949 when the Soviet Bloc lost its influence there. In a self-critical report from the 1960s from a commission established by the Czechoslovak communist party's central committee, it was asserted that Czechoslovakia's anti-Zionist strivings after 1949 were actually the most active within the whole Soviet Bloc.[20] Special attention was directed towards party functionaries of Jewish origin and myths about the Jews' significant role in 'the worldwide imperialist conspiracy', as well as their participation in ideological and political subversion against socialist states. Once again the Jews began to feel threatened, this time in communist Central Europe.

The Stalinist anti-Semitic wave culminated in the trial against the earlier leader of the Communist Party of Czechoslovakia, Rudolf Slánský, who had been arrested in November 1951. The trial was a sensation. Slánský was the communist party's general secretary, one of its founders and a lifelong member. He had spent the Second World War in Moscow. Immediately after having helped the communist revolution to victory in his homeland, and just six years after the end of the war, he was accused of conspiring against Czechoslovakia and its regime. All who took the opportunity to follow this trial live on the radio in Prague could hear 'the traitor' Slánský confess his treason towards the communist movement and at the same time point out his Jewish origins.

A total of fourteen previously high-ranking communists were prosecuted in the Slánský affair. Eleven of them had Jewish origins.[21] They were forced to confess to high treason against the government in Prague, espionage for the benefit of the West and sabotage of the socialist economy. Even if it was not true, they confirmed that the Gestapo, Zionism, international capital and Western intelligence agencies had stood behind their activities against the Czechoslovak state. Eleven of them, including Slánský, were sentenced to death and executed. Three received sentences of life in prison. 'Anti-Semitism played a certain role in earlier trials that Soviet advisors directed in the new countries governed by so-called people's democratic regimes. But never before had it played such a central role as on this occasion,' wrote the Czech historian, Karel Kaplan, about the trial.[22] Another historian, Igor Lukeš, added: 'Before it seized the power in February 1948, the Communist Party of Czechoslovakia denounced any form of bias against Jews as a manifestation of Nazi ideology. The trial changed all that'. So while Slánský's parents and two brothers had died as the result of their Jewish descent during the Nazi dictatorship, Rudolf Slánský died for very

similar reasons, but under the regime he himself had actively built as a coun-
terpoint to Nazism.[23] As Kaplan pointed out, the Slánský affair was the largest
political trial in Europe against leading communist functionaries after the war.[24]

An illuminating example of how the Czechoslovak communist propaganda
worked during the 1950s was the opening of an exhibition in Auschwitz-
Birkenau. It was intended to honour the memory of the Czechoslovak victims
by, among other things, presenting a long list of the names of Jewish citizens
deported from Czechoslovakia to the death camp. However, the chairman
of the communist-controlled, *Svaz protifašistických bojovníků* ('The Union of
Antifascist Fighters'), protested strongly against this. In his letter to the Ministry
of Education in Prague he explained his standpoint by stating that the aim of
the exhibition was to show the horror of the Nazi crimes: 'With all respect for
the victims it is, however, not in our interest to glorify such groups that pas-
sively and without any resistance went into the gas chambers.'[25] Despite protests
from the League's Jewish members, no lists were exhibited in Auschwitz.

Such claims about passive Jews going into the gas chambers without resistance facilitated the impression that the Jews had died voluntarily. At the same
time, the Czechoslovak communist regime 'forgot' the fact that there were many
Jews in the resistance movement both within and outside Czechoslovakia. The
whole logic was, however, diametrically different when it came to the consideration of Czech non-Jewish victims. A similar discussion would never have
been allowed about the brutally murdered inhabitants of the Czech village,
Lidice, for example, who were exterminated in revenge for the assassination
of Reinhard Heydrich in 1942. The very thought of questioning whether the
Lidice inhabitants could or could not defend themselves, or what resistance
against the Nazis they attempted, would have been perceived as completely
inappropriate.

At the official ideological level, the uncompromising attitude continued, though it cannot be said that everything to do with the Holocaust was
pushed aside. Whatever could be used as charges against 'the fascists', who, it was
claimed, were behind the Second World War, was put forward. However, if the
facts had to do with the Holocaust, a sort of de-Semitisation was demanded.
For instance, Kraus and Kulka's book on the Auschwitz bestiality, *Továrna na
smrt,* continued to be published in new editions. Before the end of the 1960s
it had been published six times in total, five of which after 1948. In 1957 it
was published in East Germany and the following year in Hungary. However,
the authors and their fellow prisoners were no longer Jews but 'political prisoners'. In their estimations of the number of victims murdered in Auschwitz-
Birkenau (according to them the total was 3.5 million) the authors did not
mention the ethnicity of those killed, with one exception. They wrote only
about different nationalities, for example 2.3 million 'Poles and Russians', who
for unclear reasons were counted together. The fact that most in this group, as in
all other groups, were Jews, was not stated. The only exception where Jews were

specifically mentioned comprised information about American victims – here the authors mentioned '2,000 Jews with American citizenship'.[26]

The development during the 1950s not only erased the victims' ethnicity but also changed the perpetrators' clearly defined national features. It was no longer solely 'the Germans' who were deemed responsible for the Second World War in the way that they were during the first post-war years. Now one was forced to distinguish between the progressively orientated Germans in the *Deutsche Demokratische Republik* (DDR) and the 'reactionary, neo-Nazi, revanchist' Germans in the *Bundesrepublik Deutschland* (BRD), i.e., West Germany. The war was now to be comprehended as a product of fascism, of an 'open terrorist dictatorship' exercised by 'financial capital's most reactionary forces'.[27] The question of guilt in regard to the Second World War was no longer depicted within the framework of the 1940s, but rather that of the Cold War. Fascism defined in the communist understanding could be interpreted as the creation of American capital creation but also, paradoxically, as the Jewish product of 'cosmopolitan' capital.[28]

The literature of individualisation

These ideological frameworks followed the logic of Stalinist communism. However, as soon as the political pressure eased somewhat after Stalin's death in 1953 and after the twentieth party congress in the Soviet Union in 1956, there developed a new, parallel perception of the Second World War and of the Holocaust in Czechoslovakia: a perception that could be summed up as the *individualisation* of the war and the Holocaust. The most prominent actors in this new process were at first Czech authors and later also filmmakers, who together lay the foundations of a subculture which balanced on the borderline between the officially permitted and the forbidden. Literature and films gradually attained a special place within the Czechoslovak historical culture, as there was no equivalent process for school books or in the public political debate.

Naturally, the authors and filmmakers concerned needed to take the regime into account, but at the same time they attempted to circumvent the official interpretation of the Second World War, including the Holocaust, as much as possible. In doing so, they focused on main individuals who did not fit into the large historical contexts of meaning. The works gave no clear answers, but aroused several unpleasant questions for society and the regime. Nonetheless, the creators were not prevented from continuing their artistic activities and being published by official state agencies, or from having their films presented by the only official state film company in Czechoslovakia at that time.

One of the first examples was the author, Josef Škvorecký. In 1958 his new way of portraying the Second World War by means of individualisation and de-ideologising in the novel, *Zbabělci* ('Cowards'), ignited a heated debate.

The story in Škvorecký's book takes place during the last days of the Second World War. Because it was clear that the country would be liberated even without what was officially termed the Prague Uprising of the Czech people in May 1945, Škvorecký questioned through his protagonists' actions not only the exclusively heroic interpretation of this event but also the solely positive picture of the Red Army's actions in the Czech territory. His protagonists want to live, not fight. For this Škvorecký had to endure harsh criticism from official authorities and was even forced to leave his work as editor of a world literature journal.[29] He was still able, however, to publish new books, including one about the Holocaust in which Jews were described as Jews and nothing else.[30]

The author who wrote almost exclusively about the Holocaust was Arnošt Lustig, himself a Jew who had survived it. His first book on the subject, *Noc a naděje* ('Night and hope'), was published in 1957 and contains seven narratives set in Theresienstadt. The first of his two most noted books was *Dita Saxová* from 1962. It describes a girl unable to live a normal life when she has returned from a concentration camp, who resolves her trauma by committing suicide. The second book was *Modlitba za Kateřinu Horowitzovou* ('A prayer for Kateřina Horowitzová' 1964), whose subject is another Jewish woman who decides to die actively fighting the Nazis.

In 1958 another Czech author, Jan Otčenášek, attracted attention with his short novel *Romeo, Julie a tma* ('Romeo, Juliet and the darkness'). This story of the tragic love between two young people highlights the fact that certain non-Jewish Czechs had collaborated with the Nazi regime. A young man, Pavel, wants to save a Jewish girl, Hana, who has refused to join the transport to Thereisienstadt. When he attempts to hide her they fall in love with each other, but Hana thinks that she represents a threat to her lover, particularly when the neighbours find out about her presence. She tries, therefore, to escape, but is shot dead by the Nazis immediately after leaving her precarious security. The story was made into a film by the director Jiří Weiss in 1960. Weiss, one of the four Czechoslovak directors personally struck by the Holocaust, was forced to cut an 'anti-Czech' scene, in which pressure is exerted on Hana by Pavel's neighbours, who fear for their lives.[31] However, the film still won six international awards at diverse film festivals in the West, making it one of the most successful Czechoslovak films internationally.

The author, Ladislav Fuks' first novel, *Pan Theodor Mundstock* ('Mister Theodor Mundstock'), tells the tragicomic story of a single individual hunted by history: a Jewish man who in the middle of the war practises his deportation to a concentration camp. He is unable to benefit from his training during the deportation itself. When leaving his home for transport to the camp he is run over by a car before arriving at the station. This book, from 1963, was welcomed by the critics, and was later filmed and translated into several languages. Another novel by the same author, *Spalovač mrtvol* ('The cremator'), concerned the Holocaust and received much attention. It is interesting that none of the aforementioned men: Fuks, Otčenášek or Škvorecký, were Jews, yet they demonstrated much interest in the Holocaust in their works.[32]

At the end of the 1950s, the cultural arena was given more freedom. The Jews themselves gained the possibility of honouring the memory of the Holocaust under more favourable circumstances than earlier. As already noted, the Pinkas Synagogue in central Prague was restored as a memorial site in 1959, two years before the Eichmann trial. The terms genocide or Holocaust were not used then, however. Instead the site was dedicated to the 'victims of the Nazi persecution'. Even so, the names of 77,297 Jews from Bohemia and Moravia who had lost their lives during the Second World War were written on the Synagogue's walls. Their placement in the Synagogue showed clearly that it was a question of Jewish suffering. The link to the Holocaust was stronger here than in Theresienstadt, where the memorial from 1947 was presented as 'The monument of national suffering'.

A relatively extensive production of noted literary works at the end of the 1950s and in the early 1960s laid a good foundation for Czechoslovak film artists. These artists created films that received a special place in the Czechoslovak historical culture between 1960 and 1968, before the more liberal, reformist-communist thinking was crushed by a Soviet-led invasion. The war now took centre stage, with about thirty films portraying the years 1939–1945 being made during the 1960s. The communist ideological interpretation of the Second World War was supplemented by alternative interpretations of the war. Fiction writing and above all filmmaking received a role as 'history teaching's, the media debate's and the substitute for many other things'[33] when their interpretations did not receive a place in official Czechoslovak historical culture.

Films of the new wave

Films about the Second World War were a backbone in 'the Czechoslovak new wave', as it was referred to internationally. In time, war films became absolutely the most successful of all films made in Czechoslovakia between 1945 and 1989. The new wave comprised eleven war films in total.

The Czech film historian Petr Koura's opinion is that the large number of films about the Second World War did not actually correspond to a particularly great interest in the war as such among the directors of the new wave: 'In films belonging to the new wave, the war events were often just a side-scene in the portrayal of the dramatic struggle between an individual and the totalitarian political system – in other words the theme that had during the 1960s specifically become very topical.'[34] As Koura also points out, the war was used in different experimental ways that had previously been seen as completely impossible.

The first of the films of the new wave to deal with the Holocaust was *Transport z ráje* ('Transport from paradise'), from 1962. This film was based on a short story by Arnošt Lustig and directed by Zdeněk Brynych, who openly professed himself to be an adherent of Alfred Radok's artistic style. Like *Daleká cesta*, *Transport z ráje* is set in Theresienstadt, the Nazis' 'exhibition paradise', where Jews from a number of European countries were forced to pretend how good their lives in Nazi camps were. The film's protagonists learn to live their daily lives as normally as possible. The film contains both humorous and erotic scenes, which was unusual in films concerning the Holocaust. This was the case not only in the 1960s but also when Roberto Benigni's Oscar-winning film, *La vita è bella* ('Life is wonderful'), was discussed at the end of the 1990s.

The individualised psychological perspective made it possible to touch upon other taboos as well, for example, the fact that a certain humanism existed among the perpetrators. For Czechs this was a very sensitive subject, which I discuss further in connection with *Schindler's List*. Another taboo was the question of the Jewish self-governing role and responsibility in Theresienstadt and in the whole context of the Holocaust.

Another of Lustig's literary works, a short story with the title *Tma nemá stín* ('The darkness has no shade'), was filmed in 1964 by the director Jan Němec. This led to yet another film about the Holocaust's complex problems, *Démanty noci* ('The diamonds of the night'). This film of sixty-five minutes contains almost no dialogue; the camera tells the story of how two Jewish boys manage to escape from their train transport and what problems they encounter during their escape and their struggle to survive. Among other things they wrestle with their own hallucinations, an element of the story which gave the film's creators extensive possibilities for experimentation. The boys are captured by a group of old Sudeten German commandos, but it is not at all evident if they are finally murdered or not. The director lets them 'wander about' from nowhere to nowhere, something that also has great symbolic value in relation to the post-war era.[35]

Another film belonging to the new wave and presenting a new view of the Holocaust, a view infused with new moral questions and a manifestly humanistic message, was ... *a pátý jezdec je strach* ('... and the fifth horseman is fear'), once again directed by Zdeněk Brynych. It deals with a Jewish doctor's dilemma when preparing to help a wounded member of the resistance. Helping would mean breaking the rules and risking his own life; not helping would result in the man's death and the doctor's subsequent wrestling with a guilty conscience. The wounded man finally receives help from the doctor, who is then exposed by a collaborator among the neighbours. The doctor commits suicide, however, before he can be punished. The creators' own thoughts about the communist society of the 1960s are seen most clearly when the protagonists speak of the relationship between the individual and totalitarian society, about it being impossible to capture people's thoughts. The filmmakers even reflect upon who can actually be seen as a hero: 'The hero is someone who dies unnecessarily while others live unnecessarily'.[36]

The most important work of the new wave was the Slovak film, *Obchod na korze* ('The shop on Main Street'), based on Ladislav Grosman's novel of the same name from 1965. *Obchod na korze* became important not only within the Czechoslovak context. Directed by Jan Kadár and Elmar Klos, it won an Oscar for best foreign film in 1966 and was the first film about the Holocaust to receive an Oscar award.[37]

As with Radok and Weiss – and the director Juraj Herz, who in 1968 had filmed the already mentioned, *Spalovač mrtvol* ('The cremator') – Kadár had been personally affected by the Holocaust. In the film, he and his colleague, Klos, projected the tragedy of six million Jews into a drama enacted in a single small shop in a Slovak small town during the Second World War. The ordinary farmer, Tono, receives a worthless shop of sewing articles from a pro-Nazi relative, confiscated from its original Jewish owners. The problems begin when Tono realises that in order to run the shop he must fire Mrs Lautman, an old Jewish widow, who owned the shop before him and is too old and confused to understand the circumstances. She is of the understanding that Tono has sought work and that she has employed him, and he is too decent to tell her the truth. On the other hand, he fears the regime, and when the Slovak authorities decide that the Jews must leave the town, he panics. When forcing the old lady to hide in order to save her as well as himself, he accidentally kills her. Without showing a single drop of blood or a single shot, the film gave non-Jewish Slovaks a strong impulse to examine their view of the Holocaust. An 'anti-hero', who is against the Holocaust, becomes a murderer. With the film, the clear dividing line between the Holocaust's perpetrators and passive onlookers had thus been erased.

Just two years after *Obchod na korze* had been awarded an Oscar, another Czechoslovak film about the Second World War received the same distinction. The film, *Ostře sledované vlaky* ('Closely watched trains'), directed by Jiří Menzel, takes place at a small Czech train station passed by German armoured trains transporting weapons to the front. The film was not about the Holocaust, but rather a portrait of another typical 'anti-hero', the young and sexually inexperienced train dispatcher Miloš Hrma, who unsuccessfully struggles with erotic challenges. After his first night with a woman he feels that he has become an adult man; shortly thereafter he becomes a hero when he manages to blow up an important train. The both comical and dramatic development reaches its tragic end precisely when the young man has begun to enjoy his adult life – he loses it. The success of *Ostře sledované vlaky* represented a symbolic peak of the relatively liberal period which ended with the Warsaw Pact's 1968 invasion of Czechoslovakia.

Most of the aforementioned films utilised a moral history usage of the war and the Holocaust, sometimes in combination with an existential usage.

Figures 2 and 3 *The Shop on Main Street* was the first Czechoslovak film and the first film about the Holocaust ever awarded an Oscar, in 1966. This picture shows the main 'hero', the carpenter Tono Brtko (Jozef Króner), when he – while drunk – parodies 'The Führer'. Ateliery Bonton, Zlín, archive

Through their moral questions, they debated, among other things, passive and active resistance to dictatorship. They questioned what consideration to others one should show when attempting to save oneself, and they challenged the Czech and Slovak conscience, both in relation to the totalitarian society and to the Jewish tragedy. The existential needs were demonstrated above all by those directors who had been personally affected by the Holocaust. The films did not show partiality towards any clear ideology or political alignment and they asked new questions, often without attempting to offer any concrete answers. The protagonists in these stories strive for a personal liberation that could end their current lack of freedom. The American film closest to the Holocaust view of the new wave films is *Sophie's Choice* from the early 1980s.

The new attitudes of authors and filmmakers, reflected in the aforementioned historical-cultural products, played an important role in society at the time and managed to at least partly compensate for the Holocaust's absence from the official communist ideology, from the communist historical narrative and from textbooks produced by the communist system.[38] The development of Czechoslovak film production from the early 1960s until the 1968 Prague Spring was even more interesting as it did not correspond at all to the Soviet development in relation to the Holocaust during the de-Stalinisation period.

The only Soviet film that can be mentioned in this context is *Pomni imja svojo* ('Remember your name'), which was not released until the 1970s. Its message was, however, completely different than that of the Czechoslovak films. It dealt with Auschwitz but, as the American historian, Denise Youngblood, has pointed out, 'based on the film alone, one would believe Auschwitz was built as a laboratory for Josef Mengele's medical experimentation on cute, blond, Russian children'.[39]

At the end of the 1960s, however, the Czechoslovak liberal version of tolerance towards the parallel subculture was over, and the new era known as 'normalisation' replaced the earlier reform attempts.

The communist normalisation

The normalisation regime, which reintroduced the old rules from the end of the 1940s and start of the 1950s, prohibited all the aforementioned films focusing on the Holocaust complex of problems, including the most successful film, *Obchod na korze*, and almost all of the new wave films. Even *Daleká cesta* was officially prohibited. The ideological use of the Second World War once again took over, which was tantamount to a new ideologically controlled non-use of the Holocaust. In order to steer public life in a desirable direction, the communist party's central committee adopted a document entitled *Poučení z krizového vývoje ve straně a společnosti po XIII. sjezdu KSČ* ('Learning from the crisis development in the party and society after the Czechoslovak communist party's 13th congress') in December 1970. This document became a binding directive for the cultural sphere as well, including schools and all similar institutions until 1989.

The Holocaust was not given any space in the relatively comprehensive interpretation of Czechoslovakia's history, which *Poučení* presented in order to avoid any possible future 'misunderstandings'. The Jews were mentioned only once in connection with the 1968 Prague Spring: 'The Zionist powers, a tool of international imperialism, played an important role in the fight against socialism in Czechoslovakia.' The names of seven important Zionist representatives were listed, among them František Kriegel, earlier a member of the highest party leadership and the only Czechoslovak communist leader who in 1968 refused to sign the Soviet-Czechoslovak agreement legalising the invasion of Czechoslovakia.[40] Anti-Jewish propaganda reached its peak after 1977 when *Charta 77*, the new group opposing 'the normalisation regime', was founded, and when its declaration was published in Western media. The communist party's daily newspaper, *Rudé právo*, immediately stated that *Charta 77* had been written by 'a small group belonging to the almost bankrupt Czechoslovak reactionary bourgeoisie and certain collapsed circles which had organised the counter-revolution in 1968' and 'who on the order of anti-communist and Zionist centres delivered material to certain Western news agencies'.[41]

The Pinkas Synagogue, the most important Jewish memorial site in Prague, was as already mentioned also closed during the 'normalisation period', after having been damaged by groundwater flooding in 1968. It was not reopened until 1992 and not fully restored until 1996. The memory of the Holocaust was missing both in textbooks and among the important events officially celebrated or commemorated by the Czechoslovak state.[42]

The exceptions to this rule were very few. Perhaps the most important was the Jewish journalist and author, Ota Pavel (Otto Popper), who, during the early 1970s, published two emotionally strong and poetic autobiographies about his and his family's life during the Holocaust.[43] After 1977, Czechoslovak film and literature were hardly affected by the wave of increasing interest in the Holocaust in the West. Neither the television series, *Holocaust*, nor Claude Lanzmann's film, *Shoah*, were distributed. However, William Styron's novel, *Sophie's Choice*, was published in two successful editions in 1982 and 1985, though the debate over its contents was limited and focused more on America's post-war problems than the heroine Sophie's wartime experiences in Central Europe.[44]

At the same time, the communist author most promoted by the regime, Alexej Pludek, was given a free hand when publishing his anti-Semitic works, particularly the novel, *Vabank*, from 1974. In this book he presented the Prague Spring as 'a phase in the Zionist-imperialist strivings to destroy socialism and control the world'. Pludek never became a generally popular author, however, and with the absence of possibilities for publicly expressing alternative opinions it is unclear how these attacks were perceived by the public. It was, therefore, above all an aversion to Jews steered from the top down and the general forgetfulness that became the clearest traces left to post-communist Czechoslovakia as the heritage of the communist period.

Notes

1. See, for example, Flanzbaum, *Americanization of the Holocaust*, 4–5; or Tim Cole, *Selling the Holocaust*, New York: Routledge, 2000, 7.

2. Novick, *Collective Memory*, 207–38.

3. Klas-Göran Karlsson, 'The Holocaust and Russian Historical Culture: A Century-Long Perspective', in Klas-Göran Karlsson and Ulf Zander, eds, *Echoes of the Holocaust: Historical Culture in Contemporary Europe*, Lund: Nordic Academic Press, 2003, 209ff.

4. See Herf, *Divided Memory*, 106–200; or Michael C. Steinlauf, *Bondage to the Dead*, New York: Syracuse University Press, 1997, 43–89.

5. Peter Mayer, Berbard Weinryb, Eugene Duschinsky and Nicolas Sylvain, *Jews in the Soviet Satellites*, New York: Syracuse University Press, 1953, 98–112.

6. See, for example, the latest study on Jews in Bohemia and Moravia: Rothkirchen, *The Jews of Bohemia and Moravia*, 284–88; or the newest book about the history of the Slovak Jews, Ján Mlynárik, *Dějiny Židů na Slovensku*, Prague: Academia, 2005, 338–44.

7. Helena Krejčová, 'K některým problémům židovské menšiny a českého antisemitismu po roce 1945', in Jerzy Tomaszewski and Jaroslav Valenta, eds, *Židé v české a polské občanské společnosti*, Prague: Karlova univerzita, 1999, 67–77.

8. See Ješajahu Andrej Jelínek, *Židia na Slovensku v 19. a 20. storočí*, Bratislava: Judaica Slovaca, 2000, 79–96; Mlynárik, *Dějiny Židů na Slovensku*, 303–44.

9. Radka Čermáková, 'Poválečné Československo. Obnovený stát ve střední Evropě', in Blanka Soukupová, Peter Salner and Miroslava Ludvíková, eds, *Židovská menšina v Československu po druhé světové válce. Od osvobození k nové totalitě*, Praha: Židovské muzeum v Praze, 2009, 23-35.

10. Erich Kulka, *Židé v československé Svobodově armádě*, Prague: Naše vojsko, 1990, 13.

11. Ota Kraus and Erich Kulka, *Továrna na smrt*, Prague: Čin, 1946.

12. Jiří Weil, *Život s hvězdou*, Prague: ELK, 1949.

13. This novel was later published in English, with the same title and with an introduction by Philip Roth. Jiri Weil, *Life with a Star*, London: Penguin Books, 2002.

14. Zdeněk Hedbávný, *Alfréd Radok. Zpráva o jednom osudu*, Prague: Národní divadlo, 1994, 156.

15. See Jiří Cieslar, 'Living with the Long Journey. Alfréd Radok's Daleká cesta', *Central Europe Review*, http://www.ce-review.org/01/20/kinoeye20_cieslar.html.

16. For more, see Ilya Altman, 'The History and Fate of The Black Book and The Unknown Black Book', in Joshua Rubenstein and Ilya Altman, eds, *The Unknown Black Book: The Holocaust in the German Occupied Soviet Territories*, Bloomington: Indiana University Press in association with the United States Holocaust Memorial Museum, 2010.

17. Vladislav M. Zubok, *A Failed Empire: The Soviet Union In The Cold War From Stalin to Gorbachev*, Chapel Hill: The University of North Carolina Press, 2007, 56.

18. Laurent Rucker, *Stalin, Israel a Židé*, Prague: Rybka Publishers, 2001, 236–37. The French original title is: *Staline, Israël et les Juifs*, Paris: Presses Universitaires de France, 2001.

19. See Klas-Göran Karlsson, 'Russian Nationalism, Antisemitism, and the Ideological Use of History', in Karlsson and Zander, *Post-War Battlefields*, 315–42.

20. 'Zpráva komise ÚV KSČ pro dokončení stranické rehabilitace', in: *O procesech a rehabilitacích*, Prague: Florenc, 1990.

21. See Ministerstvo spravedlnosti, *Proces s vedením protištátneho spikleneckého centra na čele s Rudolfom Slánským*, Prague: Orbis 1953.

22. See Karel Kaplan, *Zpráva o zavraždění generálního tajemníka*, Prague: Mladá fronta, 1993, 203.

23. Igor Lukeš, 'The Rudolf Slansky Affair: New Evidence', *Slavic Review* 1, 1999, 161

24. In 1963 the Czechoslovak Communist Party itself dismissed as false all charges against Slánský and the other thirteen who were prosecuted.

25. See Kulka, *Židé v československé Svobodově armádě*, 12.

26. Kraus and Kulka, *Továrna na smrt*, 225.

27. Václav Kocourek, ed., *Populární politický slovník*, Praha: 1962, 79.

28. 'Cosmopolitanism' would, according to the communist ideology, help the USA and its financial capital to win control of other countries by convincing them to give up their national sovereignty and national interests. Ibid., 124.

29. See Michael Špirit's comments on the latest Czech edition in Josef Škvorecký, *Zbabělci*, Prague: Nakladatelství Lidové noviny, 2001, 447–68.

30. This was Josef Škvorecký's collection of short stories, *Sedmiramenný svícen*, published in 1964.

31. See Petr Koura, 'Obraz holokaustu v českém hraném filmu', in Jiří Holý, ed., *Holokaust – Šoa – Zaglada v české, slovenské a polské literatuře*, Prague: Karolinum, 2007, 230.

32. Jan Otčenášek also contributed, however, to the official ideological use of history when he, at the beginning of the 1960s, wrote a screenplay for the film, *Reportáž psaná na oprátce*, about a communist resistance hero, the journalist, Julius Fučík, whose biography was adapted to the system's ideological framework. The film was first shown in 1961.

33. Agáta Pilátová, 'Tváří v tvář dějinám i sobě samým', *Film a doba*, 1966, 530–32. Quoted from: Jiří Rak, 'Film v proměnách moderního českého historismu', in Kopal, *Film a dějiny*, 28.

34. Petr Koura, 'Obraz nacistické okupace v hraném českém filmu 1945–1989', in Kopal, *Film a dějiny*, 231.

35. See Jiří Cieslar, *Kočky na Atalantě*, Prague: AMU, 2003, 457.

36. Koura, 'Obraz nacistické okupace v hraném českém filmu 1945–1989', 234.

37. Mason Wiley and Daien Bona, *Inside Oscar: An Unofficial History of the Academy Awards*, New York: Ballantine Books, 1987.

38. Kamenec, 'Reflections on the Holocaust', 163.

39. Denise Youngblood, *Russian War Films: On the Cinema Front, 1914–2005*, Lawrence: Kansas University Press, 2007, 171.

40. *Poučení z krizového vývoje ve straně a společnosti po XIII. sjezdu KSČ*, 19.

41. 'Ztroskotanci a samozvanci', *Rudé Právo*, 12 January 1977.

42. See, for example, Frankl, 'Holocaust Education', 176–89.

43. Ota Pavel, *Smrt krásných srnců* (1971); *Jak jsem potkal ryby* (1974).

44. Instead of concentrating on the traumatic European wartime past (Sophie and the Holocaust, her Polish father who sympathised with the Nazis but was killed by the Germans, etc.) the Czech edition's epilogue presented the novel rather as the history of a great author's birth when he analyses the American conscience. The reader learns that in this book Styron actually presents a late account of America's conscience in relation to fascism and Nazism. The story's narrator and one of the three main heroes, Stingo, sees a clear parallel between the Nazi relation to 'inferior races' and the relationship between white and black Americans. See Radoslav Nenadál, 'V osidlech minulosti' (Epilog), in William Styron, *Sophiina volba*, Prague: Odeon, 1995, 688–94.

CHAPTER 3

The Holocaust's uneven return

Czechoslovakia towards dissolution, 1990–1992

This chapter concerns the memory of the Holocaust during Czechoslovakia's 'Velvet Divorce' between the years of 1990 and 1992. I wish to show how the Czechoslovak communist narrative in these years was quickly replaced by two dominating national narratives – one in each of the two republics – and analyse what position the Holocaust attained in the Czech and Slovak historical culture respectively. I focus on the different main actors behind their respective narratives and illustrate how their use of history in relation to the Holocaust reflected diverse future expectations.

The road to Czechoslovakia's partition began about six months after the Czechoslovak Communist Party had lost its power in December 1989. On 29 December Václav Havel was elected as Czechoslovakia's new president. Two wholly new political movements were created as bearers of the new political power – one on each side of the common Czech-Slovak border. In the Czech case it was the *Občanské fórum* ('The citizen forum'), and in the Slovak case the *Verejnosť proti násiliu* ('The public against violence').

Initially their goals were perceived as lying very close together, and many thought that the future looked 'Czechoslovak'. The Czechoslovak-adapted Czech national-liberal narrative did not appear to have any clear challenger. Masaryk statues, Masaryk streets and Masaryk squares experienced a new boom overnight, at the same time as prominent communist figures lost their earlier right to be 'immortalised' in this way. Gottwaldov, the town which during four decades bore the name of the first Czechoslovak communist president, Klement Gottwald, retook its old name Zlín, which it had prior to the start of the communist period.[1] Even if Masaryk enthusiasm was not as great in Slovakia, a number of towns there had their streets and squares named after Milan Rastislav Štefánik, Tomáš Masaryk's close collaborator during the First World War and one of the main architects of the Czechoslovak state in 1918.

However, the first crisis with the problematic Czech-Slovak history in the main role occurred as early as in the spring of 1990 when the federal parliament in Prague was to reach an agreement on the country's new name. According to the ideas of the Czech members, the old name – the Czechoslovak Socialist Republic – could be simply changed by removing *Socialist*, which would give Czechoslovakia the same name, the Czechoslovak Republic, as it had had in the interwar period. However, parliament's Slovak members thought a new and more just name was demanded, as the interwar state's name did not indicate any Czech-Slovak equality but rather confirmed the Czechs' dominance in the country. According to the Slovak conception, the country should thereby be called Czecho-Slovakia. The hyphen, in what started to be called 'the hyphen war', gained great significance.[2] The cracks soon became wider and more visible on several different fronts, which proved that it was a matter of much more than a few particular details. This meant that not even the temporary compromise on the country's new name – the Czech and Slovak Federal Republic – could save the situation and brake or prevent Czechoslovakia's dissolution.

Even the two leading movements, *Občanské fórum* and *Verejnosť proti násiliu,* were soon affected by manifest internal cracks. *Občanské fórum* was divided into two movements: a liberal, led by previous dissidents and certain influential intellectuals from *Charta 77*, and a conservative, led by a group of radical economists. This division had, however, no great influence on the now-dominating interpretation of the past in the Czech case; while the liberals kept themselves to the national-liberal narrative, the conservatives used history very little, focusing instead on the future. Through the absence of a clear right-left perspective, which had not yet come into being, the first republic's ideals seemed to correspond to everybody's expectations. The liberal group's most well-known representative was Václav Havel; the conservatives were led by the Finance Minister and later Prime Minister, Václav Klaus. Under the latter's leadership a new conservative party with the name *Občanská demokratická strana*, the 'Civic Democratic Party' (ODS), was created and became the most important Czech political party until 1998.

The Slovak movement, *Verejnosť proti násiliu*, splintered in 1991. This led to a marked weakening of liberal political tendencies and a strengthening of left populism that cleverly exploited many Slovaks' fear of the radical economic reforms advocated by the right-wing economists in Prague. A new political party was established, the *Hnutie za demokratické Slovensko* ('The movement for a Democratic Slovakia' [HZDS]). Led by Vladimír Mečiar, who after

Czechoslovakia's breakup became Slovakia's Prime Minister, the HZDS dominated Slovak politics until 1998. The political scientist, Shari Cohen, describes this movement with the term 'history-less nationalists'; bureaucrats who lacked their own clear ideological profile, and who therefore demonstrated a significant ideological flexibility when concerning, above all, tolerance towards extreme nationalist demands.[3]

The primary challenger of the HZDS on the Slovak stage during the period 1990–1992 was *Kresťanskodemokratické hnutie*, the 'Christian Democratic Movement' (KDH), led by the previous dissident Ján Čarnogurský. He was Slovakia's Prime Minister between 1991 and 1992, shortly before the dissolution of Czechoslovakia. As I will demonstrate, it was the KDH which, of all the political organisations in Slovakia, stood closest to the Catholic Church there and highlighted the religious aspect of Slovak politics.

The final decision on Czechoslovakia's dissolution came in connection with the parliamentary election in the summer of 1992, when the ODS won in the Czech part of Czechoslovakia and the HZDS in Slovakia. The latter got its new constitution as early as a few months before the country officially began to exist. It was based on national foundations rather than the principle of citizenship.[4]

What was striking about the Czechoslovak post-communist development was the complete absence of a political party with plans including the continuation of a united Czechoslovak state. Also lacking was a democratic ideology which could have overcome the most difficult Czech-Slovak complications in Czechoslovakia's history and pointed to a common future.[5]

But when and how did the Holocaust enter the Czech and Slovak debates? Did it do so at all? And how did it relate to the Czech national-liberal narrative and the Slovak national-Catholic narrative?

Slovakia: the Holocaust as an irritant to nationalism

The Slovak debate about Jozef Tiso, wartime Slovakia and the Holocaust began rather as the result of a strong offensive from the aforementioned diaspora than as an initiative of domestic political powers in Czechoslovakia. Since the 1970s the diaspora had made its voice heard mainly through the Slovak World Congress (SWC). The diaspora's most active users of history, who at the same time were Tiso's most dedicated defenders, had a manifest advantage as they – in contrast to everyone living in Czechoslovakia – could develop their historical narrative relatively freely in the West long before 1989. According to the diaspora's own information, during the post-war era in the USA and Canada alone there were more than twenty Slovak intellectuals – historians, journalists and others – intensively engaged in Slovak history and producing a number of books on the subject. They wrote about modern history as well as earlier

Figure 4 Two Slovaks on their way from Jozef Tiso's grave in Bratislava where they took part in a ceremony glorifying the 'founder of the first Slovak nation state'. Their idol Tiso was the President and 'Führer' of that state. Photo: ČTK, Czech News Agency, Jana Mišauerová

epochs. However, most in this group were already dead when communism collapsed.[6]

The first opportunity for domestic and foreign-based Slovaks to honour Tiso's memory together occurred in April 1990 in German Bavaria. The participants were forced to stay outside Slovak territory, as they did not know how the domestic authorities would react. However, all those who so wished could, for the first time since 1948, freely travel to what at this time was still West

Germany, whether they came from Canada, Australia, Italy or Czechoslovakia. It was also the last time the ceremony had to be held outside Slovak territory.

During the Cold War it became a tradition among Tiso's supporters living in exile to meet regularly – always in April – in Altötting, Bavaria. It was here, in the monastery of Konrad the Holy, that the American army arrested Jozef Tiso on 6 June 1945, when he attempted to hide during his escape. He was shortly thereafter handed over to the Czechoslovak authorities. However, the April date for the meetings to Tiso's memory was not chosen on the basis of the arrest or extradition, but rather as a reminder of the day Tiso was executed: 18 April 1947. The execution took place in Bratislava, but the Slovak capital was closed to the diaspora between 1948 and 1989. The 1990 commemoration was attended by a few hundred people.

An important precondition for the diaspora's success in Slovakia was the fact that it, at least initially, managed to convince the new political elites that it was a serious political partner in deliberations on how the Czechoslovak political system should be reformed after communism's collapse. A group of leading Slovak politicians visited, for example, the diaspora's main centre in Toronto, Canada, in May 1990 when the SWC opened its first congress since the fall of the Berlin Wall. A member of the delegation was Alexander Dubček, then speaker in the Czechoslovak Federal Parliament and at the same time the most well-known Slovak politician in the world. He was accompanied by Milan Čič, Prime Minister in the Slovak government, and Rudolf Schuster, Chairman of the National Council in Prague's Federal Parliament.[7]

This visit from politicians at the highest level of government did not prove that all the mentioned politicians identified with the diaspora's programmes and plans, but gave, however, a clear signal that the SWC was a legitimate partner in the political process. A similar signal from the Czechs was received as early as February 1990 when Czechoslovakia's President Havel arrived in Toronto for his first official Canadian visit. There he received a medal which the SWC usually awarded to those who 'had contributed to the flourishing of the Slovak nation'. In the same month the general secretary of the SWC, Dušan Tóth, became a member of Havel's advisory group, consisting of Czechs and Slovaks living abroad but having close relations with Czechoslovakia. Antony Roman, a parliamentary member from Canada and a relative of the recently deceased co-founder of the SWC, the main sponsor and general secretary, Štefan Roman, was among the group's members. Other members of the advisory group were Tomáš Baťa, from a well-known family of shoe manufacturers; the film director, Miloš Forman; and the French political science professor, Jacques Rupnik, part of whose life had been spent as the child of French diplomats in Czechoslovakia.

As far back as during the Cold War, the SWC had adapted its ideological history usage to fit its main goal – to fight for a 'Slovak Slovakia'.[8] The Holocaust was used in the narrative, but to a small degree and without much attention from the surrounding world. The use of history was focused, above all, on defending the memory of Jozef Tiso. What was most important, it seemed, was not to question the Holocaust as such, but rather to present it as a German crime which in Slovakia was supported solely by a few German-friendly radicals whom Tiso, against his will, was forced to keep in the government so as not to enrage the Germans too much.[9] A key figure in this context was the Prime Minister, Vojtech Tuka, who on the grounds of his political sympathies for Hitler and his Hungary-friendly stance was described as both a 'fascist' and 'Hungarian'.[10] Just as important was proving that Tiso was at first unaware of what awaited the Jewish Slovaks when they were deported, and then, when he learned of the real purpose of the deportations, did his best to stop them.

The attitude towards the Jews was problematic, above all for the diaspora's radical section, comprising those activists who at the beginning of the 1990s became known as the most prominent and at the same time most experienced history users: Jozef Kirschbaum, Milan Ďurica and František Vnuk.[11] I will return to them later. In general, questions regarding the Slovaks' attitude to Jews were not perceived in the diaspora as among the most important.[12] During the 1970s a Slovak with Jewish origins, Eugen Löbl, actually served as the Vice Chairman of the SWC. During the Stalin era Löbl had been sentenced in the Slánský process to prison for life, despite having been an active communist functionary and fighting against the Slovak regime in the Second World War from his exile in London.[13]

Another example touching upon the Jewish history is a statement by Štefan Roman. In his capacity as Chairman of the SWC he directly compared, in a political use of history, the Slovak diaspora's destiny with the Jewish struggle for their own state, when speaking at the celebrations for the SWC's ten-year anniversary.[14] There is, however, very little research on the moderate section of the diaspora and its relationship to the Jews. The radical representatives' position became, on the other hand, evident when it emerged at the start of the 1990s. Prior to communism's collapse, the diaspora needed to transmit the signal that it was a question of a democratic organisation whose thinking stood in sharp contrast to that of the communists.

That being said, there were strong direct links between the Slovak Second World War regime and the SWC of the 1970s and 1980s. Among the founders of the SWC were certain prominent persons from the wartime Slovak state; most notably Ferdinand Ďurčanský and Jozef Kirschbaum. The leadership of the SWC never dissociated itself from the Tiso regime and its complicity in the Holocaust of Slovak Jews. Certain leading personalities within the SWC itself went so far as to admit that the influence supporters of the Tiso regime had within the organisation was too great to allow condemnation of that part of Slovakia's history.[15] The Czech historian, Jan Rychlík pointed out that an 'inability (or perhaps even impossibility) of breaking the connections with the Slovak war state, and particularly to clearly condemn its responsibility for deportations of Slovak Jews, complicated not only the Congress' relations to the Czechs but also to Slovak Jews'.[16]

The two most important names in this connection were, as noted, Ferdinand Ďurčanský and Jozef Kirschbaum. The most controversial of them was Ďurčanský, who during Czechoslovakia's first partition in March 1939 was Tiso's Foreign Minister and who participated with him in the negotiations with Adolf Hitler. He was sentenced to death as a war criminal in 1947, but the sentence could not be carried out as Ďurčanský was already in exile. He subsequently lived in Austria, Switzerland, Italy, Argentina and West Germany. As one of its main members, he could contribute to the establishment of the SWC before dying in 1974.

The other person behind the creation of the SWC, and who actively served Tiso's regime, was Jozef Kirschbaum, previously General Secretary of *Hlinkova slovenská ludová strana*. Later in the war, Kirschbaum acted in the capacity of Slovak diplomat in Italy and Switzerland. He was convicted as a war criminal and sentenced to ten years' prison followed by a further ten years in a punishment camp, but managed to emigrate and remained in the West throughout the Cold War. He lived in Toronto and was able to return to Slovakia after communism's collapse. With the help of some nationalist sympathisers, principally Tibor Böhm, Czechoslovakia's General Prosecutor in 1990, Kirschbaum was granted amnesty.

The SWC's most important and powerful man, Štefan Roman, could not be perceived as manifestly divergent in his attitude towards the Tiso regime, either. Roman could not be linked to the regime in the same way as Ďurčanský and Kirschbaum, because during the war he already lived in Canada, where he arrived, aged sixteen, in 1937. After the war he experienced great successes as a businessman in the mining industry, making through his company a large fortune with the help of which he could sponsor a number of diaspora activities. In 1971, soon after the formation of the SWC, Roman praised Tiso as 'a man who confirmed his love to the nation by the highest sacrifice'.[17]

Until the 1980s the thought of an independent Slovak state seemed an unrealistic dream for the diaspora. Central Europe's political destiny was decided by the interests of the two contemporaneous great powers and, above all, the ideology of one of them: the Soviet Union. However, following the Iron Curtain's fall, prospects changed radically. Slovakia's independence was no longer an impossibility, which gave the diaspora's view of Tiso and his Slovakia both a new relevance and strengthened the future dimension. Tiso was no longer a subject for nostalgists, but was also needed as an attractive historical figure for the future. More than in the past, the diaspora's history-usage concentrated on disproving assertions about Slovakia's Holocaust guilt and Tiso's involvement in the mass murder of Slovak Jews. Only a morally pure Tiso could be utilised to politically unite Slovaks in the fight for 'a Slovak Slovakia' and attract new, young adherents who had been educated in the communist period.

In relation to the Holocaust, two people from the diaspora distinguished themselves with their use of history within the radical Slovak nationalism. The aforementioned František Vnuk and Milan Ďurica both belonged to the diaspora's elder generation, but neither of them was directly involved in Slovakia's politics during the Second World War.[18] During their childhood they had experienced the interwar period's Czechoslovak Republic, and both lived in Tiso's Slovakia during their teenage years. They also emigrated soon after the Second World War.

After communism's collapse, Vnuk, who became the Vice Chairman of the SWC after Štefan Roman's death in 1988, began to publicly assert that the blame for the Holocaust could by no means be placed on Slovakia. 'The tragedy that during the war struck all Jews in all countries in the German sphere of influence struck even Slovakia', he declared. According to him the country had had insufficient strength to resist Hitler. At the same time, however, the Slovak authorities stopped the deportations in 1942 'as soon as they ascertained that the Jews were not being grouped in labour camps but sent to death camps'.[19] That is when Slovakia, according to Vnuk, became 'the safest country for Jews in the whole Central European region', and 'the Slovaks – from President Tiso to the last man out in the countryside – did a lot more for the Jews than has hitherto been acknowledged'.[20]

In other words, while the Slovak regime was, on the one hand, not powerful enough to resist German pressure, it could, on the other hand, independently stop the deportations as soon as the true nature of the concentration camps became known. However, Vnuk did not explain how this was possible when the time difference between the two decisions implemented in 1942 – to initiate the deportations and to halt them – was just a few months. In a newspaper interview on another occasion he dismissed the assertion that Hlinka's party, the HSLS, was totalitarian, prohibiting and liquidating all other Slovak parties and opponents. According to Vnuk, the HSLS was a party 'which in a democratic way expressed the nation's will'. He said in the same interview that the Holocaust 'was a tragedy which saddens us and which we must condemn'. But just a few sentences further on, Vnuk described anti-Semitism in Slovakia during the Second World War as the Jews' own fault. The Jews, as he expressed it, 'did not help the Slovaks when they before the war were struggling for their national freedom and for their rights'.[21]

Milan Ďurica was also of the opinion that Slovakia was a victim of the Holocaust rather than a co-perpetrator. As he wrote in 1989, the Slovak war state comprised the golden era in the Slovak nation's historical development, and only did for Germany what it was absolutely forced to.[22] In Tiso's defence, Ďurica collected testimonies from German agents, which, according to him, proved that the Germans perceived Tiso as undependable. This further proved, according to Ďurica, that Tiso fought for Slovakia's and not Germany's best interests during the war.[23] Already before presenting his collection of German quotes about Tiso in Slovakia, Ďurica published a similar collection about Jozef Kirschbaum in order to prove his innocence. Ďurica's conclusion regarding Kirschbaum was as follows:

> The German documents examined here show that Kirschbaum ... was a man with a clean record as a Slovak patriot and as a Catholic of conviction. He never compromised with his principles and the interests of the Slovak nation, nor its right to an independent life based on its spiritual tradition and as a member of the family of Central European nations. Only few Slovak public figures of those eventful and often critical times can look with pride at the portraits of themselves in German documents as can Kirschbaum.[24]

When he, at a conference in Bratislava in 1992, presented his work on how undependable Tiso was in the eyes of the Germans and how patriotic he therefore actually was, Ďurica claimed that both Western and communist historians had misunderstood Tiso's relation to the Third Reich and national socialism. On this and several other occasions, Ďurica asserted that Hitler had deceived Tiso and that the latter was not conscious of the true nature of the deportations. When he understood that it was a question of exterminating those deported, Tiso wanted to resign, according to Ďurica. However, as Ďurica emphasised, it was the Jews themselves who wished him to remain, as they feared that some evil and Nazi-friendly politician would replace him.[25] However, any concrete sources for this statement were not mentioned.

Ďurica's view of Tiso was almost identical to Vnuk's. When Tiso was 'deceived' by Hitler and 'persuaded' by the Jews to keep his post as the Slovak President, he was – as both Ďurica and Vnuk presented him – a relatively naive man who could be deceived and manipulated. However, the same Tiso appeared as a clever strategist and very determined politician who would compromise a little in certain tactical matters, but who would never compromise in his strategic goal to do what was best for Slovakia. This gradually became a general perception of Tiso among adherents of the Slovak national-Catholic narrative. An organised defence of Tiso began at the start of the 1990s by such groups as *Priatelia prezidenta Tisu* ('President Tiso's Friends'),[26] and *Spoločnosť Jozefa Tisu* ('The Jozef Tiso Society'), who wished to exonerate Tiso and his regime from 'Czech-Bolshevik' charges.[27]

Anti-Semitic stereotypes

In its explanations regarding Tiso's relations to the Jews and in defence of his actions in connection with the Holocaust, the Catholic-nationalist narrative combined two types of Slovak anti-Jewish stereotypes. The first consisted of anti-Semitic accusations up until 1945, i.e., from the anti-Semitic argumentation existing before and during the Holocaust. The second contained anti-Jewish assertions from the post-war, post-Holocaust period. In both cases at least part of the blame for the Holocaust was placed upon the Jews themselves, i.e., upon the victims rather than the perpetrators. The intention of externalising Holocaust responsibility and toning down its course in Slovak territory can therefore be characterised as an ideological history usage, the goal of which is to utilise history to justify power relations in the Slovak state during the Second World War.

František Vnuk's assertion that the Jews in some way deserved their fate, or at least could not expect any assistance from Slovakia during the Holocaust, as they 'did not help the Slovaks when they were fighting before the war for their national freedom and their rights', brought to the fore an important aspect of Slovak anti-Semitism in the interwar era. Its basis was the accusation that the Jews were not loyal members of Slovak society, a claim originating in the nationalism of the interwar period and the Hlinka party's ideology. Those defending this claim did not problematise this argument; neither did they take into consideration the complicated but continuously ongoing development in the national question.

The foundations for the nationalist conception of Jews as a foreign element in Slovak society derived from the pre-1918 period, when the interest among Jews for Slovak culture was relatively low.[28] The distance between Jews and Slovaks prior to 1918 was substantial even from a religious perspective, as religious life was polarised. As Kristian Gerner has pointed out, the ideological-political mixture of Hungarian-hostile Slovak nationalism and the Catholic faith was in itself an effective breeding ground for anti-Semitism.[29]

Emphasising this tension from Austria-Hungary, without taking into account the development after 1918, meant that one ignored information showing that the gap between the two groups was decreasing during the interwar era, which could primarily be interpreted as the Jews' increasing desire to adapt themselves to the new conditions.[30] Even so, the Chairwoman of the Tiso Society, Elena Kozánková, claimed in 1992, without putting forward any evidence, that 'most of the Jews said they were of German nationality, which actually meant that Germans deported other Germans from Slovakia during the war'.[31]

The politically and nationalistically motivated anti-Semitism, which blamed the Jews for their attitude to Slovakism and their assumed striving for political domination of the world, went hand in hand with an anti-Semitism based on social aspects during the interwar era. The Jews were blamed for stealing from the Slovak people and intentionally causing them to drink too much.[32]

There was also a religious anti-Semitism, which saw the Jews as the enemies of the Catholic Church. Milan Ďurica was especially keen on trying to exonerate both Tiso and the Slovak Catholic Church from charges of religious anti-Semitism. Tiso's Catholic faith was not a factor strengthening his willingness to collaborate with Germany in order to effect the deportation of Jews from Slovakia, he pointed out. Ďurica claimed that his Catholic faith, on the contrary, was a factor encouraging Tiso to save the Jews as soon as he realised what the deportations actually involved. However, no answer was given to the question why Tiso needed to save the Jews from his own regime, which prepared the anti-Jewish legislation; a legislation that, according to the legislators themselves, was a Slovak activity and, moreover, one of the harshest in Europe. When Ďurica externalised the responsibility for the Holocaust and presented the killing of Jews as forced by Germany and as German treachery against Tiso, his argument was that the 'awakened' Tiso tried to save the Jews from death by conferring upon certain Jews and their families, so-called president's exemptions, which would facilitate their non-deportation. According to Ďurica, Tiso granted in total 9,000 exemptions, thereby helping to save 30,000 Jewish lives.[33] However, Ďurica could not present any proof at all that there really were 30,000 Slovak Jews who survived the Holocaust because of the president's exemptions or who survived it by any means.[34]

Ďurica's main contribution to a historical view that trivialises the persecutions and the Holocaust, came in the mid-1990s, when his work on Slovakia's history was introduced as an official textbook in Slovak schools. The book was entitled *Dejiny Slovenska a Slovákov* ('Slovakia's and the Slovaks' history') and was published after Czechoslovakia's division. This book summarises the Slovak diaspora's most extreme attitude. Through its historical breadth, which encompasses the whole epoch between the birth of Christ and the 1900s, a detailed summary of the Slovak national-Catholic historical narrative is presented.

Dejiny Slovenska a Slovákov contains Ďurica's clearest statements on the question of how he perceives the Jewish suffering in the Second World War as well. The picture of the Holocaust given by the Jews is, according to him, exaggerated. In Ďurica's book, he does not deny the existence of the concentration camps, where the Jews were forced to wait for further transportation to their deaths, but they are described as 'companies of economic character which primarily worked for the state'. When analysing the conditions in one Slovak camp, he asserts that 'it was the most modern company in Slovakia of its kind', where the Jews lived so well that 'Jewish dentists even received gold to use when they filled their patients' teeth, something that was completely impossible for a large majority of the Slovak population'.[35]

The book, which represented the most manifest example of the Holocaust's trivialisation during the whole period, attracted much attention when it was approved by the Slovak Ministry of Education as teaching material for Slovak upper secondary schools. Ninety-thousand copies were printed. The Ministry, which at that time was controlled by the extreme nationalist *Slovenská národná strana* the 'Slovak National Party' [SNS]), used financial resources from EU funds, intended to support the development of democratic education in the post-communist countries in East and Central Europe.[36]

The storm arrived after criticism from certain historians and Jewish organisations. Two professional historians who led the History Department within the Slovak Academy of Sciences published a detailed criticism of certain points in Ďurica's book in the newspaper *Práca*.[37] The government party's spokesman, however, described the book as 'a scientifically based work which deserves admiration and respect from all Slovaks'. Criticism came from the EU as well; the European Commission member, Hans van den Broek, requested the Slovak Foreign Minister, Zdenka Kramplová, to arrange that a book defending the deportation of Jews during the Second World War disappear from the shelves of Slovak bookshops. The Ministry of Education dismissed the criticism as incompetent and as interference in Slovakia's internal affairs. According to the Ministry, the scandal was a matter of 'a serious attempt to internationally discredit Slovakia'.[38] When the Prime Minister, Vladimír Mečiar, visited Holland in June 1997, he promised that Slovakia would not use the book in schools after 1 July the same year.[39] The Minister of Education, Eva Slávkovská, explained, however, that the book would stay in school libraries, where all students and pedagogues would have the possibility to read it.[40] The book remained in bookshops and a new edition was published in 2003, this time without state funding and official subsidies.

The national-Catholic narrative's diffusion in the media during 'Czechoslovakia's Velvet Divorce' was made easier by the media's attentiveness towards certain extreme statements by domestic nationalist politicians. Stanislav Pánis was a parliamentary member in both the Czechoslovak Federal Parliament in Prague and the Slovak Parliament in Bratislava, and represented in both a nationalist Slovak party. In February 1992 he went so far as to directly deny that the Holocaust had taken place, neither in Slovakia nor internationally. The statement was made during an interview with Norwegian TV and was therefore not originally meant for the Slovak public. However, the interview was broadcasted on Slovak TV as well, and could therefore be watched in the entire country, which aroused a significant number of reactions. Pánis asserted that 'technically it was impossible to murder as many as six million Jews in the concentration camps'. He added at the same time that he hoped that 'the truth about the Holocaust one day will emerge', which, according to him, meant that everything taught until then was a lie.[41] Pánis was the highest-placed person on the Czechoslovak political stage between 1990 and 1992 to openly deny the Holocaust.[42]

Mild nationalism and its silent sympathisers

The fact that the Catholic-nationalist narrative, which to a great extent was imported to Slovakia by the Slovak diaspora, attained such a significant position in the Slovak public debate at the beginning of the 1990s was not only due to the active support the diaspora received from the domestic extreme nationalist political circles. Two other important factors in this success were a 'discreet' support from those forces which could be termed mild nationalists, and a passive resistance from those who did not concur with the Tiso-friendly national-Catholic narrative but did not manage to answer it with a convincing independent alternative.

What all 'discreet' nationalists had in common was that they, despite supporting the national-Catholic narrative, displayed a 'softer' position in relation to the Holocaust of Slovak Jews. They did not deny the Holocaust but still gave silent support to the diaspora and defended Tiso's actions. The Holocaust was seen as a kind of accident or temporary deviation from the otherwise good path Slovakia had started to follow.

The examples I first and foremost wish to present here are the interpretations of the 'Christian Democratic Party' (KDH), and its leader, Ján Čarnogurský, Slovak Prime Minister from 1991 to 1992, and the Slovak Catholic Church. But even the organisation, *Matica Slovenská*, and the representatives of the leading political party HZDS can be placed in this group.

Čarnogurský's family had personal links to the wartime Slovak regime. Čarnogurský's father, Pavol Čarnogurský, was a member of the Hlinka party and of the Slovak Parliament during the war. He was still living at the start of the 1990s and openly expressed his support for the Tiso regime even then. His book on the subject was published in 1992.[43] Despite this, Ján Čarnogurský was one of the foremost activists, who in October 1987 signed a protest against how the communist regime had treated the memory of the Holocaust. A total of 24 Slovak opposition members, mainly intellectuals, expressed in this protest their dissatisfaction with the fact that Slovakia lacked 'a worthy monument which would remind about the greatest collective tragedy in our history', i.e., the Holocaust of Slovak Jews. 'Anti-Jewish measures and above all the deportations of Jewish inhabitants from Slovakia conflicted with those principles that we would wish to see as fundamental principles for Slovakia's future – everybody's equality regardless of race, tolerance, freedom of religion, democracy, respect for laws, love between people', the document stated. In this tone the Jews were described as 'our Jewish fellow humans and brothers', and 'deep sorrow and genuine apology' was expressed for all that had taken place. There was no doubt that the blame for the oppression and the deportations of the Jews was placed upon the domestic regime: 'Deportations and other anti-Jewish measures were in Slovak hands', the document established.[44] Although Čarnogurský was only one of the authors, his signature demonstrated that he identified with the uncompromising tone.

Even after becoming Slovakia's Prime Minister after the collapse of communism, he gave a speech focusing on the Holocaust at a 1992 conference on the Holocaust in Banská Bystrica. Čarnogurský's role and official position on this occasion made him choose his wording more carefully. However, he still reminded the audience of the Slovak responsibility, though in a very unclear formulation: 'Slovakia's anti-Jewish actions came about during strong

German influence. But we cannot lay all responsibility solely on Germany. We must *examine* the Slovak responsibility for anti-Jewish measures.'[45] This was, however, only on an occasion when a group of historians had gathered to discuss the Holocaust in particular. When he as a politician spoke to 'ordinary Slovaks', Čarnogurský did not use the Holocaust as an example that should define the future's moral values, as the declaration he himself had signed had made so clear.

As Prime Minister, Čarnogurský did not openly criticise the regime that had sent the Slovak Jews to death. The same applied to other members within the party. Čarnogurský did not declare himself to be either against the diasporal interpretation of the Holocaust or against those voices wishing to exonerate Tiso's memory. Because he was the first politician at the highest level in Slovakia who forwarded the demand that the Czech Republic and Slovakia sign a common agreement as 'two sovereign nations' – which could be perceived as two sovereign nation states – and as his party in 1990 had written into its programme a demand that Slovakia as a 'sovereign' country should enter the European house, the KDH's political line was in practice incompatible with the tendency to maintain Czechoslovakia as a federation. At the same point in time, the KDH even created the impression that it stood very close to the diaspora – especially when Čarnogurský during the 1990 election campaign appeared before the voters hand in hand with the new leader of the SWC, Marián Šťastný.[46] Šťastný explained that most members in the SWC thought 'Christian Democratically, Slovak and nationally'.[47]

Any open defence of Tiso and his actions against Jews was, on the other hand, not presented by Čarnogurský or the KDH. When again a member of the government – this time a Minister of Justice – after the division of Czechoslovakia, Čarnogurský questioned in a decisive way his earlier uncompromising position in relation to the Slovak guilt for the Holocaust. On Čarnogurský's initiative, Jozef Mikuš, who was a known anti-Semite and nationalist from the Second World War and, moreover, one of the founders of the SWC, received a high Slovak distinction 'for his long struggle to give the Slovaks an own state'.[48]

The contrast in opinions between 1987 and the beginning of the 1990s was even greater in the man who had become one of the Slovak Church's highest representatives, Ján Chryzostom Korec. He as well had been among those who in 1987 signed the protest against the communist regime ignoring the Holocaust of the Slovak Jews. But Korec was at the same time the man who as early as 1990, as the very first Church representative, publicly honoured Jozef Tiso's memory by unveiling a memorial plaque in Bánovce nad Bebravou. Any explanation of how he could first accuse Tiso's regime and then defend its highest representative was, however, never given. Nonetheless, Korec's action after the fall of communism coincided with the way many leading members of the Catholic Church expressed their appreciation for Tiso's personality, and gave their support for

Czechoslovakia's partition. On the other hand, they did not get involved in the discussions about the deportations and the Holocaust during the war.

Signs of the Church's attitude towards Tiso were manifested, inter alia, during various ceremonies to Tiso's memory, as when in March 1991, almost exactly 52 years after the proclamation of the Slovak war state, a cross on Tiso's grave in Bratislava was consecrated. Two years later, also at Tiso's grave and on a similar occasion, the Catholic priest, Ladislav Šimončík, explained that 'it was not Tiso who was the criminal but those who executed him and in this way insulted the whole Slovak nation and its right to an own state'.[49] Moreover, the Church's highest representatives made it abundantly clear that they gave their support to the nationalists and their conception of the Slovak nation as a compact entity in which Catholicism would play a dominant role. In a pastoral letter expressing the Church's official attitude on the eve of the first free election in 1990, which was read out in all Slovak churches, it was emphasised that all Church members had a duty to vote for such movements that would ensure that people in Slovakia would live 'in accordance with Christian rules corresponding to God's will'.[50] The following year, in March 1991, another public document was published, directed principally at all Christian Slovaks, in which the leading Slovak bishops – including archbishops, Ján Sokol, Ján Chryzostom Korec and Dominik Hrušovský, who served as 'bishop for Slovaks living abroad' – declared that 'our nation is mature enough today to not let itself be politically manipulated by others'.[51]

Like Čarnogurský's Christian Democrats, which the Church stood very close to, particularly during the period 1990–1991, the Church never directly referred to the Holocaust in either a national, religious or any other context. Moreover, its leading representatives, with their Tiso-friendly stance, were never forced to explicitly explain how they viewed the Holocaust. Even when the fiftieth anniversary of the start of the deportations was commemorated in 1992, this complex of problems was met by almost complete silence from the Church.

Those 'history-less' politicians who led the *Hnutie za demokratické slovensko*, which after the 1992 parliamentary election became Slovakia's dominating party, matched in their relation to the Holocaust that which the aforementioned Shari Cohen describes as the opportunistic freedom 'to jump from idea to idea and from party to party'.[52] In the very few cases I have found, Slovakia's highest official political representatives spoke of the Holocaust in extremely cautious terms when the subject could not be avoided. This primarily concerned a ceremony in Nitra in October 1992 where Vladimir Mečiar participated in the capacity of Slovakia's new Prime Minister, together with the Slovak Parliament's new speaker, Ivan Gašparovič, and the Israeli ambassador in Bratislava, Yoel Sher.[53] The ceremony was dedicated to the 6,000 Jewish inhabitants of the town Nitra who had exactly fifty years earlier died in Nazi extermination camps. Mečiar and Sher together unveiled a memorial plaque reminding about the Holocaust. While Mečiar did not speak at all at this ceremony, Gašparovič condemned in his speech 'the fascist regime which caused the tragedy' and reminded listeners that 'our nation has never caused any aggression or violence'. 'Therefore Slovakia fought at the end of the Second World War against the greatest evil of the 1900s – against fascism', Gašparovič emphasised.[54] It was manifest that these two, at the time the highest representatives of the new Slovakia, officially tried to express sympathy for the 6,000 Holocaust victims, while never accepting 'fascism' as Slovak or admitting their own nation's guilt.

With a standpoint of this kind among the leading politicians, it was never possible to initiate a debate that could effectively call into question the claims about the Holocaust which the most radical users of history stood behind. That Mečiar would actually have wanted to do such a thing is doubtful – very soon after Czechoslovakia's dissolution he and his HZDS party entered into a coalition with the ultra-nationalist Slovak National Party.

Matica Slovenská had, historically speaking, great cultural significance for the Slovaks' apprehension of the Slovak national identity during a long period of its existence. It was an organisation whose task was to maintain and develop the Slovak language and culture. Matica was founded in 1863 during the contemporaneous nationalist wave in Europe and became a product of the so-called Slovak national awakening. During the communist period, Matica could not be regarded as an independent political actor, but after 1989 it began to engage itself intensively in the Slovak political arena and utilised its trust amongst the public to give support to the goals of the diaspora and the nationalists. As recently as 1990, Matica demanded a new law that would confirm the Slovak language's dominance in Slovakia. As no other language would be regarded as official there, such a law would adversely affect Slovak Hungarians, Czechs and other minorities as well. The proposal additionally conflicted with the Czechoslovak federal law, which regarded both the Czech and Slovak languages as equal official languages in Czechoslovakia.

As Shari Cohen has pointed out, Matica's position in Slovak society was important to the diaspora's radical nationalists. With its great historical-cultural prestige, Matica was one of the most important actors in the political debate outside the Slovak Parliament, while at the same time not as subject to strong state control as ordinary political and state organisations. Matica's leadership expressed its support for the SWC's general policy, but did not engage itself in the discussions surrounding the Slovak regime's repression of the Jews during the Second World War.[55]

In conclusion one can say that the difference between the radical and the moderate nationalists' standpoints in relation to the Holocaust consisted of an active denial of guilt for the Holocaust, on the one hand, and silence regarding the question of guilt and the Holocaust in general, on the other. I have not been able to find any explanation of why the moderate nationalists did not want or did not dare to use the Holocaust as actively as the radicals, despite the fact that both groups' nationalist goals and their relation to Tiso were not far from each other. However, because the first tendency, radical nationalism, was strongly linked to the diaspora, while the second tendency, the moderate nationalism, was connected to the domestic political forces, the difference can be understood as two, in several respects, different historical cultures. The first was shaped in the diaspora in Canada and the USA and the second in Slovakia and Czechoslovakia. We do not know enough about the Slovak diaspora's place in North American historical culture to be able to draw concrete conclusions. That being said, the situation in Slovakia from this perspective resembles Ukrainian nationalism, which was also to a great degree dominated by the Ukrainian diaspora in the United States and Canada (the Slovak diaspora has, however, received much less attention in the North American context than the Ukrainian). Even in Ukraine, the diaspora was followed by domestic forces, including the 'history-less' communist opportunists. The narrative uniting these forces was developed within another historical culture than the one it was used in, which led to the domestic – in this case Slovak – actors being able to take over the narrative's main features and adapt them to their own aims.[56]

The insufficient opposition

The national-Catholic narrative became successful to a great extent because of the lack of any other competitive historical narrative that could present a credible alternative and which at the same time could link the Slovak future to something other than nationally dominated values. Neither the Slovak Jews, liberally orientated intellectuals, Slovak historians nor any other actors could offer such a narrative.

The Jewish subculture was almost completely absent from the Slovak historical culture during the last decades before 1989. This was first and foremost due to the system's attitude towards the Jews and the very limited number of them left in the country after the war. It is difficult to say with certainty how many Jews there were in Slovakia during the 1980s and beginning of the 1990s, but according to estimates they numbered between 3,000 and 7,000 in a country with about five million inhabitants. Even the highest estimates put the Jewish proportion of the population at no more than two per thousand. Taking this into account, it seems hardly surprising that Jewish historical culture was as good as invisible. The Jews' participation in the public debate was minimal; their voice weak.[57]

Jewish representatives participated in various ceremonies commemorating the fiftieth anniversary of the deportations, but never received comparable attention to that received by the diaspora and its sympathisers in the Slovak mass media. The Holocaust began to be highlighted in the form of various memorial plaques at those places where the deported were moved to before their journey to death, or where they had earlier lived. Between March and October

1992 such plaques were installed at seven different places, which during the war had served as collection points for the deported Jews: Bardejov, Poprad, Komárno, Nové Zámky, Košice, Liptovský Mikuláš and Nitra. But there was still no memorial or museum that could make the memory of the Holocaust more visible in a larger context, and which could be visited by school groups and other young people. Neither were there historical-cultural products such as books or films that could draw the public's attention and at the same time problematise the Holocaust and the Jews' position in Slovak society in a manner that could be compared with the influence of the film, *The Shop on Main Street.*

Despite the small number of Jews and their very limited public activities, there were, according to certain studies, relatively strong anti-Semitic feelings in early post-communist Slovak society. It was to a great degree a question of an 'anti-Semitism without Jews'. In 1991, the sociologists, Zora Bútorová and Martin Bútora, found that as many as 42 per cent of Slovaks thought the Jews had 'too strong an influence in political and economic life'.[58] A year later the figure had risen to 53 per cent.[59] Both sociologists confirmed that the stereotypes mentioned earlier in connection with the interwar era's and post-war period's anti-Semitism remained in Slovakia in the 1990s. It concerned above all the perception of the Jews as 'economically superior' and 'politically too powerful', 'conspiratorial' and 'anti-Slovak'.[60] A similar picture was given by Gila Fatranová who, however, also emphasised the importance of the long-term and, at the start of the 1990s, still-present religious conception of the Jews as the enemies of Christianity.[61] The clearest expression of anti-Semitism consisted of attacks against Jewish cemeteries, as in Trenčín in 1991.[62]

An influential group of intellectuals that could take over the political power and could be linked to a particular historical narrative, like *Charta 77* in the Czech part of Czechoslovakia, did not exist in Slovakia. No liberal group could challenge the national-Catholic historical narrative and its interpretation of the Holocaust, which to a great degree was due to the special character of the Slovak opposition during the communist era. There was no narrative that could not have been dismissed by the nationalists as either 'communist' (at least if one's point of departure was the communist narrative) or 'less Slovak' (if one used the Czech national-liberal narrative). Slovakia consequently lacked its own anti-nationalist and liberally directed narrative that could point society towards a democratic development. The liberal tradition was relatively weak in Slovakia, where nationalism had always been constructed in opposition to first the Hungarian and then the Czech liberal tendencies.[63] The Catholic-nationalist narrative helped the nationalist forces and all others who gave the partition their direct or indirect support for creating and legitimising an independent Slovakia. A competing narrative expressing a new need to legitimise Slovakia's democratic development and future goals did not begin to crystallise until later. I will discuss this in a later chapter on the 'Museum of the Slovak National Uprising' and its relationship to the Holocaust.

Even the Slovak professional historians' contribution to the discussions surrounding the nationalists' treatment of the Holocaust was problematic. The official Slovak historians' situation was limited by the former regime through them being isolated from broader international historical research in general and Holocaust research in particular. Almost all the Slovak professional historians that were still active at the beginning of the 1990s, received their education and were active during the post-1948 communist regime. Some worked within the framework of the communist ideology with enthusiasm; some had problems getting their works published. Ivan Kamenec, for example, wrote his study of the Holocaust in Slovakia, *Po stopách tragédie*, at the end of the 1960s, but it was not published until the start of the 1990s. Others could not write under their own names after having opposed the 1968 invasion. This was, for example, the case with Lubomír Lipták. A few even positioned themselves, after having been active in the communist party, in active opposition against the regime, one of them being Ivan Jablonický, who within the opposition signed the same protest against the Holocaust's absent memory as Ján Chryzostom Korec and Ján Čarnogurský. But almost all of them had to adapt themselves to the totalitarian regime's demands and aims during at least a period of their lives.[64] As Kamenec admitted at the 1992 historians' conference in Bratislava, particularly historians dealing with the modern age could not see themselves solely as victims, but even as the regime's either direct or indirect co-architects – however with varying responsibility.[65] Historians who went against the national-Catholic narrative, therefore, became simple targets for the diaspora's members, who did not have a similar encumbrance in relation to communism. Moreover, it was unclear who could actually be regarded as professional historians. The diaspora's foremost representatives within the field of history, like Vnuk and Ďurica, were presented as historians with professional merits, which gave their conclusions a kind of scientific legitimacy.

It is, however, also important to point out that the opposition to the national-Catholic narrative on the part of the Slovak historians was strongest among those historians engaged in modern history, i.e., Slovakia's development during the 1900s, and who therefore first and foremost criticised the diaspora's glorification of the Slovak war state and its leader. The difference, and the tension, between the two groups was substantially less noticeable when concerning Slovakia's history before the 1900s. A new version of Slovakia's older history, which did not actually stand so far from the diasporal interpretation, was developed in Slovakia as early as during the last years before the collapse of communism.[66]

When just about everybody in the intellectual debate could be accused of strong ideological components in their research, who could actually be apprehended as a 'true scientist'? The public's criteria for what could be perceived as scientific history usage were unclear.

This doubt was expressed in 1992 when the Slovak Academy of Sciences decided to compensate for deficiencies in the research on Jozef Tiso. There was

no scientific Tiso biography on the Slovak book market that could be presented
as an alternative to the diaspora's interpretation of the first Slovak president's
ideas and politics. The Academy therefore organised a conference on Tiso in
Častá-Papiernička near Bratislava in May 1992. The conference bore the name
Pokus o politický a osobný profil Jozefa Tisu ('An attempt to clarify Jozef Tiso's
political and personal profile'). The fact that Ďurica, Vnuk, Kirschbaum and
some others associated with the diaspora's interpretation of Tiso and the Slovak
war state were invited, suggested that the organisers did not dare to exclude
the diaspora's representatives from the scientific circle, even if they – especially
on the grounds of their interpretation of the Holocaust – had been perceived
as 'extreme-right historians'.[67] Another conference in Banská Bystrica, which
solely concerned the Holocaust and was organised with the help of Slovak-
Israeli and Czech-Israeli historians in the same year (more about this later),
chose a completely different approach and it took place strictly without the
diaspora's participation. It was unthinkable that the diaspora's representatives
could be sitting side by side with Israeli Holocaust historians. However, the
price for this was that this conference received a lot less attention than the
meeting in Častá-Papiernička.

In Častá-Papiernička, Tiso's radical supporters were placed in the same category as Slovak researchers. Over a hundred people gathered there, both from
Slovakia and the Czech Republic and a few other countries. The historian
Dušan Kováč, who opened the conference as the representative of the Slovak
Academy of Sciences' Historical Institute, observed that the contributions were
of 'varying quality', without specifying what he meant. He added at the same
time, though, that 'bad contributions sometimes turn up at various conferences'.[68] This meeting lacked a counterpart in the Slovak post-communist
situation.

Jozef Kirschbaum, who about fifty years earlier had been a leading politician
in Hlinka's party, could thus freely defend Tiso's actions in March 1939 when
Slovakia separated from the rest of Czechoslovakia. He described 14 March
1939 as 'a day when the Slovaks constituted themselves as equal members in a
group of European nations' and when they 'identified themselves with Tiso's
person'.[69] Milan Ďurica and František Vnuk presented their contributions: *Dr.
Jozef Tiso v hodnotení Hitlerových diplomatov a tajných agentov* ('Dr Jozef Tiso in
reports written by Hitler's diplomats and secret agents'), and *Retribučné súdnictvo
a proces s Jozefom Tisom* ('The retaliation trials and the trial of Jozef Tiso'). Vnuk
maintained that during Tiso's time as Slovakia's highest leader 'not a single individual was executed in Slovakia'. 'It is impossible to avoid the thought that the
retribution trials in Slovakia where – both theoretically and formally – Slovaks
convicted other Slovaks were groundlessly cruel and disproportionately unjust.'
Vnuk then suggested: 'it is time to see these tragic events from a national and
humane perspective', and made clear that an examination of Tiso's trial 'could
become a pilot case for a delayed yet unavoidable enquiry from a perspective of

justice, European culture and ethics'.[70] When such statements were published in the Slovak press they were often simply introduced as 'debate contributions from a scientific conference'.[71] Contributions from Academy historians were, however, also characterised in the same way. Readers could thereby get the impression that all the opinions were 'scientific' and of equal value.

The professional historians' defensive position in relation to the diaspora's offensive did not mean that they had not published any works on Tiso and the Holocaust. Ivan Kamenec published two books about the Slovak state under Tiso. The first, a short work entitled *Slovenský stát*, dealt with the state and its regime in general terms and was published in the Czech Republic and in the Czech language.[72] The other, already mentioned, *Po stopách tragédie*, which solely concerned the Holocaust, was written more than twenty years earlier, but could not, due to political censorship, be published in the pre-1989 period.[73] Kamenec was also co-editor of another book on Tiso's Slovakia, *Vatikán a Slovenská republika 1939–1945. Dokumenty* ('The Vatican and the Slovak Republic 1939-1945. Documents'), in which letters and documents were presented demonstrating that the Vatican criticised Tiso and his politics, not least those relating to the Holocaust.[74] Last but not least a study, written by Ladislav Lipscher, was published in Slovakia entitled *Židia v slovenskom štáte 1939-1945* ('Jews in the Slovak state 1939–1945').[75] But none of these works were able to receive as much attention in the media and among the general public as the diaspora's and nationalists' own interpretations at this time. Such a development led Lubomír Lipták to directly admit the historians' loss: 'Our enemies look like giants in our eyes. But this is only because we are on our knees.'[76]

The Czech Republic: their Holocaust is not ours

The situation in the Czech lands, Bohemia and Moravia was different to that in Slovakia. During the Second World War they were occupied by Germany. The question of war guilt and responsibility for all war crimes was seen as clear and simple: all guilt was German. The government of Czech citizens which, under the leadership of Germany, helped the Third Reich to govern the Protectorate of Bohemia and Moravia, was 'forgotten', and after the Second World War its existence was hardly mentioned in any of the main narratives. Moreover, the Protectorate's Czech President, Emil Hácha, who during the entire war served the German occupying power, died just after Germany's surrender and there-fore was never put on trial, as opposed to Jozef Tiso. He did not become an important symbol for the Czechs, and his actions during the war never polar-ised Czech society and Czech historical culture in the same way as Tiso did in Slovakia. There was no group of Czechs wanting to defend Hácha in the same way as the Slovak diaspora wished to defend Tiso. A Czech diaspora abroad whose war nostalgia could be compared with the SWC's use of history was completely absent.

At the same time it is important to point out that the Czechs' view of Hácha was never as categorical as that of Jozef Tiso, despite both having actively served Hitler's Germany. While Tiso was unequivocally condemned on the Czech side, Hácha was viewed with significantly less Czech radicalism; some even felt sorry for him because he 'sacrificed' himself and cooperated with the Germans in order to in actual fact help the Czech nation.[77] The communist ideological history usage after 1948 contributed to the fact that Hácha and the Czech Protectorate government, which was subordinate to the German *Reichsprotektor*, were either perceived as non-Czech or almost completely forgotten, like most of the controversial questions regarding the Czech attitude in the Protectorate of Bohemia and Moravia.[78] However, in the only Hácha biography published after the fall of communism, it was observed that 'cooperation with the occupying power was only a tactic to attain a higher goal: the free state, the Czechoslovak Republic's regeneration'.[79] This argument was in fact very similar to the one used in Tiso's defence in Slovakia.

However, the Czechs' relation to the Jews differed from the Slovak's. In the Czechs' behaviour towards Jews there were no violent group actions such as pogroms, either during the interwar period or the post-war era. The Czechs did not contribute to the Holocaust in any way that was similar to the repressive Slovak legislation, and had no organisation whose role in the deportations of the Jews to the extermination camps could be compared with Tiso's Slovakia. As there was relatively little in this context that could provoke the general Czech self-image, the Holocaust was not directly felt to be a 'national burden'.[80]

At the start of the 1990s the silence surrounding the Holocaust of Czech and even Slovak Jews among those who had earlier participated in developing the communist narrative was hardly surprising. A manifest example comprised articles published in *Rudé Právo*, the newspaper that gave most space to history in its pages and which was previously the Czechoslovak Communist Party's official paper. In an article from March 1992, in which the fiftieth anniversary of the commencement of the Slovak deportations was highlighted, only factual information could be found. A few leading Slovak politicians were pointed out as being chiefly responsible for this action. The writer of the article did not attempt to connect the Slovak deportations to the Holocaust. This was thought to lie outside the very clearly demarcated main subject and outside the time frame.[81] When *Rudé Právo* later published another article about the Holocaust – this time more generally orientated – the Holocaust was described solely as a German crime in the Third Reich and the occupied territories, primarily the Polish. Despite the Czech countries also having been occupied, the paper gave no room to the Holocaust's connection to Czech history. It was only briefly mentioned that 272,000 of those Jews living in Czechoslovakia in 1938 lost

Figure 5 The memorial of those Czech Jews who were murdered during the Holocaust. The names of more than 70,000 victims are written on the walls of the Pinkas synagogue in Prague. Photo: Tomas Sniegon

their lives during the war (there was no distinction made between the Czech countries and Slovakia). The Holocaust was treated as a phenomenon that took place between 'Germans' and 'Jews'.[82]

The Holocaust was also missing when the newspaper later in the same year interviewed various historians about the Czech-Slovak relations' historical background, concentrating on Czechoslovakia's coming partition. This was the case even though one of the interviewees, Ivan Kamenec, had just published his aforementioned book on the Holocaust in Slovakia.[83] Even when the Czech archbishop, Miroslav Vlk, was interviewed about the situation in the Czech Catholic Church, the tension that at this time surrounded the question of Jozef Tiso and the Slovak Catholic Church was completely ignored.[84]

The Holocaust was also conspicuously absent from the national-liberal narrative, above all, by members of *Charta 77*, the movement that became known for its fight for human rights. Even the example of Czechoslovakia's first President Masaryk could have been utilised in this context, despite him having died just before the start of the war. Masaryk became internationally recognised because of a very well-known legal case and his battle against Czech anti-Semitism. At the turn of the century, Masaryk publicly defended a Jew, Leopold Hilsner, against false charges of the ritual murder of a young girl, who was actually murdered by her own brother. Hilsner was sentenced to death twice in a lower as well as a higher court. Thanks to Masaryk's isolated initiative, which met strong reactions from the public, Hilsner was first sentenced to life in prison and later, after more than fifteen years, acquitted in 1916. As the historian Ezra Mendelsohn has emphasised, during the interwar period Masaryk was 'the only dominant politician firmly identified with the campaign against anti-Semitism'.[85] However, Masaryk's fight against anti-Semitism never became an important component of the national-liberal narrative.

If the Jews were mentioned within the narrative's framework, it was primarily as proof of Czechoslovakia's unique character in Central Europe during the interwar period, and the Czechs' well-developed democratic culture – nowhere else in the region did the Jews receive as generous opportunities, according to the narrative. This interpretation, making anti-Semitism an exception rather than a rule in Czech society, received support among even non-Czech researchers. Mendelsohn noted in his study of the Jews in East and Central Europe that anti-Semitism was marginal in Czech politics from as early as the nineteenth century which, in his view could be explained by factors such as the Czech intelligentsia's anti-clerical traditions, scepticism towards Habsburg institutions and traditions among Czechs generally, and Czech society's relatively well-developed social structure.[86] As Kristian Gerner points out when describing the Czech Jews' identity as 'a secularised Jewish identity in the Jewish enlightenment's anti-nationalist spirit', the Jews in the Czech lands needed neither to be assimilated nor acculturated.[87] The rich Jewish cultural tradition was well known, particularly in the capital city of Prague. This positive aspect can still, however, be problematised. The Czech historian, Kateřina Čapková, points to Czechoslovakia as the only country in Europe making it possible for Jews to choose 'Jewish' as a nationality, and this was not only a result of the authorities' benevolent relation to Judaism. By making it possible for Jews to identify themselves as such, the Czechoslovak authorities actually wanted to decrease the number of Germans in the republic (those Jews choosing Jewish as their nationality could not at the same time be counted as Germans in the statistics). One did not even need to be a Jew to choose Jewish nationality – almost anyone who wished it could do so.[88] This could, in other words, be interpreted as political tactics rather than coming from a cultural and democratic standpoint.[89]

Prior to 1989 the national-liberal narrative's main bearer, *Charta 77*, issued more than 570 different documents and statements – spread by the Western mass media – which actively debated diverse contemporary and historical events in Czechoslovakia. The only document dealing with the Holocaust and the memory of it was entitled *Kritika devastace židovských kulturních památek a zamlčování úlohy Židů* ('Criticism of the Jewish cultural memorial sites' dilapidation and the concealment of the Jews' role'), and published in April 1989. The Holocaust was used against the communist regime and its attempt to 'forget' the Jews' role in history. But it was never used in the same way as during 'the new wave' of filmmaking in the 1960s, i.e., as a shocking example of repression against the powerless individual. It was instead emphasised that *they*, the

Jews, also had the right not to be forgotten. The ethnic lines were clear, but the official standpoint of *Charta 77* of how they perceived the Jews' place in the Czech national-liberal narrative remained unclear, due to the fact that it was rarely mentioned at all.[90]

The indistinct relationship between the leading Czech intellectuals and the Holocaust continued even after 1989. Since becoming president at the end of 1989, Václav Havel formally pointed out the importance of remembering the Holocaust, both during his visit to Israel and at the time of the Israeli President Herzog's visit to Prague and Theresienstadt in 1991. Besides this, Havel had a short meeting with the French director of the film, *Shoah*, Claude Lanzmann, when he was present at the film's premiere in Prague in May 1991. This was the first time Lanzmann's film could be seen in Czechoslovakia. *Shoah* was, however, shown at only one cinema in Prague in association with the French Institute in the capital city. Claude Lanzmann's film was never shown to a larger public, via, for example, Czechoslovak television.

Jiří Dienstbier, a journalist and dissident who after 1989 became Czechoslovakia's Foreign Minister, displayed the same attitude, when he together with his Israeli counterpart, Moshe Arens, re-established the countries' diplomatic relations in 1990, which had been severed in 1967. But neither Havel nor anyone else demonstrated any personal engagement in the subject by, for instance, using the Holocaust in various domestic political debates, including the Czech-Slovak debate. The discussions in Slovakia were seen as an internal Slovak matter.

Why had the Holocaust never become a burning question in the joint relations between Czechs and Slovaks? It could, of course, from a Czech point of view, be used as a simple illustration of the Czechs' superiority and 'the Slovaks' democratic immaturity' in the same way the author, Ludvík Vaculík, did when he used the Tiso regime's other aspects as examples. By such means it would also be possible to reject the Slovak nationalists' charges against the Czechs and their dominating position in Masaryk's Czechoslovakia, and thereby undermine the nationalists' credibility. The Holocaust as a warning example could easily have compromised both the Hlinka party's image as a 'warrior for the nation's interest' and the SWC' demands of the early 1990s.

The explanation – or at least an important part of it – can be sought in the fact that there had never been a three-part relationship between Czechs, Slovaks and Czechoslovak Jews which could have linked together Czechs and Slovaks with the Jewish tragedy in a single debate. In order to better understand this aspect one can, as an illustration, bring forward a situation between the two dominating peoples in former Yugoslavia, and compare the Holocaust's place in the relation between Czechs and Slovaks with how the Holocaust was used in the relation between Serbs and Croats. There were many similarities between the two countries of Czechoslovakia and Yugoslavia: both were created after the First World War; both were constructed as Slavonic border areas (Yugoslavia united southern Slavs, Czechoslovakia western Slavs) in ethnically very sensitive regions. In both cases the larger and dominating nation's territory was occupied by Germany in the Second World War, while the smaller nation was for the first time in history allowed to create its own nation state, though only in the capacity of Germany's vassal. Both had pro-Nazi regimes during the war – the Croatian and the Slovak – and the Catholic religion as one of the most important foundations. In both these examples the Jews were subjected to the Holocaust and both countries became communist after the Second World War. Even so, at the start of the 1990s the Holocaust appeared in discussions between Serbs and Croats but was hardly visible at all in discussions between Czechs and Slovaks. Why?

That which manifestly separates the two cases is that Slovaks and Czechs – as opposed to Croats and Serbs – did not kill each other during the war. As Kerstin Nyström points out, the Holocaust began to be used in debates between Croats and Serbs at the start of the 1990s, not as a memory of the killing of Croatian and Serbian Jews in itself, but above all in connection with the memories of the Croats' and Serbs' violent conflict during the Second World War.[91] The side perceived as most guilty of the Holocaust in the Balkan case was the Croatian movement Ustaša (which in the Slovak case, taking into account the absolute power of the Nazi-friendly nation state, could be likened to the Hlinka party) seen as responsible for 'the Holocaust of Serbs' in the Croatian state. The Hlinka party could not, however, be accused of 'the Holocaust of Czechs'.

It was therefore not necessary at the beginning of the 1990s to fear that the nationalism dominating the early Slovak post-communist development could escalate into a threat to the Czech minority in Slovakia. Following the conscious non-use of the Holocaust during the greater part of the communist epoch, and especially after the normalisation period, the Slovaks were in the Czech historical culture often ascribed a collective guilt for having destroyed the Czechoslovak interwar democracy with their nationalism, though not for having carried out genocide and war crimes against another nation or ethnic group. In other words, the Slovaks became traitors in the eyes of Czechs, but not murderers. And as the Czech historical culture did not pay attention to 'its own' Jews, it became even easier to 'look away from' the Slovak Jews' fate in the Second World War.

The Czechs who lived in exile during the post-war period also did not show any manifest interest in the Holocaust, with the natural exception of the relatively few who emigrated to Israel and had themselves survived the Holocaust. In contrast to the situation in Slovakia, there was no group that could be classified as a Czech diaspora. The Czech mass emigration – like the Slovak – took place in two waves: the first at the end of the 1940s in connection with the communist takeover of power, and the second at the end of the 1960s, related to the violent termination of the Prague Spring movement. The difference between these two Czech waves did not, however, consist of different views of the Second World War as in the Slovak case. During the first late-1940s wave many Slovaks fled not only from Communist rule but also because they feared revenge and punishment for their wartime actions. Most people who fled from the Czech part of Czechoslovakia did so because they did not want to accept Communist rule.

Any clear and uniform view of the Holocaust was thus absent among the exiled Czechs, as most of them abroad feeling the need to comment on this question expressed an adherence to the national-liberal narrative in which the Holocaust had hardly existed.[92] In this respect there was a certain similarity between the Czech exile and the Slovak non-nationalist exile, i.e., the Slovak exiles who did not belong to the diaspora and who saw the national-liberal narrative as Czechoslovak.[93] How little the Holocaust meant to Czech exiles can perhaps be best illustrated by Pavel Tigrid, one of the most influential Czech intellectuals who left Czechoslovakia at the end of the 1940s. Tigrid was among those who during the early Cold War established the Czech section of Radio Free Europe. He additionally started a journal entitled *Svědectví* ('Testimony') in 1956, which was first published in the USA and subsequently in Paris. Both these media had an important role among Czech exiles and even for those who managed to read *Svědectví* and listen to Radio Free Europe illegally in Czechoslovakia itself. After having returned to Czechoslovakia at the beginning of the 1990s, Pavel Tigrid first became President Havel's advisor and then Minister of Culture.

Tigrid's most well-known book was *Kapesní průvodce inteligentní ženy po vlastním osudu* ('An intelligent woman's pocket guide to her own fate'), first printed by the most important Czech exile publishing company, Sixty-Eight Publishers in Toronto, Canada. Due to foreign radio transmissions the book attracted a lot of attention, even prior to the fall of the Iron Curtain when interest in history grew strong concurrently with the increasingly greater openness in the Soviet Bloc of the time. Shortly thereafter, in 1990, the book was re-published, this time in Czechoslovakia itself. It became one of the very first non-communist summaries of Czechoslovakia's modern history published in post-communist Czechoslovakia.

Kapesní průvodce inteligentní ženy po vlastním osudu is composed as an imaginary conversation between an old man and a young woman taking place outside Czechoslovakia. The man is to give the woman a 'historically motivated' answer to the question of whether she should remain outside Czechoslovakia's borders or return and seek her future in her homeland. The man refuses to give a direct answer, but tries to explain to her why the situation is the way it is. The simple plot was consequently just the framework for a number of lessons on Czech and Czechoslovak history. The fact that this book was a summarising alternative to the communist narrative was the main factor behind its success.

The term *Holocaust* did not appear on any of the book's 570 pages. The Nazi genocide during the Second World War was mentioned only fragmentarily when Tigrid, without further references or explanations, noted that there had been 78,154 Czech victims of the Nazi terror.[94] Neither were the Jews mentioned when the author wrote of Reinhard Heydrich, one of the Holocaust's primary architects, who was killed in Prague in 1942. The focus was placed – again – solely on Czechs and the Czech nation: 'The basis of Heydrich's plan was to either germanise or physically liquidate almost all Czechs. This meant genocide.'[95] The Holocaust's absence here was strange for two reasons: firstly, Tigrid wrote his popular history of Czechoslovakia in exile, outside communist censorship, and secondly, he was himself born in 1917 in a Czech-Jewish family. However, according to certain sources from the time of the Second World War, Tigrid converted to Catholicism when he lived in exile in London and his political orientation became for the most part Christian Democrat.[96]

The major question in the Czech context is whether the absence of the Holocaust among those regarded as the national-liberal narrative's support-ers can also be seen as a non-use of history – in other words, something that in the Czech case above all characterised the communist historical narrative. It is not usual to automatically link together the ideological use of history with defence of the liberal values among parliamentary-democratic societies, to which the Czech Republic and Czechoslovakia wanted to be counted after the fall of communism. And one does not immediately think of ideological history usage in relation to *Charta 77*, when observing these human rights activists challenging the communist ideology.

However, the situation is considerably more complicated than this. It is, firstly, difficult to demarcate which relationship to the Holocaust and which use of history should be seen as typical for the liberally orientated elites, not only in the Czech Republic but also in the far more developed and stable Western democratic societies. As the historian, Tony Kushner, shows in his study on the Holocaust and the liberal imagination, not even the USA and Britain could demonstrate any 'typical' liberal way of how to deal with the Holocaust and its memory.[97]

It should also not be forgotten that *Charta 77* did not construct their version of the national-liberal narrative as a 'purely' liberal one, but rather as a mixture of various tendencies and ideologies, whose sole common connective link was a demand to be rid of the communist party's dominating role in society and introduce a more pluralistic political system and market economy. The Czech historian, Milan Otáhal, characterises this mixture using the questionable term 'non-political politics'.[98] However, despite the indistinct profile, certain Charta members perceived their movement as a blend of above all two main currents – the Catholic and the 'non-dogmatic Marxist'; the latter, however, having its roots in earlier Czechoslovak Marxist-Leninist ideology.[99]

Soon after its establishment there were no fewer than thirty historians among the Charta members, of whom most were previously civil servants within the Academy of Sciences and other official structures governed by communist ideology. They lost their jobs after the final collapse of the Prague Spring for repudiating the Warsaw Pact's invasion of Czechoslovakia. Some of them, like Jan Křen, Ján Mlynárik or Jaromír Navrátil, had important roles as historians shortly after the fall of communism, but they showed even then little interest in the Holocaust. The insufficient attentiveness towards the Holocaust could be understood in a certain relation to the respective ideologies they were influenced by prior to changing their political standpoint. Ideological factors were therefore manifestly present even within Charta, which indicates a non-use of history in this case also. Even the relation between the Holocaust and the national-liberal narrative with its national framework can be seen as ideologically characterised: interest in the Holocaust was lacking here in the same way as interest in Emil Hácha's government and the whole Czech aspect of the Protectorate's activities: in fact everything that did not concern the Czech role as Germany's unequivocal victim.

Even the group of radical conservative economists who were not Charta members before 1989 but in certain other aspects gave their support to the national-liberal narrative could, in relation to the Holocaust, be apprehended as adherents of a non-use of history. The economists joined a non-use of history in a number of respects, above all on the domestic politics stage when they attempted to turn the public's attention towards the future instead of the past. The group's ideal was expressed by its main representative, Václav Klaus in the following way: 'What we need is a positive *economic* ideal. We need this in order to be able to move ourselves from waiting to active enterprise, in order to in the economic sphere be able to distinguish between the correct and the false values.'[100] It was obvious that the need to remember the Holocaust in such a context was minimal.

Concluding remarks

The Slovak diaspora, which adapted the Holocaust to the heroic nationalist image of Jozef Tiso, became the most dominant actor in relation to the Holocaust in Czechoslovakia in the 1990–1992 era. All other actors were marginal. While the diasporal and nationalist interpretation made the Holocaust visible within the Slovak historical culture, the Nazi genocide of Jews and other groups remained a non-subject in the Czech historical culture. The development initiated after the Stalin era, which, despite the official attitude, highlighted the Holocaust in Czechoslovak literature and films, primarily in an individualised form, was not renewed during the first years after the fall of communism. The Holocaust was no longer needed as a metaphor for the individual's fight against a totalitarian power. However, it was not the powerless Jew who at the start of the 1990s was portrayed as the war's victim, but 'the ordinary

Czech' and even 'the ordinary Slovak'; something which will be shown even more clearly in the following chapters.

Because the Holocaust was one of the major war crimes of which the Tiso regime was guilty, the nationalists wished to move focus away from the question of Tiso's personal responsibility and guilt, and also to exonerate the 'Slovak nation'. The pressure from the outside world was at the same time minimal – even Stanislav Pánis's attempt to deny the Holocaust was met with very little opposition in the developed democracies of the West. An equally weak foreign reaction was inconceivable when the Europeanisation process got started a few years later.

Notes

1. For more about this process, see, for example, Zdeněk Hojda and Jiří Pokorný, *Pomníky a zapomníky*, Prague and Litomyšl: Paseka, 1996, 192–243.

2. Leff, *The Czech and Slovak Republics*, 129–32; and Sarauw, *Together We Part*, 54–58.

3. Cohen, *Politics Without a Past*, 6.

4. Lubomír Kopeček, 'Proměny moderní slovenské politiky', in Lubomír Kopeček, ed., *Od Mečiara k Dzurindovi. Slovenská politika a politický systém v prvním desetiletí samostatnosti*, Brno: Masarykova univerzita, 2003, 19.

5. Lubomír Kopeček, 'Stranický systém Slovenska', in P. Fiala and R. Herbut, a kol., *Středoevropské systémy politických stran. Česká republika, Maďarsko, Polsko a Slovensko*, Brno: Masarykova univerzita, 2003, 163–64.

6. Mark Stolarik, 'Slovak Historians in Exile in North America, 1945–1992', *Human Affairs* 6, 1996, 34–44.

7. The federal parliament during the era of Czechoslovakia comprised two chambers: *Sněmovna lidu* and *Sněmovna národů* (the People's chamber and Nations' chamber). The latter was divided into two sections – the Czech national council and Slovak national council. After having served as the Slovak national council's chairman, though still before 1993, Schuster was appointed Czechoslovakia's last ambassador to Canada. After the country's partition he became the second president in the history of an independent Slovakia.

8. Rychlík, *Rozpad Československa*, 52–56.

9. One of the first books in Tiso's defence was published as early as 1947 by Konstantín Čulen, who worked as a functionary in the Hlinka party during the war. Soon after the war's end Čulen emigrated to North America and became active as a journalist within the diaspora. See Čulen, *Po Svätoplukovi druhá naša hlava*. One of the last publications before communism's fall was a book of memoirs written by Karol Murín, Tiso's former private secretary, with the title *Spomienky a svedectvo* (Hamilton, Ontario, 1987). Among other such authors were Jozef Paučo, who during the Tiso regime was editor-in-chief of the newspaper, *Slovák*, the Hlinka party's and Slovak government's official paper during the Second World War, and Fraňo Tiso, former Slovak ambassador to the Soviet Union between 1939 and 1941. After 1950 Jozef Paučo lived in the USA, and Fraňo Tiso in Canada.

10. Vojtech Tuka had been active in the Slovak nationalist movement and the Hlinka party since as early as the 1920s. In 1929 he was sentenced as a Hungarian spy by a Czechoslovak court to fifteen years in prison, which led to strong protests from the Hlinka party. Tuka was released in 1937 and immediately became active once more in Slovak politics. He participated at Tiso's side in the negotiations with Hitler and became both Slovakia's prime minister and, after 1940, foreign minister. The conviction for espionage for Hungary from the interwar period began to be used by Tiso-friendly Slovaks against Tuka after the war as proof of his treasonable character.

It was claimed that he acted behind Tiso's back and carried out independent politics which were in actual fact against Slovakia and Tiso. See, for example, Ján Smolec, 'Slovensko sa na fašismis iba hralo', in Hoffman, *Zamlčená pravda o Slovensku*, 145.

11. Rychlík, *Rozpad Československa*, 54.

12. Jozef Špetko, *Líšky kontra ježe. Slovenská politická emigrácia 1948–1989*, Bratislava: Kalligram, 2002, 103–4.

13. As a functionary with Jewish origins, Löbl was an exception within the SWC. He was set free in 1960 and all charges against him were dismissed as false in 1963. Löbl emigrated from Czechoslovakia after 1968 and died in 1987. As an economist who stood close to the SWC's main sponsor, Štefan Roman, he was not regarded as among the most radical within the SWC. His presence in its leadership suggests that there were diverse currents within the organisation.

14. See Jozef Kirschbaum, ed., *Desať rokov činnosti Svetového kongresu Slovákov*, Toronto: SWC 1981, 8.

15. See, for example, František Braxátor, *Slovenský exil 68*, Bratislava: LUČ, 1992, 140–82.

16. Rychlík, *Rozpad Československa*, 54.

17. Kirschbaum, *Desať rokov Svetového kongresu Slovákov*, 52. See also Jozef Kirschbaum, *Slovaks In Canada*, Canadian Ethnic Press Association of Ontario, 1967.

18. Milan Ďurica was born in 1925 and František Vnuk in 1926.

19. The question of why the deportations were actually stopped in 1942 when there were still several tens of thousands of Jews still in Slovakia is even now partly open and is explained by several factors, including an increasing opposition to the regime amongst the Slovak public. See, for example, Lipscher, *Židia v slovenskom štáte*, 151–60. The diasporal interpretation is, however, based solely on the assertion that it was a question of a humanitarian step when the truth became known, and that the initiative came from above.

20. František Vnuk, 'Slovenské dejiny bez ilúzií a príkras. František Bošňák – slovenský Schindler', in Hoffman, *Zamlčená pravda o Slovensku*, 522.

21. Ibid., 527–37.

22. Milan Ďurica, *Slovenský národ a jeho štátnosť*, Padova: Cleup, 1989, 27.

23. Milan Ďurica, 'Dr. Jozef Tiso v hodnotení Hitlerových diplomatov a tajných agentov', in Valerián Bystrický and Štefan Fano, eds, *Pokus o politický a osobný profil Jozefa Tisu. Zborník materiálov z vedeckého sympózia Častá-Papiernička, 5.-7. mája 1992*, Bratislava: Slovak Academic Press, 1992, 177–94.

24. Milan Ďurica, *The Political Activities of Dr. Jozef Kirschbaum in 1939–1945 as Described in Secret German Documents*, Abano Terme: Piovan Editore, 1988, 49.

25. Ďurica, 'Dr. Jozef Tiso v hodnotení Hitlerových diplomatov a tajných agentov', 194.

26. A few dozen texts in Tiso's defence, included in the Catholic-nationalist narrative – where Ďurica and Vnuk were the main representatives in regard to the use of history – were collected and published in the group's most important project dealing with history: a book entitled *Zamlčaná pravda o Slovensku* ('The concealed truth about Slovakia'). The work was published with the assistance of Matica slovenská in 1996.

27. The 'Jozef Tiso Society' claimed to be a non-political organisation fighting for the truth about the first Slovak state, and with no links to any political party. On the other hand, members could not be former communists; neither were 'atheists' accepted.

28. Mendelsohn, *Jews of East Central Europe*, 140.

29. Kristian Gerner, *Centraleuropas historia*, Stockholm: Natur och kultur, 2004, 274.

30. In 1921, 16.5 per cent of the Jews in Slovakia said their nationality was Hungarian; in 1930 the figure had decreased to 9 per cent. The relation to Czechoslovakia developed in the opposite direction – in 1921, 22 per cent of Slovak Jews felt themselves to be Slovaks (Czechoslovaks), increasing to 32 per cent in 1930. In the same year there were in total 136,737 inhabitants of Jewish faith (it was possible to state both Jewish faith and Jewish nationality) in Slovakia, which corresponded to 4.11 per cent of the whole Slovak population. Only half of the believing Slovak Jews (47.8 per cent) said their nationality was Jewish; while 7 per cent stated it to be German.

31. *ČTK*, 12 December 1992.

32. See, for example, Gila Fatranová, 'Historicky pohlad na vzťahy slovenského a židovského obyvatelstva', *Acta Judaica Slovaca 4*, Bratislava: SNM – Múzeum židovskej kultury, 1998, 9–37; Pavol Mešťan, *Antisemitizmus v politickom vývoji Slovenska 1989–1999*, Bratislava SNM – Múzeum židovskej kultury, 2000, 45–67.

33. Ďurica's opinion on this question can be found in summarised form in primarily two texts: Milan Ďurica, 'Dr. Jozef Tiso a problém Židov na Slovensku', and 'Slovenský podiel na európskej tragédii Židov'– both in Hoffmann, *Zamlčená pravda o Slovensku*, 479–86 and 490–520.

34. Among researchers the problem with Tiso's exemptions has been discussed by, for example, Gila Fatranová, who questioned the diaspora's figures and presented four sources as being the only ones documenting Tiso's activities. Fatranová established that Tiso granted a total of 250 exemptions, which could save about 1,000 Jewish lives. See Gila Fatranová, 'K deportáciam slovenských Židov v roce 1942', in Robert Büchler, Gila Fatranová and Stanislav Mičev, eds, *Slovenskí Židia*, Banská Bystrica: Múzeum SNP, 1991, 48–50. Fatranová pointed out at the same time that the exemptions were not granted for humanitarian reasons, but rather on the basis of economic interests and for a high price. This was confirmed by other Slovak researchers who, however, arrived at different conclusions regarding the exact number of exemptions. The historian, Ivan Kamenec, asserts, for instance, in his study of the Holocaust in Slovakia, that the number of exemptions was 800–1,000, meaning circa 4,000–5,000 saved people (even the family members of those receiving the president's exemption were spared deportation). See Kamenec, *Po stopách tragédie*, 127. Ladislav Lipscher provides information that 1,111 people were saved by Tiso's exemptions; this figure includes family members. See Lipscher, *Židia v slovenskom štáte*, 162.

35. Ďurica, *Dejiny Slovenska a Slovákov*, 162.

36. During the period 1994–1998 Slovakia was governed by a coalition government, as the dominant party, the *Hnutie za demokratické Slovensko* (the 'Movement for a Democratic Slovakia' [HZDS]) with the autocratic Prime Minister, Vladimír Mečiar, at its head, could not achieve its own majority. As a result of this government's character and politics, Slovakia was internationally isolated. The participation of the SNS in the government was an important cause of this isolation.

37. *Práca*, 19 April 1997.

38. *Sme*, 26 June 1997.

39. *Sme*, 2 July 1997.

40. *Národná obroda*, 4 July 1997.

41. See Cohen, *Politics Without a Past*, 158–60.

42. See, for example, Pánis's article 'Kto vlastne vraždil?', *Slovák – Slovenská národná jednota*, II, Nr. 1, 4.

43. Pavol Čarnogurský, *14 marec 1939*, Bratislava: Veda, 1992.

44. The document, marking the 45th anniversary of the commencement of the deportations, was reprinted in Ján Čarnogurský, *Videné od Dunaja*, Bratislava: Kalligram, 1997, 122–24.

45. Ibid., 208.

46. Marián Šťastný was earlier an ice hockey player for the Czechoslovak national team, but emigrated to Canada in the 1970s. He replaced Tóth in the SWC's leadership in the spring of 1990.

47. *ČTK*, 5 June 1990.

48. Jozef Mikuš was a Slovak diplomat during the Second World War, representing Tiso's regime in the Vatican State and later in Spain. After the war he engaged himself in the diaspora while in exile in the USA.

49. *ČTK*, 14 March 1992.

50. *Katolícke noviny* 19, 1990.

51. See Mešťan, *Antisemitizmus v politickom vývoji Slovenska 1989-1999*, 60–61.

52. Cohen, *Politics Without a Past*, 6.

53. In 2005 Gašparovič became the independent post-communist Slovakia's third president after Michal Kováč and Rudolf Schuster.

54. *ČTK*, 21 October 1992.

55. Cohen, *Politics Without a Past*, 134–36.

56. See Dietsch, *Making Sense of Suffering*, 111–46.

57. The voice of the Slovak Jewish minority began to first be heard a little more towards the close of the 1990s. See Ivan Kamenec, 'Problémy asimilácie židovského obyvateľstva na Slovensku', in Kamenec, *Hladanie a blúdenie v dejinách*, 312–24.

58. Zora Bútorová and Martin Bútora, 'Wariness towards Jews as an Expression of Post-Communist Panic: The Case of Slovakia', *Czechoslovak Sociological Review* 28, 1992, 97.

59. Zora Bútorová and Martin Bútora, 'A Varying Approach: Attitudes towards Jews and Jewish Issues in Slovakia', *East European Jewish Affairs* 23(1), Summer 1993, 12.

60. Zora Bútorová and Martin Bútora, *Attitudes Towards Jews and the Holocaust in Independent Slovakia*, New York: American Jewish Committee, 1995.

61. Gila Fatranová, 'The Viability of Anti-Semitic Manifestations', in Raphael Vago, ed., *Anti-Semitism at the End of the 20th Century*, Bratislava: Judaica Slovaca, 2002, 125–37.

62. For more about manifestations of anti-Semitism in Slovakia, see Mešťan, *Antisemitizmus v politickom vývoji Slovenska*, 155–69.

63. See Dušan Kováč, *Dějiny Slovenska*, Prague: NLN, 2002, 146; and Špetko, *Líšky kontra ježe*, 36–43.

64. Cohen, *Politics Without a Past*, 95–96.

65. Ivan Kamenec, 'Ako sa vidíme sami a ako nás vidí verejnos', *Historický časopis* 39(4–5), 1991, 488–91.

66. See Gil Eyal, 'Identity and Trauma: Two Forms of the Will to Memory', *History & Memory* 16(1), Spring/Summer 2004, 13–19.

67. See Hlavičková, 'Wedged Between National and Trans-National History', 285.

68. Introduction by Dušan Kováč in Bystrický and Fano, *Pokus o politický a osobný profil Jozefa Tisu*, 12.

69. Ibid., 113.

70. František Vnuk, 'Retribučné súdnictvo a proces s Jozefom Tisom', in Bystrický and Fano, *Pokus o politický a osobný profil Jozefa Tisu*, 289–90.

71. A number of the contributions were published in full, in, for example, the magazine *Výber*.

72. Ivan Kamenec, *Slovenský štát*, Prague: Anomal, 1992.

73. Kamenec, *Po stopách tragédie*.

74. Kamenec, Prečan and Škorvánek, *Vatikán a Slovenská republika 1939-1945*.

75. Lipscher, *Židia v slovenskom štáte 1939-1945*. Lipscher was one of those exiled Slovaks not belonging to the diaspora.

76. Lipták, *Storočie dlhšie ako sto rokov*, 155. The text reprinted in this book was first published in 1990.

77. See Tomáš Pasák, *JUDr. Emil Hácha (1938–1945)*, Prague: Horizont, 1997, 10.

78. I also analyse this complex of problems in the chapter on the Holocaust of Roma, Porrajmos, in relation to the Czech authorities' responsibility concerning the repression of Roma from Bohemia and Moravia.

79. Pasák, *JUDr. Emil Hácha (1938-1945)*, 255.

80. Cf. Rothkirchen, *The Jews of Bohemia and Moravia*, 303–5.

81. *Rudé Právo*, 26 March 1992.

82. *Rudé Právo*, 4 July 1992.

83. *Rudé Právo*, 21 November 1992. Interview with Ivan Kamenec and the Czech historian Robert Kvaček. The same thing also applied to other interviews with historians, for instance, with Vilém Prečan and Jindřich Pecka, published in *Rudé Právo*, 27 October 1992.

84. *Rudé Právo*, 16 November 1992.

85. Mendelsohn, *Jews of East and Central Europe*, 139.

86. Ibid., 138–39.

87. Gerner, *Centraleuropas historia*, 274.

88. Kateřina Čapková, *Češi, Němci, Židé? Národní identita Židů v Čechách*, Litomyšl: Paseka, 2005, 27–53.

89. A total of 180,855 people in Czechoslovakia stated in 1921 that their nationality was Jewish. Among Czechoslovakia's 13,613,172 inhabitants there were at this time 354,000 Jews. In other words, more than 50 per cent of the Czechoslovak Jews chose Jewish nationality. See Rothkirchen, *The Jews of Bohemia and Moravia*, 29. Nationality was not the same as citizenship – even those choosing another nationality than Czech/Czechoslovak were Czechoslovak citizens.

90. Blanka Císařovská and Vilém Prečan, *Charta 77: Dokumenty*, Prague: Ústav pro soudobé dějiny AV ČR, 2007.

91. Kerstin Nyström, 'The Holocaust and Croatian National Identity. An Uneasy Relationship', in Karlsson and Zander, *Post-War Battlefields*, 259–88.

92. I have found no research at all on the memory of the Holocaust among 'exiled Czechs' and therefore consider that the subject has hitherto been treated as marginal. Even the most recent studies published in English, such as Heitlinger's book *In the Shadows of the Holocaust*, 125–42; and Rothkirchen's *The Jews of Bohemia and Moravia*, give almost no attention to this question. Even those Jews who emigrated from Czechoslovakia during the communist era cannot be seen as a uniform group because, as Heitlinger points out, it was not at all difficult for them to identify themselves with and adapt to their new countries.

93. See Špetko, *Líšky kontra ježe*, 106–16.

94. Pavel Tigrid, *Kapesní průvodce inteligentní ženy po vlastním osudu*, Toronto: Sixty-Eight Publishers, 1988, 268.

95. Ibid., 262.

96. See, for example, Tomáš Pěkný, 'Pavel Tigrid 1917–2003', *Roš Chodeš* 3, 2003.

97. Kushner, *The Holocaust and the Liberal Imagination*.

98. Milan Otáhal, *Normalizace 1969–1989: Příspěvek ke stavu bádání*, Prague: ÚSD AV ČR, 2002.

99. Milan Hübl, *Svár dvou pojetí českých dějin*. Informace o Chartě 77, červenec-srpen 1984. See also: http://www.sds.cz/docs/prectete/epubl/mhk_kpnd.htm and http://www.sds.cz/docs/prectete/epubl/mh_sdpcd.htm.

100. Václav Klaus, *O tvář zítřka*, Prague: Pražská imaginace, 1991, 37.

CHAPTER 4

Schindler's List arrives in Schindler's homeland

Oskar Schindler as a problem of Czech historical culture

Schindler's List, one of the most important but also most controversial films on the Holocaust, came to Europe in February 1994, two months after its first release in the USA. At the time of its first European showing in Vienna on 16 February 1994, this Steven Spielberg film was already well-known and widely discussed as a successful Hollywood project, awarded with three Golden Globes in the United States. Only a few weeks later, *Schindler's List* also won seven Academy Awards. Soon after showing in Vienna, the film opened in Germany and Poland, two countries strongly connected to Oskar Schindler's life. In Germany, *Schindler's List* opened on 1 March 1994 in Frankfurt, the city where Oskar Schindler spent the last sixteen years of his life.[1]

In the Czech Republic, the film had an official premiere on 10 March in Prague, with President Václav Havel as one of the prominent members of the audience. In this respect, the importance of the Czech opening was similar to the one in Frankfurt, where German President Richard von Weiszäcker supported the event. In the Czech case, however, the film was previewed the day before in the little town of Svitavy, German Zwittau, where Oskar Schindler was born on 28 April 1908.[2] At the time of his birth, Zwittau belonged to Austria-Hungary. In 1994, however, it was a part of the newly created Czech Republic. During Oskar Schindler's lifetime, the town was included in two other states – the Republic of Czechoslovakia (1918–1938 and later 1945–1992) and the Third Reich of Adolf Hitler (1938–1945). Thus, by the

Notes for this section begin on page 131.

age of 37, Schindler had already had Austrian, Czechoslovak and German citizenships.

Among the more than three million Germans in Czechoslovakia between the wars who had never lived in German territory, but who spoke German and not Czech or Slovak as their mother tongue and kept German culture alive, Oskar Schindler was by no means exceptional. Most of these Sudeten Germans[3] were forced to leave Czechoslovakia soon after the war. They were punished by Czechoslovak authorities and people for their earlier support of Adolf Hitler's Third Reich and its terror and violence against Czechoslovakia.

The great success of *Schindler's List*, however, made its main hero a 'Good Nazi', symbolising German goodness that contrasted sharply with the image of collective guilt of all Germans for the Holocaust. Furthermore, it started a new and extensive discussion about this former public taboo. Suddenly, Oskar Schindler became the most famous Sudeten German in the world. Almost fifty years after the end of the Second World War, his glorification provoked new and strong feelings in his homeland, the Czech Republic. As the film story approached the real world, the past once again approached the Czech present.

In the film, Schindler's real roots were never properly mentioned. Even though he was taking 'his' Jews from Cracow to 'Czechoslovakia', and his hometown Zwittau, he identified himself in the simplest possible way in a single dialogue with his accountant during the very first meeting between the two men: First, the accountant says to Schindler: 'By the law, I have to tell you, Sir, I am a Jew.' 'Well, I am a German', Schindler answers. In fact, not only Spielberg, but even a great majority of viewers and reviewers outside Czech borders, did not care about Schindler's real origin. *Schindler's List* was a story of the Holocaust. In this context, nothing else was important. In the Czech context, however, this ethnic dimension could not be ignored. As I am going to show, it became the main focus.

The task of this chapter is to analyse how *Schindler's List* and its Sudeten German hero fit into the Czech identity-building of the 1990s. In Czech historical culture, Czech-German relations in the past were highlighted during most of this period. On the one hand, groups in the post-Communist Czech Republic indicated very soon after the Velvet Revolution that they wanted to clean its image and right the wrongs of the past. According to one very early initiative of President Václav Havel, the Czechs should even send their excuses to the Sudeten Germans for crimes and unnecessary violence during the transfer of the Czech Germans in 1945. While a general transfer[4] of German minorities from Central and Eastern Europe to Germany and Austria was approved by the Allied powers at Potsdam in 1945, the Czechs considered this officially agreed framework insufficient and too slow. Already before the Potsdam Conference, they organized a more radical and violent, so called wild, transfer of the ethnic Germans. Havel's main political ideas of 'life in truth' and 'victory of truth and love over lie and hatred' could not be harmonised with a continuous traditional

Figure 6 A memorial dedicated to Oskar Schindler in his hometown Svitavy, in German Zwittau. The house where Schindler was born in 1908 is seen here as well. However, a memorial plaque to honour Schindler could not be placed directly on the house since the owner in 1994 refused to accept it due to Schindler's ethnic origin and Nazi past. Photo: Tomas Sniegon

picture of innocent Czechs, seen more or less implicitly as German victims. In this idea, the Czechs were supposed to humanise their future by uncovering and discussing unpleasant moments of their own history and seeking reconciliation with their victims. Here, thanks to Schindler and the Holocaust, one such opportunity had appeared.

On the other hand, there were voices both inside and outside the Czech Republic that feared a newly growing influence of the reunited Germany in Europe and in the world. For these voices, any 'amnesty' for Nazi crimes during the Second World War was unacceptable. In the Czech context, such an opinion, perceptible especially among the oldest generations, was combined with a fear that the once-expelled Sudeten Germans could return and claim back their former properties. In such a context, even the 'good German', Schindler, despite his help to the Jews, became a problematic and threatening figure. But who was Oskar Schindler? Who were the main protagonists in this dispute of Czech historical culture, and what role did the Holocaust actually play in this process?

Oskar Schindler created by Steven Spielberg

Schindler's List begins as the story of an unimportant businessman, gambler and womaniser, who at the right time sees an opportunity that only war can offer. He forces some Jews to do business with him under, for them, very unfair terms. With the golden badge of the Nazi Party, NSDAP, on the lapel of his suit, he once says to his wife: 'In every business I tried, I can see it was not me who failed. Something was missing . . .'. That something was the war.

Played by Liam Neeson, Oskar Schindler is far from the loser he once used to be. He is a strong man, always under strict self-control. He calmly observes the drinking and homicidal Nazis as if he was not one of them. He quietly blackmails the Jews as if he did not desperately need them. Everybody seems to be just a part of his game and he likes to be the one who decides what the next move is. He conducts his plan and nothing seems to stop him; not even the otherwise strictly totalitarian and bureaucratically pedantic Nazi regime.

It takes almost four years of the war for him to finally start to become aware. A shock from witnessing the total devastation of the Cracow ghetto in March 1943 begins to turn his priorities upside down and makes the former 'Mr Black' into 'Mr White'. Suddenly, the war means 'never the good, always the bad', as he once opens his heart to his accountant, Icchak Stern. Oskar Schindler starts to act; he keeps his mental strength, but becomes human. Rumours about his goodness spread quickly among the Jews when he creates a haven at his factory, Deutsche Emailwarenfabrik, and when he learns that his workers are in danger, decides to save them by moving from Cracow to Brünnlitz (Brněnec) near his hometown of Zwittau. The romantic hero fears nothing: kissing a Jewish woman and girl in public at his own birthday party, and spraying water to thirsty Jews in a train in front of a crowd of SS guards. He is driven by a mighty force to save Jews. Oskar Schindler and Icchak Stern put together a list: 'Schindler's List', which contains about 1,200 names. The man who had previously said he had so much money he would never be able to use

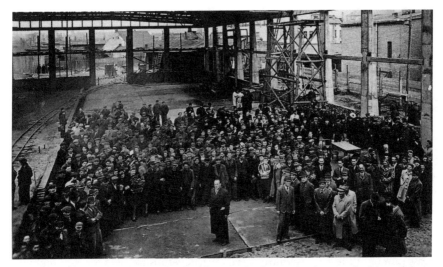

Figure 7 Oskar Schindler and 'his' workers in the factory in Cracow. Archive of Town Museum and Gallery in Svitavy.

it during his lifetime, now spends a fortune buying Jewish prisoners, who for other Germans in his surroundings are worthless. 'The list is an absolute good,' Icchak Stern concludes when they finish compiling it, 'the list is life.'

Schindler's new factory in Brünnlitz treats the workers even better than the one in Cracow. In order to keep the Jews safe, the company fakes military production. Instead of producing the goods that the army desperately needs, Schindler buys the production of others and pretends he made it himself. The text on the screen confirms: 'For the seven months it was fully operational, Schindler's Brinnlitz munitions factory was a model of non-production. During this same period he spent millions of Reichmarks to sustain his workers and bribe Reich officials.'

At the end of the war, however, Schindler is bankrupt but has managed to fulfil his mission. He is happy, though also self-critical: 'I am a member of the Nazi party. I am an ammunition manufacturer. I am a profiteer of slave labour. I am a criminal,' he admits in his final speech to 'his' Jews. Finally, he takes off his golden badge of the NSDAP. If he had sold even this, he could have saved two more Jewish lives. Only then does he start thinking about himself again and leaves the stage to save his own skin.

Schindler's identity according to Thomas Keneally

Steven Spielberg based his film on a novel, *Schindler's Ark*, written by the Australian writer, Thomas Keneally, and first published in 1982. Unlike Spielberg, Keneally indeed dealt with Schindler's Sudeten German origin. Furthermore, according to Keneally's version, 'there were signs that he wasn't *right thinking*, though he paid well, was a good source of scarce commodities, could hold his drink and had a slow and sometimes rowdy sense of humour'.[5] He also suggested that Schindler was 'disaffected with National Socialism',[6] though he mentioned that he, indeed, 'was wearing the Hakenkreuz, the swastika emblem of Konrad Henlein's Sudeten-German Party'. He also claimed that:

> ...they did not take it too seriously; it was something young Czech Germans were wearing that season. Only the Social Democrats and the Communists did not sport the badge or subscribe to Heinlein's party, and, God knew, Oskar was neither a Communist nor a Social Democrat. Oskar was a salesman. All things being equal, when you went into a German company manager's office wearing the badge, you got the order.[7]

Already by the beginning of the war, in Keneally's understanding, Schindler had taken a political position that could be understood as morally right or at least morally almost non-controversial: 'Whatever his motives for running with Henlein, it seems that as soon as the military divisions entered Moravia he suffered an instant disillusionment with National Socialism.' And more:

> ...he seems to have expected that the invading power would allow some brotherly Sudeten Republic to be founded. In a later statement he argued the new regime's bullying of the Czech population and the seizure of Czech property appalled him. His documented acts of rebellion would occur very early in the coming world conflict, and there is no need to doubt that the Protectorate of Bohemia and Moravia, proclaimed by Hitler from Hradschin Castle in March 1939, surprised him with its tyranny.[8]

While trying to understand Schindler's motive for rescuing almost 1,200 Jewish lives during the Second World War, Keneally began with a look at the Schindlers' family history. Here, he found more about the national identity of the Schindlers as well as their religious background, but could not find any key in Oskar's family history to his rescuing impulse:

> Hans Schindler, Oskar's father, approved of the imperial management, considered himself culturally an Austrian, and spoke German at the table, on the telephone, in business, in moments of tenderness. Yet when in 1918 Herr Schindler and the members of his family found themselves citizens of the Czechoslovak republic of Masaryk and Beneš, it did not seem to cause any fundamental distress to the father, and still less to his ten-year-old son. The child Hitler, according to the man Hitler, was tormented even as a boy by the gulf between the mystical unity of Austria and Germany and their political separation. No such neurosis of disinheritance soured Oskar Schindler's childhood. Czechoslovakia was such a bosky, unravished little dumpling of a republic that the German-speakers took their minority stature with some grace, even if the Depression and some minor governmental follies would later put a certain strain on the relationship ...The family Schindler was Catholic.[9]

Last, but not least, we learn more about the environment in Svitavy during Schindler's childhood from the following sentences: 'Oskar had a few

Figure 8 Oskar Schindler and his family members in Svitavy, Czechoslovakia, before the Second World War. Archive of Town Museum and Gallery in Svitavy.

middle-class Jewish friends, whose parents also sent them to the German grammar school. These children were not village Ashkenazim – quirky, Yiddish-speaking, orthodox – but multilingual and not-so-ritual sons of Jewish businessmen.'[10] In these lines, there is no mention of Schindler's relationships with his Czech neighbours in Svitavy during the earliest periods of his life. We just learn a little about his depersonalised attitude to the Czechoslovak state. In his book, and in contrast to Spielberg's film, Keneally claims that Oskar Schindler's personality had already undergone great changes towards humanity, turning against the goals of the Nazi regime, before the outbreak of the Second World War.

Earlier returns to Czechoslovakia

Neither this information about Oskar Schindler, nor a later idea to commemorate his act of saving 1,200 Jewish lives during the Holocaust by building a memorial to him, came to the Czechoslovak and later Czech public as a result of an internal activity. Keneally's book was as little noticed in Communist Czechoslovakia as Schindler himself. There were only two exceptions. The first was when Israel in the 1960s started to celebrate Schindler as one of 'the Righteous', and the Czechoslovak secret police showed some activity in order to learn more about the man who had Czech Sudeten-German roots, a Nazi past, and who received awards from both West Germany and Israel.[11] The second event took place two decades later, in 1986, four years after Thomas Keneally's book was published and well-received by Western critics. The only Czechoslovak newspaper or periodical that noticed the book was the literary magazine, *Světová literatura* ('World literature'). This not very influential, but especially among Czech intellectuals very respected magazine, published a review that – while still written under a communist regime hostile to both Jews, Sudeten-Germans and West Germany – was surprisingly positive to Keneally's book and to Oskar Schindler. The article presented Oskar Schindler's identity in the following way: 'You must not forget,' the writer quoted one of the so-called Schindler's Jews, 'that Oskar had not only a German face, but also a Czech one. He was similar to The Good Soldier Schwejk. He loved making fun of the regime.'[12] The writer, Eva Oliveriusová, admitted that even for her, Oskar Schindler was a totally unknown man, but after receiving a letter from the regional archive in Svitavy, she finished her review with a note confirming that a certain Oskar Schindler really did come to Brněnec at the end of the Second World War and established a sham concentration camp. By this act, she maintained, he saved the lives of 'about 1,200 Polish citizens, mostly of Jewish origin'.

The lack of a Czechoslovak public reaction to the book and everything else about Schindler before the end of the Cold War could first of all be interpreted as a sign that the Czechoslovak Communist regime never found a reason for considering Oskar Schindler as important – and therefore even as dangerous – that it would have to focus its propaganda on his personality. Not even the success of *Schindler's Ark*, awarded the prestigious British Man Booker Prize for fiction in 1982, made the-then Czechoslovak regime take notice of Schindler.

After the fall of communism in 1989, the first initiatives to celebrate Schindler came to Czechoslovakia from Germany and Israel. In 1991, three years before the Czech opening of *Schindler's List*, the German Munich-based organisation, Ackermann-Gemeinde (AG), wrote a letter to the Svitavy town councillors and asked whether it could place a memorial plaque in honour of Oskar Schindler in his hometown. The AG was already established in 1946 as a Catholic organisation primarily uniting those Germans who were forced to leave Czechoslovakia soon after the Second World War. Within the Sudeten-German movement, the group is considered moderate, defining itself as seeking understanding, not revenge.[13] Soon after the letter from Germany, another letter came to Svitavy from one of 'Schindler's Jews', now living in Israel. This man, a long-time member of the Israeli Supreme Court, had a similar question on whether it would be possible to erect a Schindler memorial.[14] Although both ideas came to Svitavy almost two years before Steven Spielberg completed his film, no memorial to Oskar Schindler was officially approved by the City Council in Svitavy before the spring of 1994 and the international success of the film, *Schindler's List*.

The non-compromisers: 'Drive Schindler out!'

Finally, not only one but two monuments of Oskar Schindler were established in his hometown. The first, official Czech one was financed by the City of Svitavy and was made of stone and iron, while the second one, a memorial plaque, was financed by AG. The first memorial was commemorated on the same day that *Schinder's List* was previewed in Svitavy on 9 March 1994. It was not placed on the house where Schindler was born as originally planned, but in a park on the other side of the street. According to the press, the current owners of the house would not allow any memory dedicated to Schindler to be placed directly on the house, since Schindler, in their eyes, 'was a fascist'.[15]

The fact that an identical text in Czech and German is written on both these memorials, no matter whether originating from the Czech or Sudeten-German side, is very interesting. It reads: 'Oskar Schindler. To an unforgettable rescuer of 1200 fated Jewish lives.'[16] The timing of the decision by the local authorities indicates that Schindler's memorial was approved even before the citizens of Svitavy had a chance to see the film and make up their minds about

Figure 9 Oskar Schindler with his sister Elfriede and mother Franzisca in his hometown of Svitavy, Zwittau. The photo is from 1916, two years before Zwittau became included into the new-born Czechoslovak Republic. Photo: Archive of Town Museum and Gallery in Svitavy

it, and before the discussion about Oskar Schindler actually started both in Svitavy and the Czech Republic as a whole.

Thus, the first strong denunciations were related to the memorial at least as much as to the film. The strongest denunciation in the discussion that followed came from circles that frequently made ideological use of history. In August 1994, the extremist nationalist party, Sdružení pro republiku-Republikánská strana Československa ('The Assembly for the Republic-Czechoslovak Republican Party' [SPR-RSC]), represented in the Czech parliament in Prague, brought charges against those who had built the Schindler memorial plaque in Svitavy. The SPR-RSC accused them of the criminal act of supporting movements suppressing civil rights and freedoms. 'The Republicans', in the words of their party secretary, Jan Vik, considered Svitavy's native, Schindler, not as 'a venerable Nazi who had to pay for the Jews to redeem them' or 'a good Nazi with a human face' but 'a well-known Nazi hangman'. While in some contexts, the SPR-RSC stood very close to neo-Nazis and called for actions especially against the Czech Republic's Romani population, this time, according to Vik, the party considered the unveiling of the memorial plaque to be 'a celebration of Nazi bestialities' which must receive immediate and well-deserved punishment so that the Nazi and Fascist evil can be 'rooted out'.[17]

While *Schindler's List* incited the Czech extremist right to react against German Nazism, it did not provoke any strong or open anti-Semitic feelings. One of very few exceptions was an article, 'History falsified by the Oscars', in the newspaper *Republika*, published by the SPR-RSC:

> I am not going to discuss the fact that the Oscars can hardly be won by non-Jewish film directors today. I will not question the opinion of the Jews about this version of the Holocaust. It is their problem. Maybe they will one day even believe that Eichmann too was a humanist, that gas-chambers were just a fabrication of the Pan-Slavic movement and that Theresienstadt was just a peaceful camp for the scouts.

'Why is a war criminal presented as a fearless saviour of the Jews?', the author further asked. 'Why not build a monument even to Himmler, best of all directly in Prague Castle? ... To make Schindler a famous philanthropist was easy. It was enough to put the story into the hands of Mr. Spielberg, himself a Jew.'[18]

Unlike 'The Republicans', those labelled 'communists' in their relation to Oskar Schindler were not so strongly connected to the existing Czech Communist Party that considered itself the successor of the pre-1989 Communist Party of Czechoslovakia. The top official representatives of this party, in fact, did not show any public activities related to *Schindler's List* at all. While the SPR-RSC was a political party with a clear political ideology and a political platform, 'the communists' in this context were in fact first of all the people who shared a view of Oskar Schindler and of history; one that corresponded with the ideological frame of the former Czechoslovak regime between 1948 and 1989.

The first of the two basic standpoints of 'the communists' was radical resistance against any 'revision' of the facts that the Sudeten-Germans, including Oskar Schindler, were guilty of treason to the Czechoslovak state and Czech people during the late 1930s and the whole period of the Second World War. According to this version, the treason against Czechoslovakia excluded a chance that Schindler could have had a good side, or that his pro-Nazi view from the beginning of the war could have changed as he gained better knowledge about the Nazi policy against the Jews. The Czech Germans as a whole were said to deserve to be sent to Germany, including those from Svitavy, where they comprised an overwhelming majority before the Second World War. Both Thomas Keneally and Steven Spielberg were blamed for 'ignorance of the facts' about Schindler and for 'uncritically spreading the false Schindler myth'. In addition, Israel was criticised for the same thing, while the entire process of the Holocaust and the memory of the Holocaust after 1945 were left aside.

One example of this kind can be found in articles by Jiří Frajdl from the National Council of an organisation called Klub českého pohraničí ('The Club of the Czech Borderland'); a kind of Czech attempt at counterbalancing the *Sudetendeutsche Landsmannschaft*. Although the organisation defines itself as a 'non-party patriotic movement', the ideological undertone in Frajdl's articles was obvious when he wrote: 'Nobody in the world would stoop so low as to celebrate his enemy, a representative of the Nazi regime and Germanic pride.' According to the author, 'in order to please the mighty rulers of today's Czech Republic', the Czech liberal press spread Schindler's 'fairy tale-ish legend', looking for an exemplary Sudeten-German they could use for a Czech-German mutual coming-together.[19] In the openly left-wing newspaper, *Nový zítřek*, the same author wrote with sarcasm: 'Why shouldn't this criminal, swindler, liar and Nazi have his own memorial? It is sure that the right-wing politicians need some positive examples even among the members of the Henlein party.'[20]

In some basic features, 'republican' and 'communist' attitudes were very similar. First, there was a radical attitude without any will to compromise, based on a black and white ethnic division between a good – Czech – and a bad – German – side. In this scheme, there was no place for possible Czech self-reflection. Besides this, there was also a very unbalanced attitude towards the Jews and to Israel. When appropriate, the Jews were used as an argument against Germany and Germans, but when such a use had fulfilled its role, Jews and their memory of the Holocaust were denied or criticised without any deeper analysis. This, too, was the case of the only organisation of the war veterans that wanted to participate in the debate. *Český svaz bojovníků za svobodu* ('The Czech Union of Freedom Fighters'), known under the Communist period as 'The Union of Anti-Fascist Fighters', issued a special declaration. Protesting against the memorial plaque to Oskar Schindler, the members wrote in March 1994:

Schindler took part in the occupation of our territory in 1938, in the occupation of the rest of our country by military troops on March 15, 1939, in terror against our citizens and at the beginning of the World War II, when 360,000 our best citizens gave their lives on the battlefields, in the resistance movement and in the Nazi concentration camps ... During the whole war, he led a luxurious life, profiting from the exploitation of the Jews ... Today, we cannot study what led Oskar Schindler to his activity. If Israel honoured his act, let his memory stay alive in Israel and among the Jews who are spread elsewhere in the world. But why should a Czech town celebrate a German, a Nazi, an agent of the German secret service?[21]

On the one hand, Jewish victims were here included in the number of victims as 'our best citizens'. On the other hand, however, only 'Jews in Israel and elsewhere in the world' were recommended to honour Schindler's act, while Czech Jews and other Czech sympathisers with Schindler were completely missing in this declaration.

Schindler's shadow over the Czech parliament

Jitka Gruntová, a history teacher and historian of the City Museum in Svitavy, shared a categorical anti-Schindler view. She had already declared herself 'a fighter against the Schindler myth' in a very early period of the debate. As she once admitted, she did not see *Schindler's List* until 1999 at the earliest, but was already fighting the Schindler myth long before. Thus, her main targets became Keneally's book and those who 'spread the legend' and supported Schindler's memorial. Nevertheless, she too paid very little attention to the fact that *Schindler's Ark* was a novel and not a scholarly work on Oskar Schindler. While often calling for the maintenance of 'professional standards' in history as a scholarly discipline, she never recognised the dual role of history. Gruntová thus never separated history as a scholarly discipline from history as historical consciousness, used by the whole of society and supposed to satisfy many more needs than just scholarly standards. She nevertheless became the foremost Czech expert on Schindler's life, more exactly on the two periods of his life on Czech territory, i.e., from the time of his birth until the late 1930s, and the period 1944–1945 when Schindler brought 'his' Jews from Plaszow to Brněnec, near Svitavy. From a political point of view she was the most important among all those who reacted to the film, since she was a member of the Czech Parliament and used history connected to the 'Sudeten German question' even there on some other occasions.

In her book, *Legendy a fakta o Oskaru Schindlerovi* ('Legends and facts about Oskar Schindler'), published in two editions in 1997 and 2002, Jitka Gruntová presented new evidence about Schindler's personality and drew four main conclusions. Firstly, Oskar Schindler was not a man who sympathised with the Nazi regime mainly as part of a business strategy. Rather, his sympathy was genuine. In the late 1930s he worked for Germany as an agent against both the Czechoslovak Republic and Poland. Gruntová brought new evidence about how the Czechoslovak police investigated Schindler's spy activities and how Schindler himself had already confessed to them before the beginning of the Second World War. The occupation of Czechoslovakia and the outbreak of the war saved him from all possible punishment by the Czechoslovak authorities.[22]

Secondly, in her research Gruntová also studied the activities of Schindler's factory that, in fact, was a concentration camp in Brünnlitz/Brněnec (an affiliated camp to the main one in Gross-Rosen) during the period 1944–1945, when 'Schindler's Jews' were working there. She came to the conclusion that life there was by no means better than in other similar concentration camps on Czech territory. The death rate was even among the highest. She additionally showed that the opening of this concentration camp had been planned even before Schindler's decision to transport the prisoners there from Poland, and thus cannot be explained as an individual step in order to transfer a private business from one place to another. In that case, Gruntová concluded, the decision did not emanate from Schindler's good will. Schindler was not an initiator of it; he still just wanted only to make the best of the situation while the Red Army was approaching Plaszow.[23]

Thirdly, Gruntová also refused to admit that war production in Brněnec was only fictitious and that Schindler, in fact, let the prisoners fake the war production. According to her, referring to some Czech witnesses from the area, Schindler's factory in Brněnec produced normal weapons for the Third Reich until the very end of the Second World War.[24]

Last, but not least, taking the famous document called 'Schindler's List', Gruntová analysed no less than eight different versions of it that all had a direct connection to 'Schindler's concentration camp' in Brněnec. The very first one, dated 21 October 1944, was made on the basis of the number of prisoners and contained 700 names. The numbers started with 68,854 and ended with 74,695. This, according Gruntová, did not show any special selection of the prisoners. A similar case was another list, made on 12 November 1944. All the other lists were written in the following year of 1945 with two exceptions, which were undated.[25] On the basis of these lists, Gruntová defined several groups of prisoners, reaching the conclusion that only a minority of them were chosen personally by Schindler. In such cases, they were people he needed for his various interests, while others had been chosen for humane reasons.

Combining her ideological standpoint with her research, and commenting on the Schindler monument in Svitavy, she stated: 'It is a great shame that this Nazi has a monument in Svitavy.' In the same interview, she added that the fact Oskar Schindler became one of 'the Righteous' in Israel, suggested a kind of conspiracy behind his appraisal: 'In the same year, there was an Eichmann trial in Israel. It was very diplomatic to present a contradictory, i.e. good German to the world.'[26] Schindler, however, was recognised as 'Righteous Among the

Nations' by Yad Vashem in Israel some years after the Eichmann trial.[27] Paying
no attention to that, and presenting no evidence at all on the subject, she
repeated this statement several times, even in the programme 'Fakta' on Czech
Television in 1999.[28]

Thanks to her research, Gruntová indeed brought some quite new facts
to light, and gave the Czech resistance against Schindler a 'scientific ground'
as well. Presenting herself and presented by others as a 'professional historian',
she became 'the Schindler expert' of the Czech Republic. That helped her
gain a lot of attention in various media – she was questioned and quoted in
most discussions of the Schindler case, in both the daily press and television.[29]
Questioning the 'Schindler myth', as it was presented by Thomas Keneally
and Steven Spielberg, Gruntová in fact came to a similar conclusion as the
American historian, David Crowe, the author of the first (and so far, only)
complete scholarly biography of Oskar Schindler that includes all periods and
places of his life. In fact, David Crowe partly used Gruntová's research in his
work, too. Paradoxically, however, the two came to quite different conclusions
on the question of whether Schindler saved Jewish lives or not and whether
he deserved any respect at all. Crowe, indeed, considers Schindler to be a hero
who saved more than 1,000 Jewish prisoners' lives. This heroism was earned
by his willingness to risk his own life and fortune in order to get permission
to bring the Jewish prisoners from Plaszow to Brněnec. His decisive act took
place outside Czech territory (i.e., outside the then Protectorate Bohemia
and Moravia) in 1944, and had nothing to do with his Czech-German
background.

Gruntová was not formally a member of any political party, but agreed to
became a candidate for the Communist Party of Bohemia and Moravia, a successor to the former totalitarian party from the Communist period, in various
elections on various levels. In 2002, still officially politically independent, she
even became a Communist deputy in the Czech Parliament in Prague. In
her political opposition against the Sudeten-German *Landsmannschaft*, Jitka
Gruntová even became one of the three deputies who, in 2003, initiated a
new controversial Czech law praising former Czechoslovak president, Edvard
Beneš, for his contribution to the Czechoslovak state. Even though the law
does not explicitly thank Beneš for the 'transfer' of Sudeten Germans from
Czechoslovakia, its proposal was presented at a time when the Czech campaign against new activities and demands of the Sudeten-German organisation
reached its peak in the post-Cold War Czech Republic. During the pre-election
campaign to Czech parliamentary elections in 2002, the anti-Sudeten arguments played an important role and, in the 2003 presidential elections, the new
Czech president, Václav Klaus, who replaced outgoing Václav Havel, was partly
elected due to his intensive anti-Sudeten propaganda. In this way Klaus, as a
conservative candidate representing Czech post-communist capitalist thinking,
was even able to get votes from the deputies of the Communist Party, including

Jitka Gruntová. The law about Beneš was widely understood and discussed as just another demonstration of the Czech official non-compromise attitude and refusal for self-reflection on the Sudeten-German question.

In several dozen articles, published during the whole first decade after 1993 and written either directly by her, or at least containing her quotes and comments, Jitka Gruntová never placed Schindler in other contexts than the Czech-German one; never used testimonies of other witnesses but Czech ones, and never analysed him within a Holocaust narrative. She also admitted that her attitude to Schindler included even very personal, existential aspects. For instance, when interviewed for the TV documentary film, *Zatykač na Oskara Schindlera* ('Arrest warrant for Oskar Schindler'), she compared the story of her own family to Schindler's, saying:

> My father was arrested by the Gestapo on September 1, 1939. He was kept prisoned in a concentration camp. Thanks to a skilful lawyer, it was possible to ransom my father for a lot of money. My dad had to give two houses to the Third Reich, the family had to sell a car and a collection of coins. All that went to one Gestapo official that helped my father to get back his freedom. Thanks to that, I could be born. When I once told this story to my daughter a long time ago, she told me a naive infant sentence: Mom, you have to be grateful to this Gestapo-man for your very existence. I have never felt any gratitude to that man, never had any such idea. It is not about saving human lives when a man does something like this for money. What did Schindler do? He did not save people. He traded with human lives.[30]

Jitka Gruntová's categorical rejection of the 'Schindler legend' found the support of another Czech historian, Jaroslav Valenta. In the periodical, *Soudobé dějiny* ('Contemporary history'), published by the Institute of Contemporary History in Prague,[31] Valenta praised Gruntová's work. At the same time, he criticised the attention given to Gruntová's book from the side of the Sudeten-Germans.[32] Their attention, according to Valenta, was 'incompetent' and 'pseudo-historical'.[33] Gruntová, on the other hand, 'did not use her sources selectively'. Showing very clearly that even his viewpoint was primarily based on a Czech-German ethnic dimension, and that even for him the Holocaust was actually not the most important point of the Schindler story, Valenta added another criticism against a Czech historian and author of a smaller book about Oskar Schindler, Radoslav Fikejz. Pointing at Fikejz's rather liberal evaluation of Schindler's activity during the early stages of the Second World War, Valenta wrote: 'I would not expect such a hyper-tolerant attitude of declared treason from a Czech historian.'[34]

Invisible Schindler stories – fear, doubt and compromise

With regard to Czech scholars, it might seem surprising that all 'heavyweights' among the historians were completely absent from the discussion. While

there were very few of them who could be described as Holocaust researchers, many specialised in Czech-German relations. There was, for example, a
special commission of Czechoslovak and German historians, established before
Czechoslovakia's breakdown in the early 1990s by the Ministers of Foreign
Affairs, and later continuing its work, divided into Czech-German and Slovak-
German commissions. However, none of its Czech members found it worthwhile to present their opinion in connection with *Schindler's List* in the Czech
media, even though many of the discussed subjects obviously would have
been relevant even for these historians. None of the historians, who in 2002
wrote the widely discussed book, *Rozumět dějinám* ('To understand history'),
about the Czech-Germans in Czechoslovakia (actually ordered to be written
by the Czech government in its campaign against Jörg Haider in Austria and
the Sudeten-German *Landsmannschaft* in Bayern, Germany) showed any activity.
Due to this absence, any broader scholarly perspective than the one suggested by
Jitka Gruntová was missing. The reason may be that the main task for historians,
according to Czech standards at that time, was to write 'real history' based on
archive materials and source criticism, and not participate in media discussions.
For a long time, it was only Gruntová who was dealing with primary sources
about Schindler. In 1999, she was accompanied by historian Mečislav Borák,
who, however, wrote only a script for a TV documentary on Schindler. Here,
too, Borák dealt with some primary sources and witness testimonies describing a limited part of Schindler's life and his activities in the Ostrava region
near the Czech-Polish border during the late 1930s and the rest of the war.
Even Borák confirmed the fact that Schindler worked as an agent for Germany
against Czechoslovakia and Poland, but he did not reach any further conclusion
regarding Schindler's activities within the context of the Holocaust. Nor did he
question or condemn Schindler generally, as Gruntová had.

   None of these scholars recognised the problem with Schindler's legacy as
primarily one of collective memory, historical consciousness and a clash of historical cultures. There were very few – if any – interdisciplinary studies related
to history and no research studying history from just these points of view, even
though Jan Křen, a prominent Czech historian dealing with Czech-German
relations, had already in 1990 published a whole book about 'white spots in
Czech history'.[35] However, even Křen's book became primarily an appeal to
historians to make a complete critical reconstruction of some crucial periods
of the controversial Czech recent past, rather than an attempt to look at history
from any other than just a chronological perspective.[36]

   Another unexpectedly 'invisible' group in the Schindler discussion were
leading Czech politicians, including the president, Václav Havel. While the
US President, Bill Clinton, urged people to watch *Schindler's List*, Havel, who
became one of the greatest symbols of freedom-fighting and against dictatorship in the post-communist world, did not make any comment on the film
at all in order to mark his own standpoint, or to use the Holocaust lesson for

education leading to democracy and tolerance. Thus, the only public reaction from the highest political leadership of the country came in 1994 from Prime Minister Václav Klaus, the leader of the Conservative Party ODS. He did not make a voluntary choice to speak but was forced to react to the scandal provoked by the right-extremist protests of the 'Republicans' against Schindler's Svitavy memorial in parliament. In response to a SPR-RSČ's deputy in the Czech Parliament, Klaus stated that it was for the courts to assess whether the unveiling of a plaque to Oskar Schindler meant a criminal act of support and dissemination of a movement striving to suppress the rights of citizens. It was solely up to the local people to assess this specific activity of the local authorities, Klaus said, presenting the whole problem as clearly only a legal matter. Thus, even though the SPR-RSČ did not achieve any success with its activity against Oskar Schindler after all, it was impossible to see what human, political and other possible values might be connected to *Schindler's List* in the heads of those responsible for building the new Czech democratic system.

There were other groups that could be considered as likely participants in the debate but instead remained silent. Those Czech-Germans who remained in Czechoslovakia during the whole post-war period stood close to Schindler's story and could be expected to at least try to express their own view. With regard to the post-war historical context, however, the Czech-German silence was in fact not surprising at all. Reactions that could be classified as 'Czech-German' were not only missing in Schindler's case, but even in such important moments as when Václav Havel, just elected as President in the end of 1989, very surprisingly suggested for the first time that the Czechs should apologise to the Sudeten Germans for their 'wild expulsion' right after the war.[37]

The situation of the Czech-Germans in the early 1990s can be illustrated by the following facts and figures. In 1921, there were more than 3.2 million Czech Germans in Czechoslovakia; three million of them in the Czech provinces of Bohemia and Moravia.[38] After the Munich Agreement and the occupation of Czech lands by Germany, the 'Sudeten-Germans' became citizens of the Third Reich. When the transfer of the Germans was officially declared completed by the restored Czechoslovakia in the first two years after the Second World War, only 240,000 Czech-Germans were allowed to stay. This does not mean, however, that these people were seen as non-problematic by the Czechoslovak authorities and citizens. The Czech government wished to send more Germans 'home' to Germany but was not allowed to do so by the Allies.[39] Despite that, some more Germans were forced to leave anyway during the late 1940s. As historians have reminded us, among those driven out of Czechoslovakia were also German anti-Nazis and even German Jews returning from the concentration camps.[40] Official statistics from 1950 spoke about 165,000 Germans remaining in Czechoslovakia, i.e., 1.3 per cent of the population.[41] Even though Czechoslovakia gave a kind of 'amnesty' to at least part of Germany – the Eastern, Communist-led one – the ideology demonising the 'revanchist threat' from West Germany, as well as continuous distrust, made the position of remaining Czech-Germans continuously complicated during Communist rule. The number of remaining Czech-Germans decreased further during the late 1960s when many people emigrated. By the early 1990s, the German minority consisted of less than 50,000.

Sociologist, Eva Stehlíková, has observed that this remaining German minority is very heterogeneous. There is no typical 'German region' or even political and cultural agenda in the country. Perhaps more surprisingly, the Czech-Germans can hardly be described as generally pro-German. To a large extent, they have been assimilated into Czech society, and some are not even fluent in German.[42] The Czech public debate about *Schindler's List* does not seem to have had any visual effect on the life and image of the German minority in the Republic at all.

Another important minority, the Czech-Jewish one, was in some respects in a similar situation. There were not many reactions to *Schindler's List* from the side of the Czech-Jews. A possible reason might be that Jewish organisations were not very strong and influential in Bohemia and Moravia at that time, and that open manifestations of collective Jewish identity were not welcome during the long period of communist rule until 1989. Furthermore, Czech-Jews were isolated from the international debate about the Holocaust during most of the communist period and were occupied with different problems from Jews in the West. It is therefore difficult to estimate the priority given to the memory of the Holocaust among Czech-Jews right after the collapse of the communist system, and whether the silence might be motivated by their fear of possible counter-reaction or repression.

The generational aspect is relevant, too, since it is very difficult to analyse the level of the younger Jewish generations' knowledge of the Jewish genocide during the Second World War. The young Jews got their formal education in the same official schools as their non-Jewish counterparts, i.e., within the framework of communist ideology, and had no free and independent space in which they could express their thoughts, beliefs and feelings before 1989.[43] It is likely that the Jewish generations of the children of Holocaust survivors were better educated about the Nazi genocide of the Jews than other non-Jewish children in Czechoslovakia, due particularly to the histories communicated within their own families.[44] However, such a private education was not quite automatic for all Jews either, as the case of the Czech-born US secretary of state, Madeleine Albright, might suggest. Those families who could convert or manage to hide their Jewish identity during the Nazi period might have chosen to continue to do so even in the post-war era. If Madeleine Albright's Czech parents could do so during their US exile, it is even more plausible that this was the case for similar families in Communist Czechoslovakia, especially after the anti-Jewish wave of the early 1950s.[45] Even the official Czech-Jewish periodical, *Roš Chodeš*, dedicated very little space to the film. The only exception to this rule was an interview with the distinguished historian of the Holocaust, Raul Hilberg, in which he expressed his understanding for the success of the film. The interview was not originally carried out by the Czech-Jewish period-ical, but by French journalists, and translated into Czech after being published in the French press.[46]

In this situation, the chief rabbi, Karol Sidon, from Prague became, in fact, the only active spokesman of a Jewish opinion about Schindler in the Czech media. The Rabbi did not, however, stress only the 'Jewish matter' in his speeches, but primarily emphasised respect for humanity and praised the fact that – even in such very difficult times – an individual was able to save other people's lives. 'He proved that it was possible. Everybody who did a similar thing deserves a memorial because he or she would show that is possible to save the others', Sidon said during an opening ceremony when the memorial to Schindler was uncovered in early 1994.[47] Sidon held the same line more or less consistently during forthcoming years. In 1999, for example, when Czech Television made the already-mentioned documentary programme about Oskar Schindler, he said: 'He [Schindler] saved a thousand human lives and every life is very precious. It does not matter what he was like in private, no matter where he grew up or where he came from. The human lives were the only thing that mattered.'[48]

In the same documentary, however, recalling the events from 1994, Sidon disclosed some previously unknown details from the opening of the Schindler memorial in Svitavy five years earlier. He admitted that he was more or less forced to make a speech and uncover the memorial, since all other Czech guests present at the ceremony were afraid and lacked the courage to do so. 'If Schindler had not been a German but a Czech and if he had done the same thing, he would probably have been much more accepted', the Rabbi added. When, for Sidon himself, the ethnicity of Oskar Schindler was not a decisive factor, the same could be said about his presentation of the ethnicity of victims, i.e., the Jewish prisoners. Sidon did not speak about the importance of saving Jewish lives during the Holocaust, but about the importance of saving human lives during the war. Thus, he did not even stress a special place for the Jews among other victims of the Nazi regime. The all-human aspect of Schindler's act was the most important for him, which made his words acceptable in all parts of Czech society and led to no criticism and no strong reaction from other participants in the debate, including even the most extreme ones.

The last group I want to mention here as 'uncertain' or perhaps 'careful' in its interpretation of Schindler is a small group of witnesses who personally remembered Oskar Schindler or his relatives, his factory in Brněnec, and 'his' Jews from the time of the Second World War. There were some local voices that appeared in the debate with their testimonies. All of them were searched out by either journalists or researchers, which meant that their testimonies were in all cases interpreted and used by others. The messages from the testimonies, however, were not easy to decipher at all. In the most paradoxical case, one witness testimony was used both to give credit to Oskar Schindler and to disprove 'the Schindler legend'.

During the last years of the Second World War, Cecilia Niederlová lived next to Schindler's factory in Brněnec. While interviewed by the German daily newspaper, *Berliner Morgenpost*, in March 1994, she remembered the prisoners speaking very nicely about Schindler. 'They were grateful to him for their lives', she said.[49] Jitka Gruntová also met Cecilia Niederlová and used her words to prove that 'the Schindler legend' was not based on real facts. In her book, published in 2002, Gruntová wrote: 'Cecilie Niederlová says that she used to see Schindler in his office, wearing the uniform of the SS ... In 1994, she related it to many journalists, but this important testimony – confirmed even by her husband – was refused by them and considered as impossible.'[50] Niederlová's memories are further used to prove that Schindler stole 'a huge, huge amount of Jewish goods' from the Jews and stored it in his Brněnec factory.[51] There are, however, no details as to how and where the Jewish prisoners, who, after 'Aryanisations' of their properties and following three years of the ongoing process of the 'Final Solution', had travelled from Cracow to Brněnec by goods trains at the end of the war in very poor condition, got this 'huge, huge amount of Jewish goods' that was so evident even for an outsider. No matter, Niederlová is said to also question the good conditions of the Schindler Jews in the factory. When Niederlová once tried to throw an apple to a Jewish prisoner, an SS-Officer immediately ran to her and forbade her to do it.[52]

Cecilia Niederlová was not the only 'problematic' source among the direct witnesses and survivors in the Czech Republic.[53] The atmosphere of the public discussions about Schindler influenced and even scared other Czech witnesses. Some journalists wrote that people who remembered Schindler were afraid of their neighbours. 'I have not found a single witness who was not afraid of speaking about Schindler as a good man. Somebody always threatens them afterwards', the liberal daily, *Mladá Fronta*, wrote soon after *Schindler's List*'s first Czech appearance.[54] An article by Stanislav Motl in another liberal periodical, *Reflex*, mentioned one woman who was the only Czech survivor of Schindler's concentration camp in Brněnec.[55] 'A former prisoner No. 76408 does not want to let the others in the small city of Svitavy know too much about her', he wrote. His article was illustrated by a photo where 'Mrs. 76408' could not be recognised, her face was digitally masked by computer, as was the face of her husband. Nevertheless, readers got to know that the last name of the lady was Mrs Reicherová. In the article, Mrs Reicherová did not speak about Schindler at all.

Since Gruntová, too, met the same survivor in person, I later learned that Mrs Bluma Reichertová (spelled differently than in *Reflex*) changed her name a long time ago, after her marriage. Thus the name Reichertová was in fact her maiden name. Anyway, from Gruntová's work, the reader never learns what Mrs

Reichertová thought about Schindler either. Once Mrs Rechertová mentioned with some sympathy 'a man in civilian clothes' who tried to help the prisoners in Brněnec, without specifying whether it was really Schindler. Two pages later in the book, Reichertová was just quoted as saying that 'some liked Schindler, some did not'.[56]

All these indications suggest that none of the minorities or groups standing closest to Schindler's time and life on Czech territory have found it worthwhile to profile themselves clearly in the Czech Schindler debate. Neither the Jews nor the German-Czechs found the Schindler debate crucial for sharpening their own historical consciousness and collective identity. Thus, with the exception of Chief-Rabbi, Karol Sidon, they remained almost unnoticed.

Schindler? Allow him in!

Chronologically, the most positive Czech reactions to Oskar Schindler came at the beginning of the whole debate. The first of this kind focused more on the success of *Schindler's List* as a film, than on the authenticity and moral standard of Schindler's personality or other factors. For authors of these articles – mostly reviewers of the film – *Schindler's List* was taken as a work of art based on a real story.[57] Some reactions, however, almost immediately suggested that the film should be used as a 'bridge over troubled waters' between Czechs and Germans. In the days after the opening in Svitavy and Prague, the daily *Český deník* understood the film as well as Schindler's memorial as a 'step on a way to rapprochement':

> The Town of Svitavy lacks historical memory, since 90 per cent of its inhabitants have lived here only since 1945. The discussion about the act will not end by uncovering the memorial plaque. This is the moment of necessary self-reflection about new forms of relations between people speaking different languages. It is also an impulse to thinking about our own identity, about our place in the democratic community of advanced European countries ...

The daily quoted the Svitavy mayor Jiří Brídl.[58] Some authors even wanted to see the film in a broader context as a pedagogic lesson for the prevention of genocide. As an article in the liberal daily, *Reflex*, in early 1994 stated: 'It is important for us, because Schindler was a Sudeten German, it is important for the whole world because it is important to realize right now, at the time of the Serbian rage, what genocide is all about'.[59] In the summer of 1994, the daily, *Mladá Fronta Dnes*, even saw the film as the end of the old Czech perception of the ethnic Czech-German conflict and the old communist view of the problem:

> The case of a Nazi and Jew saviour Oskar Schindler could help us to learn to dif-ferentiate with criticism in our past ... It is obvious that the general condemna-tions of the Sudeten Germans cannot last forever, even though far from everybody

Figure 10 Oskar Schindler and his wife Emilia. Archive of Town Museum and Gallery in Svitavy.

will be – just because of Schindler – willing to revise the simplifying indoctrinations brought to us by the communist regime.[60]

On a scholarly level, two local historians from Svitavy with a partly similar professional background to Jitka Gruntová showed a rather more liberal attitude to Oskar Schindler and wanted to use his act, not for Holocaust research or memory, but for the purposes of improving Czech-German relations. The first of these two men was Radoslav Fikejz, whom I have already mentioned as a criticised 'non-patriot' by historian Jaroslav Valenta. The second was Milan Štrych. Both of them worked during some time as historians of the Svitavy town museum, where even Gruntová once used to work. Both Fikejz and Štrych, however, took much less part in the debate than Gruntová. In a 1994 interview published in *Týdeník*, Fikejz, then only a student of history, said:

> There are still many people in our country who understand history in terms of collective guilt ... It is important to draw a thick line between the past and the present. It is important to start in a new way and forget national aversions. I think that Schindler especially could be the one who brings reconciliation between the Czechs and the Germans.[61]

Radoslav Fikejz wrote a study about Schindler, first as a thesis at the Masaryk University in Brno. For this work, he was given an award by the Czech Minister of Education as the 'talent of the year 1997. Later, the study was published by the Museum in Svitavy,[62] but did not get as much attention as Gruntová's book in the Czech press. Nor was it available nationwide but only in the Svitavy Museum. Nevertheless, even Fikejz formulated his studies on some archive materials and interviews with the survivors, but on a much smaller scale than Jitka Gruntová. He leaned heavily on an unpublished study by the English researcher, Robin O'Neil, and came to some quite opposite conclusions to Gruntová. For instance, although both Keneally and Spielberg distorted the story, the core of it – that Schindler intended to save and in fact saved the Jewish prisoners – was real. While saving Jewish lives, Schindler did not act only as a businessman, but also as a man of honour. Fikejz also pointed out that Schindler did not need to 're-write his own history by the end of the Second World War in order to save his own skin, as Gruntová claimed, because he had had a chance to save his own life earlier in 1944, through emigration to Switzerland, but refused.[63]

Fikejz, contrary to Gruntová, was generally very enthusiastic about Schindler in his conclusions: 'Oskar Schindler became a great personality just at the same time as he managed to take over the responsibility not only for himself, but also for others. His action balanced out all the negative sides of his life'.[64] Thus Schindler's courage in relation to his prisoners overshadowed the negative sides shown during the eve and subsequent first years of the war. At the end of his work, Fikejz even touched upon one more sensitive point when he wrote: 'Not only can Oskar Schindler himself get credit for the people in Brněnec. The local population in Brněnec, too, supported the prisoners – no matter whether they were Czechs or Germans.' Schindler's life, according to Fikejz, 'overcame a presumption about the badness of the whole German nation.' Schindler's act, not Schindler's life, becomes an appeal to future generations, Fikejz concluded, combining a scholarly and a pedagogic use of history.[65]

Milan Štrych was quoted by the national liberal daily, *Lidové noviny*, as giving the same message: 'Schindler – it is our opportunity to reach reconciliation'.[66] This article was even published before the opening of *Schindler's List* in the Czech Republic. The two journalists who wrote the text finished it with the following words:

> Together with the most important thing – that human lives were saved – the case of Schindler, although still open, brought together one theme: lines are not drawn either between the nations, or between the political parties or between the religions. There are not even clear lines we carry within us. Black or white, negative or positive, everybody can in his or her life do something that matters.

A general problem with all these positive reactions to *Schindler's List* was their temporary character. As enthusiasm for the film soon decreased, so did calls to use the film for the 'democratic education' of Czech society and for a new self-reflection in terms of Czech national identity. The opponents, headed by Gruntová, were on the contrary much more consistent in the long run. With new evidence about Schindler's guilt in his relation to the Czech nation emerging, it made the initial effort to use Spielberg's film for self-reflective purposes look like a temporary effort of incompletely informed enthusiasts.

No challenge to 'the real Czech trauma'

During most of the period of my study, which means the years between 1994 and 2003, the problem of the Holocaust was pictured as secondary in the Czech debate about *Schindler's List*, if it was recognised at all. I cannot say that Schindler was condemned entirely for who he was and not what he did, since he was condemned to a large extent for his own Nazi activities. Nevertheless, his ethnic origin played a very important role in all discussions and helped in the end rather to widen the gap than bridge it. Besides, *Schindler's List* never led to crucial discussions about such questions as the behaviour of 'ordinary Czechs' during the Holocaust or the tragic history of the Czech (or former Czechoslovak) Jews, in order to prevent anti-Semitism.

Thus, the debate about *Schindler's List*, which in fact was the first extensive debate in the new-born Czech Republic initiated entirely by the Holocaust and its memory, has never become a turning point for Czech self-reflection, neither regarding the Holocaust nor the Sudeten Germans. During the first decade after the 'Velvet Divorce', the arguments against Schindler proved to be much 'heavier' than some attempts to use Schindler in order to influence Czech historical culture.

I found the need to confirm the understanding of the Czech nation as a collective victim of the much bigger and stronger German neighbour prevailing in the debate. It was accompanied by silent approval or at least absent opposition from most of the new post-communist elites and from the main groups involved. Old stereotypes, valid during the whole post-war period, seemed to be too stable in comparison to attempts to challenge them. Put differently, *Schindler's List* as a history-cultural impulse was not strong enough to successfully challenge old perceptions of history.

Notes

1. Schindler died on 8 October 1974 in Hildesheim, Germany and, according to his own wishes, was buried in Jerusalem.

2. Among those who were present in Svitavy during this preview were local politicians; the Chief-Rabbi in the Czech Republic, Karol Sidon; the German and Israeli Ambassadors; and representatives from the US Embassy in Prague. None of the creators of *Schindler's List* took part in the Svitavy ceremony.

3. The terms 'Sudetenland' and 'Sudeten German' were created by the nationalist German politicians who, after 1918, appeared on Czechoslovak territory as part of Czechoslovakia but actively opposed such a development. The expressions were supposed to stress the unity of Czechoslovakia's German population. During the ensuing years, the terms gained many political undertones: some authors distinguish between 'Sudeten Germans' and 'Czech Germans', where Czech Germans are those Germans who lived in the Czech part of Czechoslovakia outside the 'Sudetenland', i.e. the border areas near Germany and Austria. During the Second World War, when Bohemia and Moravia became an occupied Protectorate and when most of the Sudeten Germans supported the policy of the Third Reich, the official 'Sudeten district' covered only the regions in western and northern parts of the Protectorate. After the war, when most of the Germans were forced to leave for Germany and Austria, the term 'Sudeten German' mostly became a synonym for all Germans driven out from Czechoslovakia.

4. 'Transfer' is a rather neutral expression used in official documents. Many authors, however, speak about 'expulsion'. Since the same word became an organic part of the vocabulary of the Sudeten German activists, many Czech sources consequently refute it and continue to speak and write about *odsun* (transfer, displacement).

5. Thomas Keneally, *Schindler's Ark*, London: Coronet, 1982, 19.

6. Ibid., 35.

7. Ibid., 42–43.

8. Ibid., 42–43.

9. Ibid., 35–36.

10. Ibid. 37.

11. In fact, even the West German government was taken by surprise in the middle of 1960s. As Liliane Weissberg has noted, politicians there first noticed Oskar Schindler when they learned about the MGM plan to make a film about him. See Liliane Weissberg, *The Tale of a Good German*, in Yosefa Loshitzky, ed., *Spielberg's Holocaust*, Bloomington: Indiana University Press, 1997, 179.

12. Eva Oliveriusová, 'Úspěšný pokus o fúzi mýtu a literatury faktu', *Světová literatura* 1, 1986, 241.

13. Eva Hahnová and Hans Henning Hahn, *Sudetoněmecká vzpomínání a zapomínání*, Prague: Votobia, 2002, 159–61.

14. Stanislav Motl, 'Schindlerův rok', *Reflex* 12, 1994.

15. *Reflex* 10, 1999, 30. This information even appeared in several other newspapers.

16. Oskar Schindler, Nezapomenutelnému zachránci života 1200 pronásledovaných židů.

17. Czech News Agency, ČTK, 9 August 1994.

18. 'Historie falšovaná Oscary', *Politické noviny Republika*, article signed by jok.

19. Jiří Frajdl, 'Jak si svitavští radní ušili z ostudy kabát', *Hraničář*, January 1998.

20. Jiří Frajdl, 'Schindlerovské mýty ukončeny', *Nový zítřek-Levicové noviny* 12, 1997. The Henlein Party was a party uniting the Sudeten Germans against the Czechoslovak State in the 1930s.

21. Quoted according to *Týdeník*, the local newspaper in Svitavy, 9 March 1994, 2. This declaration was published and quoted in several newspapers.

22. Jitka Gruntová, *Legendy a fakta o Oskaru Schindlerovi*, Prague: Naše Vojsko, 2002, 14–19. The book was first published by Barrister & Principal in Brno in 1997.

23. Ibid., 86–130.

24. Ibid., 87–91.

25. Ibid., 63–64.

26. 'K pravdě o Schindlerovi se přiblíží až příští generace, míní historička', *MFDnes*, 30 March 1999.

27. http://www1.yadvashem.org/righteous/bycountry/germany/oskar_schindler.html.

28. In 1961, Oskar Schindler visited Israel for the first time. For more about the circumstances of this visit and its relation to the Eichmann trial, see: David Crowe, *Oskar Schindler: The Untold Account of His Life, Wartime Activities, and the True Story Behind the List*, Boulder, CO: Westview Press, 2004, 493–539.

29. In the preface of the second edition of her book, however, Gruntová described the situation during the first three years after the premiere of the film in quite different terms. According to her, 'many of our newspapers refused to publish my articles' and 'it took a long time for me to find a publishing house that had the courage to help me in my fight against windmills'. See Gruntová, *Legendy a fakta o Oskaru Schindlerovi*, 6.

30. Zatykač na Oskar Schindlera. Ceska Televize (Czech Televisison, Public Service), 1999.

31. Jaroslav Valenta, 'Kauza Oskara Schindlera v dvojím pohledu', *Soudobé dějiny* 2–3, 1998, 328–43.

32. Valenta refers to an article: F. Seebauer, 'Sowjetische Weltsicht konserviert', *Sudetendeutsche Zeitung*, 6 March 1998, 2.

33. Valenta, 'Kauza Oskara Schindlera v dvojím pohledu', 331.

34. Ibid., 337.

35. Křen, *Bílá místa v našich dějinách*.

36. For an analysis of this state of scholarly historiography, see Jan Stříbrný, 'Rezistence a válka v paměti současné české společnosti', in Július Lipták, ed., *SNP v pamäti národa. Materiály z vedeckej konferencie k 50. výročiu SNP*, Banská Bystrica: Múzeum SNP, 1994, 45–46.

37. Václav Havel was elected as Czech President on 29 December 1989 and made his suggestion repeatedly at the same time, both inside the Czech Republic and during his very first presidential visit abroad that – symbolically – led just to Germany. Havel's idea met great scepticism among most Czech citizens.

38. Zdeněk Beneš and Václav Kural, eds, *Rozumět dějinám*, Prague: Gallery, 2002, 56.

39. Karel Kaplan, *Pravda o Československu 1945–48*, Prague: Panorama, 1990.

40. For more about the situation of the German Jews, see, for example, Tomáš Staněk, 'Němečtí židé v Československu 1945–1948', *Dějiny a současnost* 13(5), 1991, 42–46.

41. Kaplan, *Pravda o Československu 1945–48*, 153–58.

42. Eva Stehlíková, 'Aktuální kontexty obrazu Němce a Německa v české společnosti', in Eva Broklová and Jan Křen, eds, *Obraz Němců, Rakouska a Německa v české společnosti 19. a 20. století*, Prague: Karolinum, 1998, 253–67.

43. For further discussion about the Holocaust as part of Czech(oslovak) school education, see Frankl, 'Holocaust Education', *Intercultural Education* 14(2), June 2003.

44. See Hamar, *Vyprávěná židovství*, 116–34 and 208–11.

45. Albright discovered her Jewish roots first when she became the US Secretary of State in 1997, and thanks to information brought by an Arab newspaper. Interestingly, her father, Joseph Korbel, did not mention the Holocaust at all when he wrote a book about the history of Czechoslovakia in the 1970s. See Josef Korbel, *Twentieth Century Czechoslovakia: The Meanings of Its History*, New York: Columbia University Press, 1977. For more information about the whole Albright affair, see, for example, Madeleine Albright, *Madam Secretary*, New York: Miramax Books, 2003, 235–49.

46. *Roš Chodeš*, May 1994, 8–9.

47. Quoted according to the *Daily Express* from 14 March 1994.

48. *Zatykač na Oskara Schindlera*, Czech TV, 1999.

49. Czech News Agency, ČTK, 4 March 1994.

50. Gruntová, *Legendy a fakta o Oskaru Schindlerovi*, 121, this quotation translated from Czech by T.S.

51. Ibid., 93.

52. Ibid., 118.

53. In this analysis, I am not studying witnesses from other countries, for example those who helped Keneally and Spielberg in making the film. Writing his novel during the Cold War, Keneally either could not or did not wish to interview Czech/Czechoslovak sources. As far as I know, Spielberg did not attempt to do so either, even if he had already started filming after the fall of Communism in Czechoslovakia.

54. Štěpánka Králová, 'Jeden ze šestatřiceti spravedlivých', *MFDnes*, 12 March 1994.

55. Motl, 'Schindlerův rok'.

56. Gruntová, *Oskar Schindler, Legendy a fakta*, 128 and 130.

57. See, for example, 'Neuvěřitelný a fascinující Schindlerův seznam', *Mladá Fronta*, 18 December 1993.

58. *Český deník*, 12 March 1994, 10.

59. 'Schindlerův seznam, *Reflex*, 13/94.

60. Martin Schmarz, 'Bez Schindlerů bychom to měli jednodušší', *MF Dnes*, 24 August 1994.

61. Fikejz in an interview 'Nemyslím si, že Schindler židy zvlášť miloval', *Týdeník*, 1994.

62. Radoslav Fikejz, *Oskar Schindler (1908–1974)*, Svitavy: Městské Muzeum a galerie Svitavy, 1998.

63. Ibid., 89.

64. Ibid., 151.

65. Ibid., 153.

66. 'Každý svého Schindlera', *Lidové noviny*, 26 February 1994.

CHAPTER 5

Pig farm as a *Porrajmos* remembrance site

The Holocaust of the Roma as a new challenge for Czech historical culture

It has already been mentioned that European institutions in their definition of 'the Holocaust' made no clear distinction between the Holocaust of Jews, *Shoah*, and the Holocaust of Roma, *Porrajmos*. When the Holocaust began to be used in the Europeanisation process as a means to combat racism and xenophobia, there were relatively few who even cared about this difference. In the Czech context, however, precisely this detail came to play a major role. The situation was further complicated when the Holocaust's Americanisation, which had otherwise focused almost exclusively on the Holocaust of the Jews to the exclusion of the Roma, entered into the discussions, this time applied to the Holocaust of Czech Roma.[1]

In 1994 Paul Polansky, an American history researcher and activist with distant Czech roots, made a, for him, very surprising discovery in the Czech Republic. When he visited the Czech village, Lety u Písku, in order to search for information about the Czechs who in 1848 emigrated as the first Czech pioneers to Cleveland, Ohio, and happened to come from Lety itself, he discovered by chance that during the Second World War there was a concentration camp for Czech gypsies in this small village, situated about 100 kilometres south of Prague. On the same site as where the gypsies had been murdered three decades earlier, a pig farm had been built at the beginning of the 1970s, i.e., during the communist era. According to Polansky the Czech attitude to the dead gypsies' memory was shameful, and he decided to contribute to improving the situation. He thought that the Czech Republic's new, post-communist authorities would share his interest in setting things right; the amends in Lety would, according to Polansky, be a part of the broad process of coming to terms with the past that was taking place in the Czech Republic after the fall of communism. As Polansky discovered, the personnel of the Lety camp during the Nazi period were not German but Czech. Even the pig farm was built in the 1970s by Czechs. The new Czech regime, which after 1989 condemned both Nazism and Communism, should, according to Polansky's conception, quite simply condemn the Czech actions of the 1940s and 1970s and build a worthy monument to those people who had died in the Holocaust of the Roma, the *Porrajmos*, during the Second World War.[2] However, to his great surprise Polansky met strong opposition from the Czech side and reactions he later described in terms of silence, ignorance and open racism.[3] He was even denied further access to the regional archive in the town of Třeboň, where up to 40,000 documents about the Lety camp were kept, according to some reports.

The subsequent battle between Polansky and Czech authorities led to the most comprehensive, heated and longest Czech debate on the Holocaust after the fall of the Iron Curtain. Instead of Jews, it was the Roma and the Lety pig farm that stood in the centre of the debate – one that began in 1994 and reached its peak in 1999. Its length and intensity make the particular ways in which history was used especially interesting, which is why I here focus on the different uses of history. I will demonstrate how different uses of history could lead to the same goal: literally all the uses could be used – and were used – to strengthen the national aspect of the dominating Czech historical narrative. I will also show how one and the same use of history could lead to completely different results. Last, but by no means least, I will demonstrate that the same actors during the debate could utilise several different uses of history to achieve their goals.

Holocaust, *Porrajmos*, *Shoah*

The question of whether the Holocaust of the Roma, *Porrajmos*, can be placed on an equal footing as the Holocaust of Jews, *Shoah*, has no obvious answer. As the discussions surrounding the questions of whether the mass murder of gypsies during the Second World War was actually race-motivated or not, and if the *Porrajmos* could therefore be classified as genocide, affected even the Czech historical debate, I would initially like to discuss this issue.

The prominent Israeli Holocaust historian, Yehuda Bauer, writes: 'Roma were not Jews, therefore there was no need to murder all of them'.[4] According to Bauer, there was no manifest 'pure' racism against the gypsies as the Nazi policy was inconsistent in its perception of them. Therefore, Bauer writes, there exists no doubt that the Holocaust was completely unique and could only be connected to the Nazi genocide of the Jews.[5] Even another leading Holocaust historian, Raul Hilberg, treated the *Porrajmos* marginally: in the three volumes of his comprehensive study of the Holocaust, *The Destruction of the European Jews*, little more than ten pages dealt with the fate of the Roma.[6]

However, the American historian, Sybil Milton, has criticised Bauer and claimed that the exaggerated preoccupation with anti-Semitism and the Jewish Holocaust's unique character 'has limited our ability to recognize the connections between Nazi ideology, German social policy, and Genocide'.[7] She calls attention to the fact that besides Jews, even gypsies and the handicapped were killed on the grounds of their genetic characteristics, as the Nazis saw all these groups as a threat to racial purity. 'In the final analysis', Milton maintained, 'all three groups were condemned for racial – not political – reasons; and, in fact, the murder of the handicapped chronologically preceded that of Jews and Gypsies.'[8]

It is, moreover, difficult to establish how many gypsies were actually systematically murdered during the Second World War. As the political scientist, Zoltan Barany, notes, the qualified estimates vary between 200,000 and 1.5 million. However, none of these figures can be documented as well as the six million in the Jewish case.[9] 'From a scholarly point of view, short of solid quantitative information – usually yielded by years of painstaking archival research – there is simply no way to safely estimate the number of the Holocaust Romani victims,' Barany concludes.

The Nazi system divided the Roma into several categories: racially pure gypsies, racially mixed ones, asocial people with a gypsy lifestyle, and so on. This made it more difficult to recognise the racist undertone in all these categories. The philologist, Ian Hancock, who intensively researched Roma culture and history, has in his detailed summary of arguments attempted to lessen the significance of the Roma Holocaust and its memory, concluding that *anti-Gypsyism* and *anti-Semitism* in the Third Reich, for the most part, led to the same result.[10]

As this discussion indicates, the question of who can actually count the Holocaust's memory as their own has in certain cases become more important than the question of what really happened in the Second World War. In contrast to the Holocaust of the Jews, *Shoah*, the Holocaust of the Roma, *Porrajmos*, has not been highlighted in the cultural and cineastic world. There are no *Porrajmos* historians who could play as important a role as Raoul Hilberg, Christopher Browning, Yehuda Bauer and other leading Holocaust historians have done. Neither are there any globally acknowledged moral authorities on the Roma side like Simon Wiesenthal or the Nobel Prize winner, Elie Wiesel.

Despite this, at the start of the Czech debate, *Porrajmos* was perceived as equal to *Shoah*; this was primarily because there were so few who cared whatsoever. As I will show, *Porrajmos* did, however, rouse a Czech reaction. Denial of the repression of gypsies during the Second World War became part of a defence against charges of Czech participation in the gypsy genocide.

The *Porrajmos* and Roma in the Czech context

Most of the 6,500 gypsies who, at the start of the Second World War, lived in Bohemia and Moravia lost their lives during the following six years: some in Auschwitz-Birkenau to which they were deported; the others within the Protectorate's borders, primarily in the two concentration camps intended for Czech gypsies – Lety u Písku and Hodonín u Kunštátu.[11] The situation in Slovakia was different, however. While the repression of Jews was one of the Slovak war state's central policies, Tiso's measures against the gypsies were never as intensive, and did not therefore compromise the Tiso regime as much as the deportations and murder of Jews had done.[12]

Only a couple of hundred Czech Roma survived the Second World War, but as early as 1947 there were, according to statisticians, as many as 16,752 Roma in the Czech lands of Bohemia and Moravia; a result of the first wave of migration from Slovakia. The second wave took place in the 1950s when the Slovak Roma came as manpower for the Czech heavy industry. In the Czech border regions the immigrating Roma from Slovakia replaced the earlier Sudeten German population.

Under communism there were social programmes which focused on the Roma and collectively recognised them as a weak social group in need of state help. This meant that the Roma could not later feel that they were collective victims of communism. On the other hand, the authorities refused to allow the Roma to develop their own lifestyle and culture and did their utmost to force them to be 'converted', i.e., to be assimilated into the majority population.[13] They were never recognised as a distinct national minority in Czechoslovakia. In this way the Roma were prevented from strengthening their relation to their own identity and thereby to their history.

In 1958 a special law prohibited the Roma from continuing their hitherto nomadic lifestyle. The uneven distribution of the Roma in the Czech lands which caused a locally very high concentration of Roma, and the enforced change of their traditional lifestyle, created a tension between Roma and non-Roma Czechs that the Czechoslovak authorities never managed to solve. In 1989 a total of almost 400,000 Roma lived in Czechoslovakia; about 145,000 in the Czech lands and 250,000 in Slovakia. Among the 10 million inhabitants of Bohemia and Moravia, the Roma at this time comprised 1.4 per cent of the population (in Slovakia it was a case of 5 per cent of 5 million inhabitants). As the ethnologist, Arne Mann, has pointed out, these figures actually represented 'qualified estimates', because the definition of who was and was not a

Roma was very unclear and sometimes subjective.[14] As Mann has emphasised, it was only after 1989 that the Roma in Czechoslovakia were first able to freely discuss questions about their identity and also participate in political life.

Shortly after communism's collapse, the first Roma political party was founded, named *Romská občanská iniciativa* ('The Roma's Citizen Initiative'). However, certain new radical political parties with extremist and anti-Roma tendencies formed during the same period, as already mentioned in a previous chapter. In addition, Czechoslovakia's partition created new problems, as some of the Roma from Slovakia intended to move to their relatives in the Czech Republic and obtain Czech citizenship; a tendency that was met with increased unease in Czech society. In a November 1993 opinion survey, more than 60 per cent of the questioned Czechs stated that they had negative feelings about the Roma.[15] In 1993 alone, during the first year of the Czech Republic's independence, five people died as the result of racially-motivated crimes of violence. The most well-known crime took place near Lety in the Písek region, where armed extremists prevented three Roma from leaving the water in which they were bathing, thus causing them to drown. According to the Czech Ministry of the Interior, from January 1993 to mid-1994 over 450 racially-motivated violent crimes had been committed.[16]

When the euphoria from the 'Velvet Revolution' had begun to diminish, Western mass media described the situation in the Czech Republic in very dramatic terms. The British newspaper, *The Independent*, described, for example, racism among the Czechs in the following way: 'If you confuse the word "Gypsies" and "Jews", it might be Germany in the 1930s. Replace it by the word "Black" and it might be South Africa some years ago.'[17]

From the Czech perspective, the question regarding the relation between the state and the Roma minority became sensitive because it called into question the new democracy's development with regard to one of its apparently strongest points, i.e., striving for respect of human rights. President Havel had, in particular, become an important symbol due to his fight for human rights during the communist regime. Suddenly it was 'his' regime that was criticised for exploiting the post-communist citizenship law in order to discriminate the Roma.

Lety, Polansky and the Americanisation of the *Porrajmos*

In the beginning Paul Polansky acted on his own. However, taking into account the development which followed, his continued engagement in 1994 can be seen as an attempt to situate the *Porrajmos* within a larger historical-cultural context – to Americanise the genocide. The starting point is that important American actors became drawn into his conflict with Czech authorities and that the same American institutions included Polansky's activity in their own

Figure 11 A crucified Romani man as a symbol of the victims of the *Porrajmos*, the Holocaust of the Roma in the Protectorate Bohemia and Moravia. This memorial plaque is placed inside a small cemetery in Černovice near the former *Porrajmos* camp Hodonín u Kunštátu. Photo: Tomas Sniegon

international operations. The year is important, taking into account what some researchers call 'the *Schindler's List* effect', by which is meant 'a readiness to suspend critical judgement' on how the Holocaust is portrayed in Steven Spielberg's film,[18] or 'the great moral paradigm',[19] which refers to The Year of the Holocaust in the USA in 1993 (when The U.S. Holocaust Memorial Museum opened and *Schindler's List* had its premiere) and its immediate results. Polansky's discoveries in the Lety archive came just a few weeks after *Schindler's List* had been awarded several Oscars. After 1994 the American engagement in the Czech Lety debate decreased substantially.

On 15 May 1994 Polansky published an article about his discoveries in Lety in a local American newspaper, *The Decorah Journal*, with the heading 'Researcher Claims Thousands of Gypsies Exterminated by Czechs'. He additionally presented his findings to the Commission on European Security and Cooperation in the American Congress in Washington. The reason he decided to inform this specific commission was his apprehension that all the countries that had signed the Final Act of the Conference on Security and Cooperation in Europe in Helsinky in 1975 guaranteed that they would preserve 'death camps' from the Second World War in their original condition as national monuments. Lety was, according to Polansky, a 'death camp' for Czech gypsies. He did not specify the relation between his own use of the term 'death camp' and the official use of the same term used in connection with the Holocaust of Jews. *Death camps* or *extermination camps* signified only a few camps which existed in occupied Poland and whose non-official categorisation in German was *Vernichtungslager*.[20]

All of this led to a meeting between Polansky and representatives of the Czech embassy in Washington, which was also attended by a representative of the Congress' Commission on European Security and Cooperation and a director of the U.S. Holocaust Memorial Museum. Polansky claimed that during the meeting he received a promise from the Czech diplomats that the pig farm in Lety would be demolished. It was at that time owned by the Czech state but subsequently privatised in September 1994, at which point the Czech state retreated from the question of responsibility for the future of this place.

In September 1994 Polansky participated as a member of the American delegation in an international colloquium arranged by the Conference on European Security and Cooperation in Warsaw. He had the opportunity of speaking before representatives of about 100 countries; his subject being the Czech government's ignorance regarding the memory of the *Porrajmos* in Lety. His critical words coincided with a broader American criticism of the Czech Republic on the matter of a new Czech law on citizenship, which inter alia made more difficult the possibility for Czechoslovak Roma, who in connection with Czechoslovakia's partition wanted to move from Slovakia to the Czech Republic, to become Czech citizens. American representatives described the Roma's situation in Central Europe as 'a humanitarian crisis'.[21]

In October 1994 the Human Rights Commission of the U.S. Congress criticised the Czech citizenship law in a comprehensive study of human rights in the Czech Republic. This was at the same time the first study of the same subject since 1988: 'The Czech Law on state citizenship lacks respect for minorities' rights and violates the norms of the Conference on Security and Cooperation in Europe ... As long as human rights are a domain just for the majority, the transition to democracy will be neither complete nor firmly anchored in the Czech Republic.'[22] The report referred to 'an American historian with Czech roots' who had recently found archive material on the camp in Lety.[23] As far as I have been able to ascertain, Paul Polansky was one of the first Americans – if not the very first – who strived, as an aspect of a generally increasing American interest in the Holocaust, to highlight the memory of the *Porrajmos* and the situation of the Roma in Eastern and Central Europe. A Czech pig farm on the site where the Roma were imprisoned and died during the Second World War was perceived as a powerful symbol in this context. My aim with the following account is to show how Czech historical culture was influenced by the American position and how the individual uses of history were applied in the Czech debate to meet Polansky's harsh criticism.

A part of the globe that has been stolen – the moral use of history

The first Czech public reaction occurred on 13 May 1995. President Václav Havel unveiled a new monument in Lety to gypsy prisoners who had lost their lives during the war years. The point in time corresponded almost exactly to the 52nd anniversary of the deportation of 420 Czech gypsies from Lety to Auschwitz-Birkenau, which took place on 4 May 1943. The ceremony to their memory was held just a few days after the European states and a number of other countries had celebrated the fiftieth anniversary of the end of the Second World War.

The pig farm was not demolished, but the monument was placed beside it. This monument, a work of the Czech artist, Zdeněk Hůla, was made in the form of a cracked globe with its top missing. While the globe under normal circumstances symbolises perfect wholeness, the damaged shape of the monument led to the conclusion that harmony could not be perfect without whatever was missing.[24]

In the context of the *Porrajmos* and its memory in the Czech Republic, the ceremony in Lety initiated the development that Klas-Göran Karlsson has characterised as the moral use of history. History was used as a moral force in the political-cultural agenda, the indignant main actors of which strived to come to terms with the earlier totalitarian communist regime.[25] One wanted, in other words, to stress that the new, democratic age did not accept the earlier way of dealing with the memory of the *Porrajmos*. The Czech moral history usage was characterised by four important aspects. Firstly, 'the moralists' were, as noted, very critical of the totalitarian legacy, this in regard to both Czechoslovak communism and German Nazism. Secondly, they also expressed certain criticism towards Czech society during the Second World War, if only to a very limited extent. Thirdly, this use of history's foremost actors, Czech politicians with roots in *Charta 77* and those who sympathised with the anti-communist opposition, attached themselves to a demand to put on trial those few Czechs thought to be guilty of the repression of Lety prisoners and who were still alive; this despite the great distance in time between the war and the 1990s. Lastly, the use of moral history culminated in a radical demand to pull down the pig farm and replace it with a worthy monument to the memory of the *Porrajmos*.

In his very first speech in Lety in May 1995, President Havel emphasised that the camp had been established by German Nazis. However, the Czechoslovak Communist state which replaced the Nazi regime after the Second World War, manipulated and transferred the Roma in a more organised way, which led to them being dispossessed of their roots. 'This unhappy legacy has still not been overcome in both parts of our society, that is to say within the Czech majority's society and the Roma minority,' Havel added.[26] When he touched upon the guilt question he admitted that 'it however was the Czech police who ran the

Lety camp and guarded the prisoners', and that 'it was Czechs in the camp's vicinity who exploited the cheap gypsy workforce'. However, the Czech guilt was immediately relativised by Havel pointing out that 'it was also however Czech doctors who took care of the prisoners' health and it was also Czechs who at the risk of their lives hid gypsy families and saved them from being deported or saved gypsy children by adopting them'. At the conclusion of his speech the Czech president summarised: 'It is our duty towards these victims and towards ourselves to admit that also the Czechs bear a certain part of the responsibility for these horrors. We know what horrors racism can lead to. We must not allow them to be repeated.'

Havel's, as well as Paul Polansky's use of history can be categorised as moral. Both Polansky and Havel criticised the consequences of the totalitarian regime and the current position regarding the memory of the *Porrajmos* in the Czech Republic. Both emphasised that the situation had to be improved. Despite this, they demonstrated that moral history usage can easily place two practitioners in opposition to each other, if they use morality linked to ethnicity and the guilt question as determining criteria in their moral- and conscience-political engagement. Polansky became Havel's most radical critic and opponent.

At the core of this conflict was the question to what extent 'the Czechs' and even Havel's own family could be considered as having any guilt in the *Porrajmos*. According to Havel the principal guilt lay on the German side, whereas Polansky thought it lay on the Czech side; he seldom commented on the guilt of the Germans. Polansky even accused 'the Czechs' collectively of being racists.[27] In his view the main concrete responsibility for the *Porrajmos* lay with the Czech officials of the Protectorate government, and not least, with Havel's family.

The background of the conflict emerged in 1999, when Polansky published a novel in the Czech language entitled *Bouře* ('The storm'). According to the author the book was 'based on findings from documents about the camp in Lety and on facts about the Czech nobility's role in the starting and running of this camp, which by its cruelty could match German concentration camps'. Here, he no longer spoke of a death camp. Polansky further explained in the preface that 'most of the events had really taken place but the people were fictitious'.[28] The structure of *Bouře* was similar to Keneally's account of Oscar Schindler. The gypsy prisoners were in time deported from Roky to Auschwitz, but were in the end saved and freed by a non-gypsy hero. Polansky claimed that it was a Czech initiative which successfully induced the Germans to establish a gypsy camp in Roky, which in the Czech language is simply a modification of the name Lety. It was asserted that it was the Czech nobility, in collaboration with the Germans, who wanted to use gypsies as a cheap workforce. Two of the Czech collaborators behind the construction of Roky, who were indirectly identified in the book, were relatives of Václav Havel and his close colleague at the time of his presidency, Karel Schwarzenberg (in the book the names were changed to Šavel and Weisenberg).[29] In contrast to a number of Polansky's earlier comments and claims, *Bouře* aroused little attention in the Czech Republic.[30]

In a similar tone to Havel, certain other Czech politicians later expressed their moral history usage. One of them was the minister, Pavel Bratinka, chairman of the government's special commission for national minorities in the Czech Republic, who at another ceremony in Lety on 12 May 1997 also honoured the memory of those victims transported from Lety to Auschwitz in May 1943. 'The Nazis prepared and carried out during the Second World War a similar genocide of Roma as they committed against the Jewish population. The Roma victims' powerlessness continued even after the war when the communist regime did not respect the memory of the Roma victims and refused to recognise the Roma's national or ethnic identity,' Bratinka said.[31]

The third aspect of Czech moral history use – the demand for a just punishment for the guards who during the war worked in Lety and in the 1990s were still living – first arose in April 1997 when the two last Czech guards in Lety who were still alive were reported by the police to the then Czech Minister of the Interior, Jan Ruml, and the Czech Chief Public Prosecutor. Behind the report stood certain well-known Czech politicians and intellectuals.

A complete list of those who signed the document was never published, but a number of names gradually became known via newspapers. Among them were Petr Pithart, then chairman in the Czech Parliament's Upper Chamber; Pavel Tigrid, former Minister of Culture (1994–1996); the author Ludvík Vaculík; and the former Deputy Prime Minister, Pavel Rychetský. The group was formed by liberally orientated intellectuals and members of the social democratic party (apart from Rychetský this applied to, for instance, Pavel Dostál and Egon Lánský) who at that time belonged to the opposition in the Czech parliament. Most of those who stood behind the police report could thereby be characterised as supporters of the Czech national-liberal narrative. There were no conservative politicians in the group (it was the conservative government which three years previously allowed the privatisation of the Lety pig farm). As I will show, the conservative politics in relation to the *Porrajmos* were above all characterised by a non-use of history.

As with Havel's reaction, which did not come until 1995, after the American criticism, the demand for justice can also be seen as a reaction to an external impulse and not a reaction initiated by Czech actors' own needs. Behind the demand for at least a symbolic punishment for the former guards stood Polansky, and later his colleague Markus Pape, who took over Polansky's initiative when he was denied access to Czech archives and began to be criticised more strongly.

Pape was a German freelance journalist who had trained as a sociologist in Germany and since 1991 was living in Prague. In 1997 he published the book, *A nikdo vám nebude věřit* ('And no one will believe you'). This book was the first complex survey of the Lety history during the Second World War and its memory.[32] Pape claimed that he had gone through 'all accessible historical sources in both state and private archives'. His starting point was practically identical to Polansky's.

The heaviest accusation Pape presented was that 'the Czechs' had been guilty of genocide against gypsies during the Second World War, as Lety was also, according to him, a death camp. In order to get past the definition problem concerning concentration camps and death camps he added that the death camp status was not official in Lety.[33] Although the survivors had testified about murders by the guards and rapes of prisoners, Pape stated that he had not found any written proof that could confirm this. But there was at the same time no proof that could exclude it, he emphasised.[34] Last but not least, he pointed out the absent memory of the *Porrajmos* in the Czech Republic/Czechoslovakia after the war and wondered how it was possible that the guards' crimes were never sufficiently investigated, and why these people were treated generously even by the communist regime that said it had zero tolerance for fascism.

Pape's book accompanied the police report and he himself was among those behind the initiative. To supplement his activity, Polansky revealed to the Czech press in September 1997 that the police report planned against the two former Czech guards would be expanded to include a third person – a Czech man who during the war had worked at the Protectorate's Ministry of Internal Affairs and had borne the responsibility for the planning of genocide against the gypsies. According to Polansky this man was responsible for five concentration camps for gypsies. However, it remained unclear which other camps they were.[35] There were two, not five, camps of the 'Lety type' in Bohemia and Moravia (for apart from Lety, there was camp Hodonín u Kunštátu) during the Second World War. However, the third person was never reported to the police.[36]

The moral history usage's fourth and last aspect – the demand to demolish the pig farm – also occurred in 1997 and received support from liberal newspapers and magazines such as *Lidové noviny*, *Mladá Fronta Dnes*, *Respekt* and *Reflex*. *Respekt* emphasised, for example, that Lety was not the Czech Roma's problem but the Czechs' own problem: 'In a country that willingly boasts of its suffering under foreign oppression (and where Simon Wiesenthal has been made an honorary doctor several times) the existence of such a pig farm is an unforgivable disgrace – this is not only in relation to the surviving Roma but a disgrace to the Czechs themselves.'[37] The pig farm's continued existence was presented as an 'absurd comedy'.[38]

During the aforementioned ceremony of 12 May 1997 in Lety, the Minister of the Interior, Jan Ruml, and a government colleague, the minister, Pavel Bratinka, converted the demand to an official promise that they would ask the Czech government to buy back the pig farm, demolish it and replace it with a 'worthy monument' to the *Porrajmos* victims. The promise thereafter became

a heated political question. Nonetheless this solution attracted new supporters among Czech politicians and intellectuals. An especially visible person in
this context was Petr Uhl who in 1998 was appointed ombudsman for human
rights by the Czech government. The situation became acute in 1998 when
the conservative Czech government led by the Prime Minister, Václav Klaus,
who had been in power since Czechoslovakia's partition, was forced to resign.
During the first six months of 1998, when the country was preparing for a new
election, the Czech Republic was led by an interim government which was not
manifestly defined either politically or ideologically. That, which earlier had not
been able to gain political support for, now became possible to carry out – on 1
July 1998, just ten days after the parliamentary election in the Czech Republic
and literally during its last hours in power, the interim government decided
without any lengthy discussions that the pig farm's owner would be forced to
sell it to the state, which would consequently have the pig farm demolished.
A new, worthy monument would be erected in Lety and the building work
would begin in January 1999. The interim government at the same time bound
its successors to reach an agreement with the pig farm's owner about the conditions for its demolition, though without determining any further concrete
guidelines.

The new government which came into power after the 1998 election, and
which for the first time since the fall of communism was formed by the social
democratic party, seemed to respect the decision, despite the pig farm's owner
making increased demands and continually raising the value of the farm. As
early as during the final phase of the election campaign, Miloš Zeman, who
after the election became the country's new Prime Minister, expressed himself
uncompromisingly when he stated that 'for a new monument to the victims
of Czech – I emphasise Czech terror against our Roma citizens, even the sum
of 600 million Czech crowns is negligible'. The 600 million was the amount
the pig farm's owner AGPI Písek demanded for the demolition at this time.[39]

At least three members of the group that gave its support to the police
report against the previous guards in Lety became ministers in the new
social democratic government: Egon Lánský, who had himself survived the
Holocaust, was now Deputy Prime Minister as was the lawyer, Pavel Rychetský.
Pavel Dostál, an intellectual with roots in the world of theatre, was appointed
Minister of Culture.[40] However, it was this new government that in the end
made the definite decision that the pig farm would remain. This was done
with reference to the new situation that arose in 1998 and 1999, which will be
further analysed later in this text. The demand to replace the pig farm with a
new monument became in the end as big a failure as the demand to place the
last surviving Czech perpetrators before the courts.

The moral history usage in connection with the situation in Lety u Pisku
became on the Czech side problematic for three reasons. Firstly, it only took
place as a reaction to foreign criticism or foreign initiatives. This was the case

in regard to the first monument which, besides, was never seen as a permanent solution, not even by those politicians who stood behind its creation. There was continued talk about the need for a new and 'worthy' monument even after this monument's inauguration in May 1995. Havel's speech in Lety must also be mentioned here – after communism's collapse all Czech politicians kept quiet about both the *Porrajmos* and the Lety camp, despite several other aspects of the Second World War being drawn attention to on different occasions. It became generally admitted on the Czech side that without Polansky's initiative the almost total Czech lack of interest in the *Porrajmos* would have continued even after 1995. A similar situation arose surrounding the initiative to prosecute the old Czech guards from Lety.

However, even the interim government's decision of July 1998 was forced by external circumstances, which was also admitted by the government members. Vladimír Mlynář, who replaced Bratinka as chairman of the government's commission for national minorities, implied in an interview in June 1998 with the very revealing headline 'The monument in Lety will not solve the problems with the Roma but it is a necessary gesture', what lay behind the sudden urgency to demolish the pig farm:

> The whole problem about Lety is to a great degree a matter of the symbolism. Not many people realise that the pig farm in Lety also has an international dimension. Its existence is mentioned in every article about the Roma's life in the Czech Republic – and there have been many such articles written lately. Two hours ago I was visited by an American ambassador and even she talked about the American opinion regarding our relation to the Roma. Next week I will be meeting the ambassadors from the EU's member states and we will be discussing the same subject. Our relation to the Roma is an international problem for this country and it is an illusion to imagine that we can become members without us learning how we can solve the problem.[41]

The Holocaust's Europeanisation – and in this case the Europeanisation of the *Porrajmos* – thus became very important in 'the Lety debate' after 1997, which, for example, the Czech sociologist, Daniela Kozlíková, confirmed in her study *Romská otázka – překážka vstupu České republiky do Evropské unie?* ('The Roma question – a hindrance to the Czech Republic's membership of the EU?'). She observed that the Czech interim government could not disregard the EU's demands for respect for national minorities and individual human rights in the so-called candidate countries when it in July 1998 took its decision regarding Lety.[42]

The Europeanisation is also the most probable answer to the question why most of the Czech politicians and intellectuals did not begin to involve themselves in the questions surrounding the memory of the *Porrajmos* until 1997, in connection with the police report against the Lety guards. While the original initiative from Polansky in 1995 and 1996 was responded to coldly by most people, the continuation of the historical-cultural discussion, in the form of Pape's book and the police report that followed, received a much more favourable response; this despite the fact that the criticism of how the Czechs perceived the memory of the *Porrajmos* was directed towards the new political elite as well, with President Havel at their head. That the Holocaust's Europeanisation appears to be the most important explanation in this context can be motivated by the fact that the Czech Republic applied for membership of the European Union in 1996, thereby becoming the focus of EU interest. In its first report of July 1997 on the Czech Republic's possibilities of becoming a new member, the European Commission evaluated the Republic in a generally positive way and declared that the country was ready to begin negotiations on the membership terms. At the same time, however, the same commission, which at this time to an increasing extent looked at the memory of the Holocaust as a common European symbol for a European identity, maintained that discrimination of Czech Roma continued and that the country had serious problems with racially-motivated criminality, the authorities' insufficient tolerance of the Roma, and their social situation. According to a study, long-term unemployment was three times higher among the Roma than among the rest of the population in the Czech Republic.[43]

Secondly, the Czech moral history usage led to virtually no concrete results in the main question, except the monument from 1995; this despite the fact that the foremost actors of this history use had sufficient power to improve the situation and that the decision to demolish the pig farm had already once been made. It was, on the contrary, the same government whose members prior to coming into power had most actively advocated the pig farm's removal, who made the definite decision to let the farm remain where it was. Also this indicates that the moral use of history in connection with Lety and the *Porrajmos* was a pragmatic question for the actors behind this usage rather than an expression of their need to really achieve the wished-for change.

Thirdly, this usage primarily reflected a more or less open conflict and tension between, on the one hand, the foreign users, i.e., Polansky, Pape, some U.S. institutions and the EU – and, on the other, the Czechs. The main victims of the *Porrajmos*, Czech Roma, ended up in the shade.

From the defence of Roma identity to that of Czech identity – the scientific use of history

The scientific use of history expresses researchers' need to discover and reconstruct historical events in order to create new knowledge and in this way contribute to inner-scientific development. Concerning the debate on *Schindler's List* I showed the close connection between the scientific and the ideological use of history in the Czech Republic during the 1990s. In the debate about the camp in Lety the situation was only slightly different.

It is important to point out that the scientific production about the Porrajmos has been very limited both in Czechoslovakia and the Czech Republic and that the Lety discussion has mainly been based on works by one researcher, Ctibor Nečas. This man therefore attained just as dominating an expert role as Jitka Grunová in the Oskar Schindler debate. It was only in the Lety debate's closing stage that a few more historians joined Ctibor Nečas.

The scientific contribution to the discussions clearly reflect two different phases, in which the Czech debate about the camp and the pig farm in Lety and about the whole *Porrajmos* developed within the Czech historical culture. The chronological demarcation of both phases is very simple – the first took place prior to Paul Polansky's strong anti-Czech attacks, and the second came after their commencement. Despite the fact that the history usage was the same in the debates, the scientific use of history played two different roles. During the first period, when Nečas was presented as a researcher dealing with the Roma's culture and history, his scientific production was orientated towards pointing out injustices in the Czech behaviour towards the Roma, which naturally included the *Porrajmos*. However, Nečas never stated his conclusions as clearly as Polansky. When Polansky entered the picture, and when Nečas had at the same time become the foremost Czech expert on the *Porrajmos*, his scientific production served far more than earlier the purpose of presenting counter-evidence to Polansky's accusations and assertions. I will document this by a few concrete examples.

As early as during the communist era Nečas questioned not only certain Czechs' attitude towards the gypsies during the Second World War but the handling of the 'gypsy question' in the first Czech Republic, as well.[44] He criticised that the Czechoslovak gypsies – as opposed to the Czechoslovak Jews – were never recognised as having their own nationality in Masaryk's first republic.[45] Moreover, in 1927 the Czechoslovak Parliament approved law number 117 'on itinerant gypsies'. The law was intended to combat 'gypsy criminality' but could be used flexibly against non-criminals, as well. In parliament the law was particularly defended by Czech and German members, who politically represented primarily the farmers' parties and parties whose programmes were built upon religious values. They demanded that the gypsies adapt their life-style to that of the majority population. The Czechoslovak law was inspired by a similar one in German Bavaria which had been passed the year before. In this way it was notably Bavaria and Czechoslovakia which had particular laws especially directed at gypsies. Other European countries like France also had laws against 'itinerant persons', but they were not aimed at a concrete, named ethnic group.[46]

The Czechoslovak anti-gypsy legislation of the interwar era continued to be developed even after the passing of this law. For example, all gypsies, not just the itinerant or criminal, became forced to register themselves with the authorities and obtain a special identity card that they had to carry permanently and use on many occasions when the non-gypsy citizens did not need to do the same. The law even attempted to prevent gypsy parents from living nomadically by legislating that their children could, in that case, be taken from them. All this could also be put into practice against non-criminal and non-nomadic gypsy families.[47]

The other controversial measure in Czechoslovakia of the interwar period came at the end of the 1930s, when Hitler's Germany intensified its oppression not only of Jews but also of gypsies. While a proportion of the German Jews found, at least temporary, refuge in the neighbouring country to the east – something used as proof of Czechoslovak democracy which could therefore stand in sharp contrast to German society's intolerance of minorities – the Czechoslovak authorities prohibited the German gypsies from seeking protection in their country in the same way as the Jews. It became increasingly important to carry the Czechoslovak gypsy identity card, as those who could not offer proof of identity were pursued by the authorities and even handed over to Germany.[48] This all took place even before the German occupation of Bohemia and Moravia on 15 March 1939.

These aspects of the first Czechoslovak Republic were not dealt with in the Czech national-liberal narrative, which the new elites highlighted before the mid-1990s. One of the reasons for that could be that criticism of the bourgeois Czechoslovakia of the interwar period was, by communism's opponents, perceived as part of the communist narrative and consequently dismissed as communist propaganda. These aspects could at the same time be ignored on the basis of the only very slight significance the Roma's history had had in all historical narratives in Czechoslovakia/the Czech Republic and Slovakia in the post-war epoch. A new 'post-communist' publication of Nečas' findings in 1994 did not lead to any great change, as his new book on the Roma's history during the Second World War – including facts about the *Porrajmos* and the concentration camp in Lety – was printed by a university publisher in Brno in 1994 in an edition of only 500 copies.[49]

In regard to the Czech attitude towards gypsies during the Second World War, Nečas brought up this question as early as in his first study on the *Porrajmos*, which was published during the communist era.[50] In the book that was published in 1994, the same year that Polansky made his first discoveries in the Lety archive, Nečas, without any attention whatsoever from the media, presented his up to then most bitter picture of the Czech relation to the Roma during the Protectorate.[51] Nečas cited Czech voices that demanded a radical solution to 'the gypsy question' and that included their demands in a letter to the Protectorate's Prime Minister, Rudolf Beran: 'Because humanity has failed we must take another route. We cannot be criticised if we are able to clear the nation's stock from such parasites as gypsies.' He also quoted the press of the time which expressed strong anti-gypsy sentiments: 'Humanity has no place here as it is too one-sided. All must of course work and everyone has the right to protect their property against such rabble.'[52]

At the start of 1995, before the monument in Lety was unveiled and before the mass media started paying attention to the issue, Nečas criticised in a newspaper interview the local population in the Lety area who allowed the pig farm to remain in place, as well: 'The local population bear full responsibility for the fact that there still exists a pig farm today in the same place where a camp was earlier.'[53] According to Nečas, many Czechs living in the region wanted to forget everything that had happened in Lety as soon as possible after the war; that is to say, before the start of the communist period. In a trial against personnel from the other concentration camp in Hodonín in 1947, no one was punished as a result of insufficient interest from the authorities. In the mentioned interview, Nečas also criticised the new elite who took over power after communism's fall: 'From my own experience I know that they almost do not care at all,' was his answer to the question of the leading Czech intellectuals' interest in the Roma's situation. These examples indicate that Nečas, during the period of time when he strived to draw attention to the *Porrajmos* for the Czech public, expressed a significantly more Czech-critical opinion than later, when the debate was internationalised. When the relation was solely about Czechs and the Roma he dared to exhort Czechs to respect the Roma's history. When the conflict attained an international connection he chose, however, to select such arguments that defended 'the Czech nation' against foreign accusations.

In 1994 Paul Polansky based his criticism on his findings in an archive in the Lety area. In other words, it should not have been difficult for Czech historians to locate his source material and test his conclusions at the same place. Polansky himself described his material investigation as follows:

> The first day I discovered a strange, deficient correspondence. The official camp diary which contained lists of prisoners did not correspond to the lists of those prisoners who had arrived at the camp. The Czech police transported to the camp in Lety thousands of Roma, but only 600 were given a number and were registered in the official camp diary. Among the documents I found papers which noted prisoners who had been shot while attempting to escape. I also discovered some files with death certificates; it was a matter of thousands. It took two days to go through them. According to these notations only eight people died of typhus. For some deaths absurd reasons were given: 'He laughed himself to death', 'He died because he could neither read nor write', 'He was so drunk that he could not live.'[54]

One could expect that the foremost *Porrajmos* historian would undertake the assignment when interest was so minimal among other historians, but there was not any polemic between Polansky and Nečas about how the American had treated the source material, and Polansky's sources were, moreover, never directly commented upon by the Czech historians. Even so, shortly after Polansky's criticism, Nečas questioned whether the killing in Lety had taken place at all. 'The prisoners were struck but there is no evidence that they were killed. I went through the register and among the causes of the prisoners' deaths there were only illnesses.'[55] Which register this was and what his view was on documents which, according to Polansky, stated exceedingly strange causes of death among gypsy prisoners in Lety – causes of death without illnesses – Nečas did not specify. Nečas did, however, criticise Polansky during the whole course of the debate, despite him admitting that there would not have been any *Porrajmos* debate at all in the Czech Republic had not Polansky put forward his criticism.[56]

In 1999, just before the final rejection of the pulling down of the pig farm, the resistance to foreign criticism culminated in the Czech Republic. Ctibor Nečas, while striving to present scientific proof, was joined by two more Czech historians. Together Jaroslav Valenta and Oldřich Sládek, Nečas organised a press conference to influence the government's decision 'in a scientifically correct direction'. At this conference they distributed a brochure published by the Czech Academy of Sciences Historical Institute.[57] In the brochure Nečas dismissed Polansky's and Pape's assertions that the Czechs committed mass murder of the Roma during the Second World War, and also their figures on the number of gypsy victims as exaggerated and lacking any evidence.[58] Any source-critical analysis of the material which Polansky and Pape had as their starting point and which he himself used was not carried out by Nečas here, either; something that suggested that he followed the line of the documents' authors when they described the causes of death in Lety. At the press conference, Nečas said he was against the remains of the dead being subjected to a new forensic examination to determine the causes of death – he insisted that typhus was the cause, and that a new examination would therefore be dangerous for those who carried it out.[59] On the question regarding the possible Czech responsibility for the Roma's deaths, Valenta added that the government in the Protectorate could not be seen as Czech and that 'the nation's core' could not be accused of those crimes committed during the Second World War. 'It is true that the government's members – at least in the beginning – had Czech origins and spoke the Czech language, but the government was not Czech in the sense of having been elected by the Czech nation and being its legal representative . . . It was the occupation power's Quisling tool.'[60]

Besides attempts to prove that the Czechs were neither murderers nor mainly responsible for the gypsy victims who died in Lety, there was a further historical argument, the weight of which increased in the debate's final stage. It concerned the claim that the pig farm was actually not in exactly the same place as where the gypsy camp had been situated earlier but 'in its vicinity'. However, any facts about exactly where the camp had stood could not be found. Certain representatives of the local authorities therefore asserted that 'no pigs tramp in Lety on the Roma's graves', at the same time as they admitted that the pig farm in actual fact covered a fifth of the original camp's grounds.[61] All similar claims referred to old, secret aerial photographs which were asserted to be stored in military archives and which could therefore not be presented.

It was peculiar, however, that the attempts to question whether the geographical situation of the site was historically correct, came only when the interim government hinted that the pig farm would be destroyed. Testimonies from the local population in Lety surfaced, in which it was very clearly remembered that the camp had actually stood somewhere else.[62]

Ctibor Nečas confirmed at the aforementioned press conference that 'it is impossible to determine the camp's original position', despite him earlier having claimed the opposite. Sládek, who worked at the archive of the Interior Ministry, confirmed on the same occasion that 'it is almost certain that the camp was not in the same place as where the pig farm is today'.[63] Any further explanation for these statements or analysis of why they came as late as four years after the first monument in Lety had been unveiled was not presented. But if all these arguments were true, no Czechs could be perceived as murderers of the imprisoned gypsies; no Czechs could be held mainly responsible and be accused of cynicism and indifference in relation to the *Porrajmos*, as one had not actually built on the site where the gypsies had died. It can therefore be noted that the named historians in the latter phase of the debate contributed to the increasing relativisation of the Czech involvement in the *Porrajmos*.

'Don't forget us' – the existential use of history

The existential use of history is an expression of a need to remember in order to orientate oneself and feel stability in a society that is undergoing rapid change or is under strong pressure. Groups finding themselves under strong external pressure can, by creating an existential use of history, try to reach an inner cultural harmonisation. Having traumatic experiences in common plays a particularly important role in such processes. Klas-Göran Karlsson speaks of these groups as 'memory societies'.[64]

Of all the Czech groups which participated in the debate on Lety and the *Porrajmos* it is, of course, the Czech Roma who comprise the most conceivable memory society in this context. The memory of the *Porrajmos* does not, however, have as natural a position in the Roma historical culture as, for example, the memory of the Holocaust in the Jewish historical culture. The Roma historical culture is far less researched than the Jewish, but it is generally known that the Roma, who have most often chosen a different lifestyle to the Jews, have not usually wished to be limited to a few specific places and territories. As Zoltan Barany has pointed out, even the Roma's relation to their own history has varied. History has, according to Barany, 'been an alien concept in Romani culture, where the dead are rarely mentioned and seldom become the subjects of commemoration.'[65] The Czech ethnologist, Eva Davidová, has also problematised this relation when describing the Roma as 'children of the moment'. She claims that 'the Roma ignore the future almost as much as they ignore the past'. The Roma's flexibility is, according to her, so great that they often conform to the religion of a country in which they currently live. The Roma following a nomadic life are seldom tied to specific places.[66]

A conception of this kind about time dimensions puts into question if there is a Roma historical consciousness at all. If the Roma's historical culture is not bound to history in the same way as many others are, what notion of the Roma's future would this reflect? And if the Roma's thoughts about the future were different, to what purpose would they use history at all? There is hitherto very little research on this topic, but if this were the case, for whom would the monument in Lety actually be intended?

When Paul Polansky began his examination of the Lety archive in 1994 and consequently his fight against the pig farm, he was assisted by some Roma. However, the general apprehension was that it was Polansky's initiative and not that of the Roma. In other words, Polansky's fight 'in the name of the Roma' could not be automatically interpreted as expressive of an existential use of history among the Roma. The same can be said about the activities that Polansky's colleague, and to a certain degree also successor, Markus Pape carried out. The debate surrounding Lety did not provide an unequivocal picture of 'Roma' as a homogenous group that could become united by a conception of how the Roma history in general and the *Porrajmos* in particular should be remembered.

At the start of the Lety debate there were two Roma political parties and more than forty interest groups, cultural associations and similar organisations in the Czech Republic. The first time the Roma's representatives involved themselves in the debate at an official level was in May 1995, when the first *Porrajmos* monument was unveiled in Lety. On the same day the Czech government's commission for minorities in cooperation with the Roma cultural museum in Brno organised a seminar on the *Porrajmos* with the name 'The unknown Holocaust'. Almost one hundred representatives of various Roma movements from the Czech Republic, Hungary, Poland, Austria and Germany participated in the seminar, but no concrete suggestions emerged on how the Lety problem should be handled in the future. When the government's representative, minister Igor Němec, who at that time was responsible for minority questions, was asked whether the monument next to the pig farm was a temporary or final measure, he replied that every monument, and there were many such in the Czech Republic, were in a way a challenge to those they were intended for.[67] Němec's words directed towards the Roma produced no reaction, despite the fact that it could be interpreted as indicating that the Czech government wished to partly give the responsibility of the memorial site to the Roma.

The largest Roma political party, the 'Roma Initiative' (ROI), did not participate in the discussions that ensued. Not until February 1999 did its representatives openly show their support for the idea of demolishing the pig farm and building a new monument in Lety, and claimed they had the support of the 'International Roma Congress', which, it was said, wanted to make the new monument a European symbol of the Porrajmos.[68] This was, however, the only reference to a foreign Roma organisation in the debate. The whole discussion between Czech Roma was otherwise enacted with the help of 'domestic' arguments. The alleged decision of the International Roma Congress was not commented on at all by other Roma participants in the debate. Thereafter the Congress refrained from involving itself in any further activities or lobbying.

The Roma's representatives in the special commission, which under the Czech government dealt with 'the Lety question', did not present any uniform opinion on how the memory of the *Porrajmos* in Lety should be handled, either. The first of them, Matěj Šarközy, initially claimed in the press that 'I and other Roma think that the pig farm must disappear'.[69] Shortly afterwards, however, another Roma member of the same commission, Rudolf Táncoš, criticised those Roma who fought for the pig farm's demolition and labelled them as 'certain activists from Prague who just want to be seen in the media'. His focus was instead directed at the present: 'Our problems must be solved at other levels – like by education, employment and the integration of the Roma minority'.[70] Also Jana Horváthová, a Roma researcher from the 'Museum of Romani Culture' in Brno, described the attempt to pull down the pig farm as a striving by 'some radical Roma and a small group of Czech politicians and intellectuals'.[71] All these signs could indicate that there was no collective will to remember the Porrajmos in a special way in order to fulfil the Roma's existential needs.

However, this was only partly the case. When the pig farm, and therefore also the Lety camp, attracted that much attention from the media and the scandal just kept growing, the Roma moved their focus to the other former gypsy camp from the Second World War on Czech territory, Hodonín u Kunštátu. The discussions on the *Porrajmos* were first expanded from Lety to both camps in 1997. To begin with, it seemed as if Hodonín could give rise to a similar scandal as that concerning Lety. It became apparent that the camp's site in Hodonín had during the communist period been converted to a 'pioneer camp', a summer camp for Czech children, and later to a camping site. The complex was privatised after the fall of communism, in 1995, in a similar way as the Lety pig farm. There was one single building left at the Hodonín camping site which had been there since the 1940s and had therefore been in use during the time of the gypsy concentration camp.[72] The situation regarding Hodonín has, however, never led to as great a scandal as the controversy surrounding Lety.

During the war, the camp in Hodonín u Kunštátu was intended for gypsies from the Moravian part of the Protectorate. As with Lety, the Hodonín camp was established in 1940 for 'asocial people' and for those who 'shunned work', Roma or not Roma. On 2 August 1942, however, the camp changed character and became a concentration camp solely for Moravian gypsies. It remained open until 30 September 1943, and during this period a total of 1,396 prisoners

Figure 12 Lety u Písku, 'AGPI Písek-production of pork meat'. In the same place, a concentration camp for Gypsies from the Protectorate Bohemia and Moravia was located during the Second World War. Photo: Tomas Sniegon

lived in its barracks. A third of them were women and children.[73] A total of 207 prisoners did not survive their time in Hodonín. Official explanations for their deaths were, above all, pneumonia, tuberculosis and typhus. The remaining prisoners were deported from Hodonín to Auschwitz.

Following the war the former gypsy camp served firstly as a collection point for Sudeten Germans, who were later punished by the Czechoslovak authorities or expelled to Germany and Austria. During the communist epoch new prisoners arrived – Hodonín became a punishment camp for the regime's opponents. The transition to a camp for children and camping site occurred, in other words, at a later point in time.

At the start of the summer of 1997, the 'Museum of Romani Culture' in Brno presented their own initiative to build a new monument in Hodonín in order to prevent the Moravian victims of Hodonín being forgotten when the focus was solely on Lety. The monument was unveiled in August 1997 during a ceremony whose objective was to remind people of the 54th anniversary of the largest transportation of gypsy prisoners from Hodonín to Auschwitz-Birkenau on 21 August 1943. As opposed to Lety, where the 1995 monument stood next to the pig farm, the Hodonín monument was not placed directly by the place where the camp was situated during the Second World War, but hidden in the woods above the old camp, next to an old mass grave where almost two hundred victims had been buried during the Second World War.[74] The monument's form was an iron cross with two Roma symbols: a wheel from a nomad vehicle and a harness. It was a creation of the Roma artist, Eduard Olah, and was to a large extent financed by donations from leading Czech politicians.[75]

It would, however, be too problematic to assert that the Roma initiative regarding Hodonín unequivocally illustrated a special Roma memory culture linked to the *Porrajmos*. The short debate on Hodonín was only a marginal one that arose as a counter-reaction to the development concerning Lety. Neither the Hodonín case nor the *Porrajmos* was presented from the Roma side as part of a historical narrative that could be characterised as Roma or Czech Roma. And the Roma did not show any interest in Hodonín until seven years after the Velvet Revolution and three years after the beginning of the Lety debate.

The extent to which the debate about the *Porrajmos* and its memory was steered by the scandals and attention surrounding Lety can be shown through two examples. Firstly, Polansky and Pape never referred to the paradoxical situation in Hodonín to strengthen their criticism of the Czech attitude towards the *Porrajmos*. In actual fact they did not participate at all in the side debate about the Hodonín camp, as their focus was upon Lety. Secondly, even a prominent representative of the Roma minority, Karel Holomek, who represented Czech Roma at the 2000 Stockholm International Forum on the Holocaust, forgot to remind people about the situation in Moravia and Hodonín when the Czechs were preparing a police report against the last Czech guards from Lety. The report concerned only the Lety personnel and no one from Hodonín, which Holomek later admitted was his mistake.[76] Holomek was a son of the only gypsy lawyer in Czechoslovakia during the interwar period and Chairman of *Společenství Romů na Moravě* ('Roma Association in Moravia'), and one of those who prepared and signed the 1997 police report.

There were exceedingly few Roma voices, if any, who linked together the need to strengthen the memory of the *Porrajmos* with a possible improvement of the Roma's lives in the present and the future in the Czech Republic. From this perspective Roma historical culture appeared fragmented and indistinct. That there were groups within the Roma minority of the Czech Republic which still experienced the *Porrajmos* as traumatic was demonstrated when Polansky published his book, *Tíživé mlčení* ('Heavy silence'), which included a few dozen testimonies from the survivors of Lety and their family members about life in the camp and life after the war.[77] However, there was at the same time neither the time nor the will to go deeper into the matter. A number of new problems arose, furthermore, which made the debate about the *Porrajmos* all the less relevant; something I will be analysing in the section on non-use of history.

The Roma were not the only ones who could be connected to an existential use of history in the context of the Lety debate. A group that also wanted to draw attention to their own history was represented by the 'Political Prisoners Association', which united people who had been repressed by the communist regime. One of its leading members, Stanislav Stránský, pointed out that there were other places of historical-symbolic significance that could be paid attention to instead of Lety, which meant that he was against the state investing large sums of money in order to particularly highlight the Roma's history: 'On the site of the former Rovnost camp near Jáchymov where dozens of people were tortured to death during the communist era there are today a camping site and summer cottages belonging to prominent people,' Stránský said to the newspaper, *Lidové noviny*, and complained: 'No one can force these people to demolish their summer cottages in consideration of the place's history. The Czech Republic has still no worthy monument to the memory of communism's victims and no one demonstrates the same striving to build such a one as people are doing in Lety.'[78] Jakub Černín, Chairman of the 'Association of Freedom Fighters', which during communism was called the 'Association of Anti-Fascist Warriors', complained in a similar way that the fight against Nazism did not get the same space in the post-communist Czech historical culture as the *Porrajmos*.[79]

In no such statement were the gypsy victims of the war considered as being equal with the Czech victims. This dismissive line of argument, that 'we' should be able to remember 'our' dead, while others should not, displayed a complete inability to remember and honour all the dead of the war, regardless of ethnicity. Nonetheless, the initiative of the Political Prisoners Association was successful. In connection with this group's activity in the Lety debate, the discussions on the need for a worthy monument for those who fought against communism intensified. In 1999, i.e., the same year that the Czech government definitively rejected the proposal that the Czech state should buy back the pig farm in Lety, demolish it and replace it with a dignified *Porrajmos* monument, the same government approved the suggestion of paying seventy million Czech crowns to reconstruct the former communist work camp of Vojna near the Czech town of Příbram and turn it into a monument of anti-communist opposition. No greater discussions followed this decision and the museum in the Vojna camp opened in 2005. The government's decision from 1999 indicated that the memory of communism was felt to be much more pressing and traumatic for the Czech politicians than the memory of the *Porrajmos*.

For Roma or without Roma? The ideological use and non-use of history

An ideological use of history is a matter of 'with the help of history constructing a relevant context of meaning, which is able to legitimate a certain power position and rationalise it by putting history in order so that mistakes and problems on the road to power are toned down, made banal or disappear'.[80] In the Czech context this ideological history usage was first and foremost expressed by the rejection of the Roma's right to their own history, and by the denial of the *Porrajmos* as an organised mass repression of Czech Roma.

The first attitude was primarily expressed by more or less racist attacks against Roma. There were not so many of these visible in the public debate, however. Taking into account that the strong tension between the Czech Roma and Czech society's non-Roma part was in other respects manifest, the limited debate was probably due to the mass media not wanting to publish such events that conflicted with existing Czech law. All the same, news reports have revealed that the problem has been far from negligible; this even in circles that were not right-wing extremist. Openly racist were, for example, arguments in the discussions about the camp and the camping site in Hodonín. The Town Mayor was forced to resign as he had in cooperation with the Roma cultural museum in Brno attempted to push through plans for a monument to the memory of Roma victims of the *Porrajmos* and even demanded that the camping site be demolished and replaced by a new monument in the same place. 'We do not want any Roma here,' explained a man from the village's administration to the media. The 1,500 inhabitants feared, according to him, those Roma who would come to Hodonín and honour the memory of the *Porrajmos* victims.[81]

The second attitude, the denial of the *Porrajmos* and the Czech camps' repressive character, was more sophisticated and its point of departure was the argumentation that the Czech historians presented as scientific evidence. This applied above all to the argument that there were no murders committed in the Lety camp, but rather that the Czech Roma died as the result of illnesses and the bad hygienic situation in the camp.

According to this logic the Lety camp was not a proper concentration camp as it, firstly, was not created through racial motives but instead intended for people who shunned work and could therefore not be fitted into society in any other way.[82] Secondly, the camp was not guarded as intensely as 'real' concentration camps, which meant that the prisoners could leave the camp if they had really wanted to.[83] Both arguments were intended to diminish, or even completely remove, the guilt of the Protectorate's authorities and of the Czech guards. This line of argument would turn the guards into victims as they were 'forced' to work in this dirty, unhealthy and therefore very dangerous environment.[84] The Czech nation would, then, be seen solely as the great victim of the war.

This argumentation was not presented by the Czech government as decisive when it in the end rejected the plans to demolish the pig farm in Lety. That it, even so, played an important role was apparent after the decision, when the discussions on the Lety pig farm continued, though on a far smaller scale. As late as 2005, one year after the Czech Republic joined the EU, the country's second president, the conservatively orientated, Václav Klaus, claimed that the Lety camp was not actually a 'real' concentration camp but 'a camp for those who did not want to work', and that it was not the guards but epidemics which killed the prisoners there.[85] In his referral to 'scientific historical proof' he was, remarkably enough, in complete agreement with the Czech communist member of the European Parliament, Miroslav Ransdorf, who used identical assertions in his argumentation.[86]

The use, which in its application was decisive in the end, consisted of the ideological history usage's special form: non-use of history. This use should be analysed as a conscious standpoint among intellectuals and political groupings that the historical dimension is to be ignored and suppressed. Instead of disturbing historical events, the society in question is to focus on current, specific socioeconomic conditions or on a bright future.[87] This standpoint was obvious, above all among those political and economic elites who made economic well-being the meaning and goal of the Czech post-communist development. Although these groups' intentions were not clearly shown in the discussion on the genocide of the Jews, they became very apparent during the years of 1998 and 1999, at the very time when a definite decision on the pig farm's future became unavoidable and when the problems between Czechs and the Roma were most clearly shown internationally as well. 'The non-users argued against the pig farm being torn down, since a step of this kind was claimed to lack 'rational grounds'.

The argumentation against demolition intensified significantly between the first government decision to pull down the pig farm in 1998, and the final decision not to do so in 1999. Most of the pig farm's defenders did not want to assert that the building of a pig farm in Lety in the communist era was correct, or openly support racist arguments that denied the Roma's right to honour those who had died during the *Porrajmos*. They instead pointed at 'a waste of resources' and made the *Porrajmos* memory an 'unprofitable business', and even tried to show that a demolition was contrary to 'democratic principles' and threatened 'private property'.

The pig farm's owner, AGPI Písek, protested most strongly against the farm being replaced by a new monument. The pressure from the interim government which wanted the farm torn down was considered unacceptable: 'If we cannot believe in democratic society's rules, the 1989 revolution was completely unnecessary. It is unthinkable to discriminate against private ownership and people in this way,' the owner said, and announced that his company would defend itself against the government in a judicial process.[88] Tomáš Sokol, who soon after the fall of communism became Czechoslovakia's Minister of the Interior and who later became a well-known lawyer, wrote a debate article, where he with powerful wording defended the inviolability of private property and warned against moral consideration in the calculations.[89] The voices calling for 'common sense' urged that the government should save the money that would be paid for the pig farm and invest it in social measures which could improve the Roma's contemporary situation in Czech society.[90] The high costs of unemployment if the pig farm were to close were also emphasised

– something that received powerful backing from the trade unions in the region as well. The farm workers' union representative, Ivan Kašpar, claimed that a closure of the farm would hit three hundred people: 'In the conflict between the government and the owner of the pig farm we will be giving our support to those defending their property,' he stated.[91] According to this appreciation, the whole conflict surrounding the pig farm was one between the government and the owner, or essentially a conflict between 'socialism' and 'capitalism', not one about how history is remembered and which values are reflected and created through this memory.

The definite government decision on 7 April 1999, which finally determined that the pig farm could remain, was an approval of arguments forwarded by those who were against history being used in the debate at all. Even more striking was that politicians, who were connected to a moral use of history while in parliamentary opposition, and who had later become members of the new government, were behind this decision. This applied above all to the aforementioned Pavel Rychetský, Egon Lánský, Pavel Dostál and, not least, the Prime Minister, Miloš Zeman. The social democratic government stated in their decision that it would not be possible for the state to purchase the pig farm and replace it with a new monument on the current budget. The government would, however, increase its support for 'putting the Roma minority on an equal footing with the Czech majority population'. Government policies would be directed towards long-term goals extending to 2020.[92] The unclear wording and the long time period meant that the fulfilment of the promises could essentially not be reached at all.

That the members of the new government abandoned their moral history arguments as soon as they took over government responsibility, supports the thesis that the moral use of history in the *Porrajmos* context for a number of Czech politicians was to a great degree a matter of political tactics. But if history was used morally in consideration of external circumstances, and particularly regarding the Europeanisation of the Holocaust, how can one explain the fact that in the end a decision was accepted – letting the pig farm remain – which by no means corresponded to these circumstances?

The explanation does not have to be complicated. At the end of the 1990s the Czech Roma themselves began to draw attention to their situation internationally by starting to leave the Czech Republic and applying for asylum in a number of Western countries, such as Canada, Great Britain, France, Finland and Sweden. This new turn of events came as early as August 1997, when a Czech television company indirectly encouraged Roma to seek happiness on the other side of the Atlantic by presenting Canada as an almost idyllic country and problem-free paradise for Roma.[93] Even before the year's end, more than a thousand Czech Roma had emigrated to Canada; during the following years the emigration continued and expanded to almost the whole Western world. According to a non-official report, in the Moravian town of Ostrava alone, where the Roma's social problems were considerable, there were about five thousand Roma who said they were willing to emigrate. Some Roma sold their properties during the preparations – but the tension increased even more when the majority were not recognised as political refugees and were forced to return to the Czech Republic.

In 1998 a new problem arose. In the Czech town of Ústí nad Labem there were plans to build a wall between private houses and an area where most of the inhabitants were Roma, because 'those who lived in the houses were disturbed by their Roma neighbours'. Matiční Street, where the wall began to be built, became known in the whole of Europe. The wall began to be described in the foreign mass media as a 'new Berlin Wall' which would separate two ethnic groups instead of two ideologies, as the Berlin Wall had done.[94]

The whole business started in May 1998, just before the extraordinary parliamentary election, when the interim government was still in power. It was already well underway when the government decided that the Lety pig farm should be demolished. The general crisis culminated during the following year and international institutions such as the Council of Europe and the EU Commission became involved in the search for a solution. The social democratic party, *Česká strana sociálně demokratická* (ČSSD), which took over power in the country after the 1998 election, observed in October 1999 that the situation concerning the Czech Roma, and especially the crisis regarding the wall in Ústí nad Labem had become a serious hindrance to the Czech Republic's EU entrance. To a considerable extent this led to the pig farm in Lety – and with it the whole *Porrajmos* complex of problems – losing its earlier position as the most important symbolic question in relation to the Roma's rights. A decision to pull down the pig farm would hardly have enabled the Czech Republic to save face internationally. In this context the Roma's history had once again become unimportant to the Czech majority population. This was confirmed when the government's decision met no strong or visible protests from the Czech public.

Czech continuity

As I have shown, all the analysed uses of history on the Czech side were above all used to dismiss charges of the guilt of certain Czechs during the Second World War, and to confirm the conception of the Czech nation as a collective victim during the war. From this perspective the results of the Lety debate were very similar to the result of the Czech discussions about the film, *Schindler's List*. In both cases it became clear that the young Czech democracy and the new Czech state were not ready to critically reassess historical developments prior to 1989, or for that matter give up a black-white, ethnically accentuated thinking, directed towards attributing to all the nation's members positive characteristics, and at the same time negative characteristics or at least negative intentions to non-members.

I have also demonstrated that the results of the different uses of history could vary – in regard to the moral use of history the results were dependent, for example, to a great extent on the users' ethnicity, as the goals of Polansky and Pape were not identical to those of Havel and others. Even the existential history use's main proponents actually stood in opposition to each other – at least according to the view presented by those Czech organisations representing communism's victims. In defence of 'the positive Czech-ness', certain Czech actors used different history uses during the course of the debate; while they could start their argumentation with a moral usage, they tended, in the end, to lean upon an ideologically accentuated non-use. Last but not least, I have shown that a history usage could be applied to reach two almost completely different goals – this in the case of the scientific history usage on the Czech side. Although the scientific use of history at the start of the 1990s indicated that the Czech innocence in relation to the *Porrajmos* should be problematised to a greater extent, at the end of the 1990s the historians contributed with their scientific proof to confirm the opposite. In this case it also becomes clear how thin the line between a scientific and an ideological history usage can be.

From the perspective of the aforementioned historical narratives it was remarkable that the result of the Czech debate on the *Porrajmos* did not change or at least strongly put into question the communist narrative's non-use of the *Porrajmos*, but rather replaced it with a new non-use. The result of the *Porrajmos* debate and its reception are therefore much more indicative of continuity in the Czech standpoint than discontinuity or the wish to manifestly change the earlier situation.

Notes

1. See, for example, Linenthal, *Preserving Memory*, 228–48.

2. There are differing ways of using the terms 'Roma' and 'gypsies'. I write about gypsies when referring to events and contexts before and during the Second World War. When dealing with the post-war era and memory of the Nazi repression of gypsies, I use the term Roma instead, and therefore write of the Holocaust of Roma and not gypsies. In the Czech language this difference is noticeable by use of the terms cikáni (gypsies) and Romové (Roma).

3. Paul Polansky, *Tíživé mlčení*, Prague: GplusG, 1998, 9–19.

4. Yehuda Bauer, 'Jews, Gypsies, Slavs: Policies of the Third Reich', in *UNESCO Yearbook on Peace and Conflict Studies 1985*, Paris: UNESCO, 1987, 86.

5. Yehuda Bauer, 'Correspondence: "Gypsies and the Holocaust"', *The History Teacher* 25(4), August 1992, 513–15.

6. Raul Hilberg, *The Destruction of the European Jews*, New York and London: Holmes & Meier, 1985.

7. Sybil Milton, 'Gypsies and the Holocaust', *The History Teacher* 24(4), August 1991, 375–87, quote 382.

8. Milton, 'Gypsies and the Holocaust', 516.

9. See Zoltan Barany, *The East European Gypsies: Regime Change, Marginality and Ethnopolitics*, Cambridge: Cambridge University Press, 2002, 107–10.

10. Ian Hancock, 'Responses to the Porrajmos: The Romani Holocaust', in Alan Rosenbaum, Ed., *Is The Holocaust Unique?* Boulder, CO and Oxford: Westview Press, 2001, 69–96.

11. At least 2,645 Czech Roma died in Auschwitz-Birkenau. Only 583 gypsy prisoners returned from the various concentration and death camps after the war. For more about this, see Ctibor Nečas, *Holocaust českých Romů*, Prague: Prostor, 1999, 173.

12. The repression of the Roma occurred in Slovakia during the whole of the Second World War, but their organised physical mass-liquidation started first when Slovakia began to be occupied by Germany at the end of the summer of 1944. For more on the Slovak situation see, for example, Július Táncoš and René Lužica, *Zatratení a zabudnutí*, Bratislava: IRIS, 2002, 51–102.

13. Anna Jurová, 'Rómovia v období od roku 1945 po november 1989', in Michal Vašečka, ed., *ČAČIPEN PAL O ROMA. Súhrnná správa o Rómoch na Slovensku*, Bratislava: Inštitut pre verejné otázky, 2002, 53–77.

14. Arne Mann, *Romský dějepis*, Prague: Fortuna, 2001, 38. After 1989 it became impossible to use 'race' as a criterion for registration in the statistics. Only 32,903 people stated that they identified with a 'Roma nationality'; in 2001 the figure was merely 11,716 inhabitants. There were diverse Roma groups in the Czech Republic that came from different regions, spoke different languages and had different lifestyles. For example, indigenous Czech Roma; Roma immigrating from Slovakia; Slovak-Hungarian Roma from the border area between Slovakia and Hungary; and nomadic Roma who came from, for instance, Romania. See Ctibor Nečas, *Romové v České republice včera a dnes*, Olomouc: Vydavatelství Univerzty Palackého, 1995, 48–49.

15. *ČTK*, 30 November 1993.

16. *Rasismus v České republice, profil, ČTK*, 15 May 1995.

17. *The Independent*, 13 January 1993.

18. Michael Andre Bernstein, 'The Schindler's List Effect', *American Scholar Magazine*, Summer 1994.

19. The term is used by Jeffrey Schandler to show how important a moral role *Schindler's List* and The Year of the Holocaust had for American thinking. See Jeffrey Shandler, 'Schindler's Discourse: America Discusses the Holocaust and Its Mediation, from NBC's Miniseries to Spielberg's Film', in Yosefa Loshitsky, ed., *Spielberg's Holocaust*, Bloomington and Indianapolis: Indiana University Press, 1997, 153–68.

20. These were Belzec, Sobibór, Treblinka, Majdanek, Auschwitz-Birkenau and Chelmno. For more on the categorisation, see, for example, Abraham Edelheit and Hershel Edelheit, *History of the Holocaust*, Boulder and San Francisco and Oxford: Westview Press, 1994, 272–95.

21. *ČTK*, 23 September 1994.

22. *ČTK*, 21 October 1994.

23. *MF Dnes*, 31 March 1995.

24. Hůla explained his view of the monument's symbolism in the magazine *Týden* 20, 1995, 60.

25. Klas-Göran Karlsson, 'Historiedidaktik: begrepp, teori och analys', in Karlsson and Zander, *Historien är nu*, 58.

26. Havel's complete speech was published in Hana Frištenská, Ilona Lázničková and Andrej Sulitka, *Neznámý holocaust*, Prague: Muzeum romské kultury, 1995, 12–14.

27. In an interview Polansky went so far as to say that the Czechs were 'the most racist nation I have ever come across'. *ČTK*, 15 December 1995.

28. Paul Polansky, *Bouře*, Prague: GplusG, 1999, 7.

29. Karel Schwarzenberg's family were forced to leave Czechoslovakia following the communist power takeover there in 1948. Until 1947 they owned a total of eleven palaces and 30,000 hectares of land there. After the 1968 Prague Spring, Karel Schwarzenberg, who was born in 1937, began to personally support the opposition against communism in Czechoslovakia and primarily the *Charta* 77 movement. In 1984 he was appointed chairman of the International Helsinki Committee for Human Rights. He returned to Czechoslovakia after 1990, where he also received

back a large part of the family's previously owned property. Between 1990 and 1992 he led Václav Havel's presidential secretariat. Following the close of the Lety debate, Schwarzenberg became engaged more and more intensively in Czech political life. In 2004 he was elected to the Czech parliament's upper chamber, *Senát*, and became the Czech Republic's foreign minister in 2007. In 2013, he became one of the two main candidates in the Czech presidential elections, but lost the final round to Miloš Zeman, the former prime minister who became the third post-communist president of the Czech Republic after Václav Havel and Václav Klaus.

30. The only newspaper that attempted to examine Polansky's information was a relatively insignificant evening paper, *Super*, in 2001; *viz.*, two years after the book had been published. The journalists wrote that 'a certain historian' had discovered facts which wholly corresponded with the book's contents. When the paper asked Karel Schwarzenberg, the former head of President Havel's secretariat in Prague, whether his family had, in fact, exploited Roma and contributed to Lety's establishment, Schwarzenberg denied all such claims. The article's writers came to the conclusion, even so, that it was Schwarzenberg rather than the unnamed historian who had lied. The problem was not examined any more closely. See *Super*, 12 September 2001.

31. *ČTK*, 12 May 1997.

32. Markus Pape, *A nikdo vám nebude věřit. Dokument o koncentračním táboře Lety u Písku*, Prague: GplusG, 1997.

33. Ibid., 118.

34. Ibid., 119.

35. *ČTK*, 22 September 1997.

36. The enquiry initiated by the police report against the former Lety guards was terminated at the end of 1998 because 'it could not be ascertained that genocide had actually been committed'. The investigators interviewed, according to official comments, a total of fifty Roma witnesses from Lety. *ČTK*, 19 January 1999.

37. 'Ten prasečinec páchne', *Respekt*, 12 May 1997.

38. 'Slunce, seno, koncentrák', *Reflex* 36, 1997.

39. *Respekt* 49, 1998.

40. Lánský, who was originally from Slovakia, was deported as a Slovak-Jewish child to a concentration camp by the Tiso regime but managed to survive.

41. 'Památník v Letech nevyřeší problémy s Romy, ale je to nutné gesto', *Lidové noviny*, 4 June 1998.

42. Daniela Kozlíková, *Romská otázka – překážka vstupu České republiky do Evropské unie?* Prague: Sociologický ústav ČSAV, 2001, 51–52.

43. See Pavel Navrátil a kol., *Romové v české společnosti*, Prague: Portál, 2003, 61.

44. Ctibor Nečas, *Nad osudem českých a slovenských cikánů v letech 1939–1945*, Brno: Univerzita J.E. Purkyně, 1981, 42–54.

45. Ctibor Nečas, *Českoslovenští Romové v letech 1938–1945*, Brno: Masarykova univerzita, 1994, 11.

46. Ibid., 18–26.

47. Ibid., 26.

48. Ibid., 29–33.

49. Nečas, *Českoslovenští Romové v letech 1939-1945*.

50. Nečas, *Nad osudem českých a slovenských cikánů v letech 1939-1945*, 42–54.

51. Nečas, *Českoslovenští Romové v letech 1939-1945*, 33.

52. Ibid., 35.

53. *Respekt* 4, 1995.

54. Polansky, *Tíživé mlčení*, 10–11.

55. *MF Dnes*, 12 April, 1996.

56. *Respekt* 4, 1995.

57. Jaroslav Valenta, Ctibor Nečas and Oldřich Sládek, *Historikové a kauza Lety*, Prague: Historický ústav ČSAV, 1999.

58. Ibid., 24 and 35.

59. 'Češi nemají na svědomí romský tábor v Letech, tvrdí historici', *Lidové noviny*, 31 March 1999.

60. Valenta, Nečas and Sládek, *Historikové a kauza Lety*, 13.

61. *Lidové noviny*, 12 February 1999.

62. *Haló noviny*, 12 February 1999.

63. 'Češi nemají na svědomí romský tábor v Letech, tvrdí historici', *Lidové noviny*, 31 March 1999.

64. Karlsson, 'Historiedidaktik', 55–57.

65. Barany, *East European Gypsies*, 103.

66. Eva Davidová, *Cesty Romů. Romano Drom 1945–1990*, Olomouc:Vydavatelství univerzity Palackého, 1995, 123–40.

67. *ČTK*, 13 May 1995.

68. *Zemské noviny*, 2 February 1999.

69. *Zemské noviny*, 7 May 1998.

70. *Zemské noviny*, 3 August 1998.

71. *MF Dnes*, 10 March 1999.

72. These facts were first made public in May 1997 by Czech television in a documentary with the Roma entitled *Ausvicate hi kher báro*.

73. For more about Hodonín's history, see Ctibor Nečas, *MA-BISTEREN-NEZAPOMEŇME. Historie cikánského tábora v Hodoníně u Kunštátu*, Praha: Muzeum romské kultury, 1997, 7–11.

74. When the monument was being planned, there was also a discussion of possibly situating it closer to the original place/camping site or even making a small museum of the only authentic building left in Hodonín dating from the Second World War. The camp site's owner, Alena Vojtová, commented on the situation in this way in the Czech press: 'When I bought this place no one thought that its history was important. No one was interested then and now suddenly everyone cares. If the Roma want to have a memory hall here I am not against it. Just let them pay for the reconstruction.' See *MF Dnes*, 30 May 1997.

75. Among the donators were both President,Václav Havel and Prime Minister,Václav Klaus.

76. *MF Dnes*, 6 May 1997.

77. Polansky, *Tíživé mlčení*.

78. 'Političtí vězni: Proč má památník v Letech přednost?', *Lidové noviny*, 11 July 1998.

79. *Slovo*, 22 January 1999.

80. Karlsson, 'Historiedidaktik', 59.

81. *Lidové noviny*, 20 November 1998.

82. See, for example, *MF Dnes*, 31 March 1999, or magazine *Veřejná správa* 19, 1999.

83. See, for example, *Haló noviny*, 12 February 1999, or magazine *Týden* 39, 2000.

84. See *Zemské noviny*, 15 March 1999.

85. Václav Klaus in an interview with the newspaper *Lidové noviny*, 14 May 2005.

86. Ransdorf, who in the communist era worked as a historian, categorically claimed that 'as a historian I know very well that people lie almost limitlessly about Lety – there was never a concentration camp there'. *Právo*, 10 May 2005.

87. Karlsson, 'Historiedidaktik', 61.

88. *Lidové noviny*, 4 July 1998.

89. *MF Dnes*, 31 July 1998.

90. See, for example, *Lidové noviny*, 5 May 1998, and *Právo*, 4 June 1998.

91. *Špígl*, 11 July 1998.

92. See, for example, *MF Dnes*, 8 April 1999.

93. The report was transmitted by TV Nova on 5 August 1997.

94. For more, see Rick Fawn, 'Czech Attitudes towards the Roma. "Expecting More of Havel's Country"?', *Europe–Asia Studies* 53(8), December 2001, 1193–1219.

CHAPTER 6

The Slovak war history goes to Europe

The Holocaust in the Slovak national-European narrative

In this final empirical chapter I examine the Holocaust's position in the new, post-communist Slovak narrative. The aim has been to place Slovakia side by side with the West European democratic countries. I call this narrative *the national-European narrative*. It was developed with the intention of creating an antipole to both the communist and the national-Catholic narrative.

The need for a new non-nationalistic Slovak historical narrative that would point towards a democratic future was evident already in the shadow of nationalism's successes prior to the partition of Czechoslovakia in 1992. However, it developed fully only during Slovakia's independence after 1993. Its contours became clear after 1998, when Vladimír Mečiar and his party the *Hnutie za demokratické Slovensko* (HZDS), which together with the Catholic-orientated nationalists had dominated Slovak politics during essentially the whole separation process, lost the parliamentary election and were forced to leave their posts. The attempts to use part of Slovakia's war history to create a kind of Slovak 'European-democratic' narrative then began to characterise the process aiming at Slovakia's entry into the EU, which finally took place in 2004.

The event that became central in a new post-communist and post-Czechoslovak use of Slovak World War history was the Slovak national uprising, in Slovak *Slovenské národné povstanie* (SNP). The uprising was a revolt against Tiso's regime and took place in the summer of 1944. During the Second World War the uprising brought about positive reactions in the anti-Nazi coalition, which led to the USA, the Soviet Union and Great Britain recognising that part of Slovakia affected by the uprising and its political leadership as their ally.[1] However, at the end of October 1944 the rebels were defeated.

The uprising's symbolic significance was of great importance following the end of the Second World War, during Czechoslovakia's reunification in 1945, the communist regime until 1989, and even in the post-communist era. As the Slovak sociologist, Silvia Mihálikova, has pointed out, no other event in Slovak history has, during the 1990s, been able to function as a demonstration of the Slovak transition from the cross (which was the symbol of Catholic nationalism) to a Slovak star on the EU flag.[2]

As early as 1992, 29 August became the Slovak national day, after a heated political discussion in parliament with very mixed starting points and strong opposition from radical nationalists. Emphasising the uprising in particular has gradually become the most direct way for the opponents of radical nationalism to dissociate themselves from the Tiso regime and the national-Catholic narrative. The symbolic significance of the national day has been portrayed in even broader terms: as a reminder of 'Slovakia's resistance to dictatorship'.[3] Parliament's decision was never accepted by the radical nationalist side with the diaspora at its head.[4]

The attitude towards the uprising has been as split among the general public as it has been among the politicians. However, as the sociologists, Zora Bútorová and Martin Bútora, have shown, the way in which questions about the uprising have been put has had decisive significance. The public opinion polls between 1990 and 1993 showed that most Slovaks saw the SNP as part of their national identity and pride. As many as 89 per cent agreed (partly or wholly) with the statement that 'by the national uprising the Slovaks expressed in a convincing way their attitude towards fascism'. However, when the term 'fascism' was replaced by 'the fascist Slovak state' only 62 per cent of those questioned agreed. And when, in a third rewrite of the question, the message was that Slovakia had clearly rejected the wartime Slovak state's legacy through the uprising, only 49 per cent agreed.[5]

In order to illustrate the main problems in the handling of the Holocaust within the Slovak national-European narrative's framework I have chosen the concrete example of *Múzeum SNP* (the 'Museum of the Slovak National Uprising'), in the city of Banská Bystrica in central Slovakia. In the post-war period it is the most important museum to have been dedicated to the memory of the Second World War. During essentially its whole post-war existence, including the period after 1989, this museum has held a dominating position among all the Slovak museums dealing with modern Czechoslovak and Slovak history. Prior to 1989 the *Múzeum SNP* was at the same time the largest museum devoted to a single historical event in the whole of Czechoslovakia.

During the communist, as well as the post-communist, era the museum's way of presenting the SNP and the Tiso regime has stood in opposition to the national-Catholic narrative. After 1989 the museum abandoned the Czechoslovak communist historical narrative and began to seek a new method of presenting the SNP when facing its continued existence. Between the collapse of communism and Czechoslovakia's partition the museum organised the first major conference on the Holocaust since 1989. After Czechoslovakia's partition, the *Múzeum SNP* opened the first permanent exhibition on the Holocaust in Slovakia. It was also behind the Slovak national exhibition in Auschwitz at the beginning of the twenty-first century. There is, in my opinion, no other example that could express the changes within the Slovak historical culture and its relation to the Holocaust in the whole period of 1993–2004 better than this museum.

The uprising

The SNP started on 29 August 1944, the same day that Germany initiated a direct occupation of Slovakia in order to halt the Soviet Union's advance towards Berlin and crush the increasing Slovak opposition to the Tiso regime. The uprising ended with the rebels' defeat about two months later. This was the most important event in which a section of Slovak society demonstrated its opposition to Tiso's dictatorship.

The uprising was led by the Slovak National Council, which was established at the end of 1943 in cooperation between illegal Slovak resistance movements and the Czechoslovak exile government in London. Until August 1944 the Council worked illegally. The most important part of the resistance was certain units of the Slovak army that turned against Tiso – during the uprising the army was called the first Czecho-Slovak army in Slovakia. On the rebels' side these resistance forces were united with the communist and non-communist opposition. Germany, together with Tiso's regime, was forced to fight against approximately 60,000 rebellious Slovak soldiers and 18,000 armed partisans.[6] The rebels received assistance from 8,400 sympathisers from 32 countries. In total the uprising took place in about a third of the Slovak territory, with 1.7 million inhabitants, which comprised roughly two-thirds of Slovakia's population at the time. This did not, however, mean that all these people gave the uprising their support, but the population's structure and conduct in this area have, never been closely studied.[7] During the two months that the uprising lasted, the rebellious Slovak unit that acted independently of Tiso's government and Bratislava presented itself as 'a renewed Czechoslovak republic'.

The uprising's most problematic aspect was the fact that it was primarily enacted between two parts of Slovak society and not between two states. The Tiso regime managed to defeat the uprising only with the help of the Germans, which led to Tiso awarding German soldiers Slovak distinctions, which demonstrated, clearer than ever, that his regime's link to Nazi Germany was crucial for its survival.

The German army and its Slovak allies burned down 93 Slovak villages in the rebel territory and murdered over 5,000 people. The rebels, who in the uprising's final phase received unsuccessful assistance from some Soviet forces and Czechoslovak soldiers arriving from the Soviet Union, killed about 2,400 people, mainly Germans and supporters of Tiso's regime; among them Catholic priests.

The increasing opposition to the Tiso regime towards the end of the war also involved opposition from the Slovak Jews, i.e., those Jews who had not been deported from Slovakia during the first deportation wave of 1942. As early as April 1944 two Jewish Slovaks, Alfred Wetzler and Rudolf Vrba, managed to escape from Auschwitz-Birkenau to Slovakia and spread information about the conditions in the Birkenau death camp and about Nazi plans to enlarge Birkenau so as to effectively be able to mass-murder those Jews who were being deported from Hungary.[8] During the final days before the start of the German occupation and prior to the uprising, Jewish revolts occurred in the concentration camps of Nováky, Sereď and Vyhne, in which there were a total of approximately 4,000 prisoners, most of them Jews.

Approximately 1,500 Jews actively fought in the Slovak national uprising itself, primarily on the partisans' side. The uprising's defeat led to the recommencement of deportations of Slovak Jews to the death camps, and a further circa 12,000 Jews lost their lives in the so-called second deportation wave, which lasted until the end of the Second World War.

The museum as a historical-cultural object

As an expression of the Slovak historical culture the *Múzeum SNP* corresponds to what Pierre Nora called a site of memory, that is to say a material-cultural trace from the past that in a purposeful manner strengthens the feeling of continuity.[9] Memory sites, which Nora also calls 'illusions of eternity', thus express no spontaneity – diverse 'imagined communities' use memory sites like museums, festivals, memorial days or monuments both as material proof and symbolic guides. As Kristian Gerner points out, it is, however, above all the *national* dimension (which is also reflected in the museum's name) that is often decisive for the memory sites' function in a society. National memory sites refer to both the state and the state-supporting people.[10] This applies in the greatest degree to the Slovak case as well.

Museums dealing with societal development belong to those historical-cultural objects that clearly reflect all three dimensions of historical culture: the political, the cognitive and the aesthetic.[11] There is thus no particular history usage that could be described as completely dominating in connection with the museums' activities; one and the same museum often combines in its activities several uses of history simultaneously. Taking into consideration the character of the museums, their creators focus on the ideological as much as the political, the existential and the scientific history usages. As will become evident, the *Múzeum SNP* in Banská Bystrica has above all combined the ideological, the political and the scientific uses of history; the latter as it has also had the status of a scientific institution.

The museum's historians have linked together the ideological use of history with the communist period. It is therefore usual that they see the museum's activities after 1989 as 'purely scientific', separated from ideological and other influences. As I will show, these historians' view of Slovakia's history including the Holocaust is, however, influenced by their historical consciousness in the same way as with all other, non-scientific history users. The American sociologist, Gil Eyal, shows that a number of Slovak historians who wanted to distance themselves from communism, but themselves had roots in this system, perceived their task as a service to the nation, this despite the fact that several of them could not be counted among the supporters of the national-Catholic narrative. In this context Eyal cites the aforementioned Jozef Jablonický, who was first a communist historian, later turned against communism and became a dissident, and after 1989 became an authority on the history of the Slovak national uprising: 'History is a national discipline'.[12]

In my analysis of the museum's activities as expressions of changes in the post-communist Slovak historical culture, I study the museum's permanent and temporary exhibitions, various conferences organised by the museum and publications written by the museum's representatives and closest advisors.

My main focus is kept on the conferences for a number of reasons. They were, firstly, organised by the museum, which meant that the museum had full control of the choice of the main subjects, when they were to take place and who would be invited. Secondly, the conferences gave the museum's foremost representatives the opportunity to explain their own intentions and further plans in connection to the museum's activities, which illustrates the procedural development within the *Múzeum SNP* and the leading personalities' historical consciousness better than if I had only analysed the individual exhibitions as end-products. The conferences were organised far more often after the fall of communism than new permanent exhibitions, and it is clearly evident that the museum's historians and their colleagues who are mentioned in this context were not passive recipients but, on the contrary, active actors who to a great degree had participated in the development of the new narrative. Thirdly, the conferences demonstrated the development of the relation between the Slovak national-European narrative and the Holocaust from as early as 1992, although the Holocaust was presented in the exhibition rooms of Banská Bystrica only later. To sum up, the explanations presented during various conferences, combined with the exhibitions' texts, design and catalogues, imparted a clear picture

Figure 13 The Museum of the Slovak National Uprising in Banská Bystrica, Slovakia. The building consisting of two parts connected by a bridge was built in the 1960s. Photo: Tomas Sniegon

of the criteria behind the selection of the comprehensive material and the line of argument, i.e., the historical meaning the material was to follow.

The history of the museum before 1989

The first attempt to maintain the SNP's memory in a special way took place at the beginning of 1946, about a year after the collapse of the Tiso regime. The Czechoslovak government in Prague, with President Edvard Beneš at its head, tried to re-establish the first republic and its parliamentary-democratic system and reconcile Czechs and Slovaks after the war. In March 1946 an initial exhibition was organised in Bratislava; one that showed how one of the main centres of the uprising, Banská Bystrica, was temporarily liberated from the German occupation and how the SNP prepared the way for Czechoslovakia's reunification.

In December 1947 the Slovak National Council, which now became the leading Slovak organ within the Czechoslovak state, decided to establish a special institute, the Institute of the Slovak National Uprising.[13] The foundation-stone was laid by Edvard Beneš. This was, however, just a prelude to the initiative of establishing a specialised museum in Banská Bystrica and organise the first permanent exhibition about the uprising. The first museum was opened in 1955.

The period after the communists' power takeover in February 1948 was characterised by Stalinist thinking. The communists who had participated in the battles were presented as the uprising's indisputable heroes. An important moment came at the start of the 1960s when the Czechoslovak state changed the museum's status from regional to national. This indicated how much weight the regime attributed to the SNP's memory at this time.

The first permanent exhibition on the SNP from 1955 was changed in 1964 in connection with the twentieth anniversary of the uprising and replaced by another. The most important change was dropping Stalinism's most obvious imprint. It was thus not a question of a changed conception of the uprising, as the communists' merit in the fight against Germany and an expression of the Slovaks' will to build a communist system.

At the beginning of the 1960s plans were also initiated for the *Múzeum SNP* to have its own building. Its foundation-stone was laid in the central part of Banská Bystrica in 1964. A new *Múzeum SNP* was opened in 1969. Due to its special modern architecture the museum building soon became the town's most well-known silhouette. The statue-like construction consisted of two main parts resembling a two-part bowl on a pedestal, which were linked together by a glassed-in bridge. The design, a work of the architect, Dušan Kuzma, had a symbolic explanation. The two separate parts did not, however, symbolise the split Slovak nation that would be bound together by the uprising/bridge. They rather symbolised two different time periods: the evil, before the uprising, and the good, consisting of the uprising itself, its intentions and the post-war development in Slovakia.[14] The building was declared a Czechoslovak national monument in 1982.

Along with the new building, which was inaugurated on the twenty-fifth anniversary of the uprising in 1969, a new and third long-term exhibition was opened. The main theme remained the same, but there were also nuances. While the difference between the first and second exhibition was that the second highlighted the Soviet assistance to the uprising in a less conspicuous way than the first – it removed everything to do with the cult of Stalin – the third exhibition once again emphasised the Soviet help; an allusion to the brotherly Soviet 'help' Czechoslovakia received by the 1968 invasion. This stress was not, however, apparent from the start, as the third exhibition's content was planned during the Prague Spring itself. It was strengthened at the start of the 1970s, but during the short time in 1969 when certain aspects of Czechoslovak reform thinking were still current, for the first time the Holocaust of Slovak Jews in connection with the SNP was drawn attention to at the *Múzeum SNP* in Banská Bystrica. The presentation of the Holocaust was not comprehensive; even so, it was completely removed after just three months when the normalisation politics branded the earlier reforms as Zionist attacks against the communist regime. The official order for the removal read as follows: 'To avoid religious themes, to avoid racist motivated reprisals', which, in other words, meant reprisals against Jews.[15]

Prior to the end of the communist period a further two permanent exhibitions were organised in Banská Bystrica – the first (thus actually the fourth) opened in connection with the thirtieth anniversary of the uprising in 1974 and the second ten years later. During this normalisation period the museum was placed under the administration of the Department of Internal Affairs, which, on the one hand meant tighter control by the regime, but, on the other hand strengthened the museum's already privileged position.

Some of the staff who worked at the museum during the normalisation period and developed the communist historical narrative stayed even after 1989. At the time of the Velvet Revolution the *Múzeum SNP* was, however, forced to find a new profile. Supporting the earlier foundations, i.e., asserting the uprising's Czechoslovakia- and Soviet-friendly character and underlining communist heroism as the decisive factor in 'the Slovak nation's' rebellion against the Tiso regime, was no longer an option.

The post-1989 development can be divided into three periods. During the first, between 1990 and 1992, the museum struggled for its continued survival and abandoned its earlier character as a communist propaganda museum. In the second phase, 1993 to 1998, the museum lost its previous Czechoslovak profile and was adapted to the new Slovak reality, at the same time a distance was kept from the national-Catholic historical narrative. During the third, post-1998 period, the museum has steered a course towards Europe.

The period of great uncertainty and the Holocaust

The beginning of the 1990s meant for many Czechoslovak museums, particularly those focusing their activities on the Marxist-Leninist interpretation of Czechoslovakia's modern history, a time of increasing uncertainty. The transitional period from planned economy to market economy brought into question not only the political content of their activities, but also a number of other factors, such as financing methods and the staffing situation. In April 1992 the situation became so tense that the Slovak museums' union held a press conference in Bratislava and stated that all Slovak museums, including the *Múzeum SNP* in Banská Bystrica, were in an acute crisis.

In the case of the Museum of the Slovak National Uprising, the reasons for this uncertainty were twofold. They were partly of general political character and similar to those of all the museums in the country. They were, however, also specific to this particular museum and concerned the changing historical consciousness and the new Slovak historical culture. As long as it was not known which political power would take over in Slovakia after 1989, it remained uncertain which historical narrative could be perceived as state-supporting. The SNP was, up to then, important above all for the communist interpretation, in which the national aspect was combined with the proletarian internationalism:

'The Slovak national uprising initiated our national and democratic revolution. In the uprising steadfastness in the progressive forces' international solidarity and first and foremost our alliance with the Soviet Union in our battle against fascism were tested, against national oppression and to secure our freedom in the world after the war.'[16] But even if the Czech national-liberal narrative had won in its Czechoslovak form, that is to say if Czechoslovakia had not been partitioned, the uprising could be utilised to give meaning to the Czech-Slovak democratic relation in the same way as had occurred soon after the end of the war. But none of these two narratives dominated in Slovak society in the years of 1990–1992, and the dominating national-Catholic narrative did not give the SNP any place in its explanation of the meaning of Slovak history.

The nationalists behind the Catholic-nationalist narrative completely dismissed the thought of 'the Slovak nation's uprising', as 'the nation', according to them, stood behind Tiso, and all in society who did not do so were exceptions, traitors or non-Slovaks. František Vnuk's summary of the Catholic-nationalist perception of the SNP could be read as early as 1990:

> The uprising cannot be linked to the Slovak nation. It was created by a few short-sighted politicians and ambitious officers together with some fanatical communists and ruthless opportunists. It resulted in the nation being humiliated and deprived of its dignity. Two months of this idiotic uprising cost about 40,000 lives. If there was a dominating actor and true winner in the uprising it was Germany.[17]

The diaspora and its allies perceived the Slovak heroism during the Second World War in a completely different way. Milan Ďurica gave his explanation of what he thought was the 'Slovak national resistance against the German Nazism' without thinking of the SNP at all. He attempted to prove that the Slovak nation – 'which in its capacity as the first Slavic nation at all that had accepted Christianity' –on the grounds of its love for God could not accept the Nazi ideology that was 'so openly hostile to Christianity'. His explanation for this special Slovak form of resistance was as follows:

> The German pressure on Slovakia was different compared to other countries lying within Germany's sphere of interest. It was therefore logical that even the Slovak national resistance would have different forms than in other countries. The German pressure on Slovakia never assumed brutal forms, it never touched the traditional Slovak national values. It concerned an imperial control in an international sense and a gradual infiltration of the inner Slovak life, which however always respected the forms of the Slovak state sovereignty.

As Ďurica made clear, the Slovak national resistance to the German National Socialism was represented by 'leading personalities in the Slovak political, cultural, religious and economic life who received broad support from a large majority of the Slovak nation's members'.[18]

Even the fact that Tiso, after the failure of the uprising, handed out high Slovak honours to German soldiers who had fought the rebels, was explained to the advantage of Tiso. In a collective article signed by 'President Tiso's friends in Slovakia and abroad', it was claimed that Tiso 'was forced by violence to travel to Banská Bystrica and reward German officers'. According to the authors it was a matter of a humanitarian act – without any references to concrete sources or any more detailed explanation it was claimed that Tiso had saved 20,000 Slovak soldiers from deportations to Germany. He further, it was said, saved three hundred Slovak hostages who were in German hands and about to be executed. According to the article he also saved three Slovak towns that would otherwise have been bombed – in all three cases it was a matter of the uprising's centres: Banská Bystrica, Zvolen and Brezno – where about 150,000 people would have died. 'Tiso felt great shame when he carried out this ostensibly shameful collaborative action. He only did it, however, to save his beloved nation'.[19]

Within the national-Catholic narrative almost all controversial matters were explained in a similar manner. There was nothing positive that the SNP could be seen as having contributed to. The criticism of the uprising went so far that the German army was sometimes presented as a victim. For example, when another diaspora member, Ján Mikula, in his contribution to the discussions condemned the murder of the members of a German military mission in Slovakia at the start of the uprising. Mikula was shocked by the fact that the partisans murdered not only German soldiers but also their women and children: 'In military history one can hardly find another example of such a crime being committed in an allied state, that a military mission with diplomatic immunity has been liquidated as if it were a case of ordinary criminals.'[20]

However, it became clear enough to the leading Slovak political elites that history writing of this sort could never win support outside Slovakia if it had been presented as the official view of Slovak history abroad. Parliament's 1992 decision to establish 29 August as a Slovak national day saved, for that reason, the museum and gave the *Múzeum SNP* a renewed – though still very precarious – legitimacy.

The museum's relation to the Holocaust was no clearer during this period. As early as January 1990, about two months after the major political changes in Czechoslovakia, the *Múzeum SNP* presented an exhibition on the liberation of some concentration camps in Europe: Auschwitz, Majdanek, Dachau, Sachsenhausen, Mauthausen and Buchenwald. The exhibition consisted of one hundred photographs from these camps. The European interest in the Holocaust had not yet reached the intensity that came after the success of *Schindler's List* and the increased attention from the EU. Neither was the actual Holocaust focused upon yet. The exhibition's aim was to point out 'human beings' humiliation by that violence born in fascism'. On the one hand the exhibition's timing corresponded to the anniversary of Auschwitz-Birkenau's liberation, the event that in the whole of Europe is associated with the memory of the Nazi genocide of Jews. On the other hand, however, the ethnicity of the prisoners was not specified. The communist language usage was still apparent when the Nazi crimes were presented here.[21]

The exhibition lasted about six weeks, and after its end in March 1990 the museum was closed to the general public and reorganised. The aim of this reorganisation has already been mentioned: to leave behind the old interpretation of the Slovak national uprising as one organised and carried out by the illegal Slovak communist party in close cooperation with the Soviet Union and Soviet partisans, and to modify the last permanent exhibition from the communist era in such a way that even non-communist forces' participation and merits as well as assistance from countries outside the Soviet Union could be presented.

The first event at which the museum focused on the Holocaust as the genocide of Slovak and other Jews took place in March 1992, when Czechoslovakia was on its way towards its final Czech-Slovak crisis. A conference entitled 'The Slovak Jews' tragedy' was held in Banská Bystrica. It was a contribution to the memory of the fiftieth anniversary of the deportations of Slovak Jews from Slovakia to the death camps.

The *Múzeum SNP* organised the conference together with Israeli historians who had their roots in Czechoslovakia of the interwar period. Some of them were internationally known: Akiva Nir, Yeshayahu Jelinek and Gila Fatran, originally from Slovakia, and Livia Rothkirchen and Yehuda Bauer from the Czech part. Other historians from Slovakia, the Czech Republic and Poland also participated. Contributions from the conference were published in Slovak in the same year.[22]

This conference was not about giving the Holocaust a new meaning, but rather supplementing the Slovak collective memory with knowledge about the Holocaust by contributions based on chronologically orientated scientific research, the main question being what had actually taken place. Robert Büchler spoke, for example, on the Jewish minority's lives in Slovakia during the interwar period; Yehuda Bauer analysed the tragedy of the Slovak Jews in relation to the German Nazi regime's general anti-Jewish politics in Europe; Yeshayahu Jelinek focused on the Slovak Catholic Church's relation to the Holocaust between 1942 and 1944; and the Czech Holocaust historian, Miroslav Kárný, spoke about the aforementioned report of Vrba and Wetzler. Also those who had survived the Holocaust had the opportunity to speak. For example, Margita Schwalbová, who as a young doctor and prisoner in Auschwitz worked there as the assistant of the infamous Josef Mengele, and Juraj Špitzer, who described life in the Slovak Nováky concentration camp and the Jewish prisoners' chances of resistance there.

Those who participated in the Banská Bystrica conference naturally discussed questions that even the diaspora included in their version of the national-Catholic narrative. However, a direct confrontation with the increasingly successful nationalist interpretation did not take place during the conference. Those taking part focused solely on their topics in concrete historical time frames and did not draw any further conclusions concerning the Memory of the Holocaust in Slovakia or within the diaspora. A typical example of this was the Slovak historian, Katarina Hradská's paper: 'The Influence of Germany on the "Final Solution of the Jewish Question" in Slovakia'. When Hradská discussed Slovakia's responsibility for the deportations that followed the failed uprising in October 1944, she pointed out that Heinrich Himmler, when Slovakia was first occupied by German troops, visited Bratislava and expressed his dissatisfaction with 'the final solution'. She stated that 'the visit itself was a warning signal to the Slovak government – Germany was dissatisfied with the slow rate of the deportations'. Hradská finally added, however, that 'the pressure from the German side did not increase' after Himmler's visit, without attempting to draw any conclusion at all about the relation between the official Slovakia and the Holocaust at the end of the war.[23]

In contrast to the Slovak Academy of Sciences' conference in Častá-Papiernička, no prominent supporters of the national-Catholic narrative participated in the Banská Bystrica conference. With one exception, no one at the latter conference reacted directly to the assertions of Ďurica, Vnuk or anyone else, and no one spoke about the memory of the Holocaust. The exception was Yeshayahu Jelinek, who wanted to refute František Vnuk's claim that the Jews during the war asked Tiso to remain in power as, if he resigned, he could have been replaced by someone who would not have protected the Jews as Tiso was claimed to have done.[24]

Despite there being a group of Israeli historians behind the conference, this attempt to 're-import' the Holocaust to Slovakia could not be compared to the diaspora's activities. Comparing the two groups, it can be perceived that the Israeli group was far less compact and lacked internal organisation. It did not demonstrate any ambitions on either the political or ideological stage and lacked the will to present a Jewish-Slovak historical narrative. Neither was the Jewish history drawn attention to and explained in this manner.[25] A manifest theme was, however, apparent in all the contributions – a demarcation line between *them* and *us*, between Slovaks and Jews. An interesting detail was that all the delegates who presented their papers – irrespective of their origins or which country they came from – spoke of *Slovak Jews* and no one of *Jewish Slovaks*. While almost everyone wanted to call attention to the long-standing Jewish ethnic group in Slovak history, no one wished to discuss the question of how the ethnic division itself contributed to genocide in general and the Holocaust in particular, or which lessons or consequences this had had in both Slovak and European post-war history.

The museum's activities in this period concerning the Holocaust cannot, in summation, be seen as directly linked to any concrete historical narrative. The main aim of the activities was to supplement the collective memory after communism. A clear future dimension was lacking. The history writing presented can, therefore, be characterised as non-narratively formed and descriptive. As

Jörn Rüsen has pointed out, descriptive history writing does not lack the three
time dimensions of historical consciousness, but the narrative character of a
historical creation of meaning is consciously pushed back.[26] Yehuda Bauer, the
only one who mentioned the Holocaust in a broader context than just the
'strictly historical', touched upon this: 'Perhaps we can learn something from
the Slovak Jews' tragedy. Perhaps we can learn that such genocide can be prevented by pluralistic and democratic international cultures and through international understanding. But you will surely agree with me that this is not a goal
for this conference but a subject for another.'[27] The Israeli side's motives for
the whole of this initiative can be viewed as first and foremost existential and
moral – not to allow the Holocaust of Slovak Jews to be forgotten in the same
way as during the earlier decades.

At the time of Czechoslovakia's partition in January 1993 the Holocaust
was still not included as part of the permanent exhibition at the *Múzeum SNP.*
The distance between the two main events in this context – the Holocaust and
the Slovak national uprising – was still great.

The search for a new meaning

In the section on changes in the Slovak historical culture during the initial
post-communist years I showed that the Holocaust was used above all by Tiso's
sympathisers, who wanted to 'reconstruct' an independent Slovakia with Tiso's
ideology as a model, and who used the Holocaust to exonerate the domestic Slovak regime of the Second World War by placing all the blame upon
Germany. This Slovak 'revisionism',[28] which did not deny the Holocaust but
focused instead on making excuses for the Slovak guilt, was until the mid-1990s
very successful. The ultra-nationalist party *Slovenská národná strana* (SNS), which
belonged to the foremost political representatives of this revisionism, became in
1994 a member of the government coalition in a regime that the political scientist, Fareed Zakaria, has described as a non-liberal democracy.[29] As the earlier
noted scandal surrounding Milan Ďurica's book *Dejiny Slovenska a Slovákov*
from 1996 indicated, the nationalists tried intensively to make their version of
the Holocaust part of the official version of Slovakia's World War history that
would be taught in schools; something with which they were partly successful.

The rebels behind the Slovak national uprising were in the national-
Catholic narrative given the blame for the second wave of deportations and
the murder of a further circa 13,000 Slovak Jews. This assertion was based on
Tiso's own words, inter alia in an answer to Archbishop Eidem in Uppsala,
Sweden, who appealed for help for the Slovak Jews; a document Ďurica cited
in his book *Dejiny Slovenska a Slovákov*: 'Until 28 August 1944 the Jews in
accordance with Slovak laws were placed either in well-organised work camps
or – if they obtained permission – were left in their earlier locations.' But on 28

August 'began a guerrilla war by partisans and diverse international organisa-tions against the Slovak state, a rebellion that Jews joined'. Therefore, according to Tiso, Jews were punished like 'all the other partisans'.[30] In other words, had the Jews not taken part in 'treachery' against the Slovak nation and its state, they would, according to Tiso and Ďurica, have been able to remain living in peace and quiet in their 'well-organised work camps' or, with the presidential exemp-tions, even through the rest of the Second World War, i.e., the last eight months between the uprising and the end of the war.

As opposed to the communist narrative, which completely ignored the Jewish participation in the uprising, the national-Catholic narrative did thus recognise the active fight of Jews against the Slovak war regime, but at the same time made them perpetrators instead of victims. They were claimed to have contributed to the Slovak 'idyll' being destroyed. Their punishment was there-fore seen as just. This amounted to a transformation in the nationalists' percep-tion of the Jews' position in Slovakia's World War history: while the Jews in the first deportation wave of 1942 were recognised as victims, with Germany as the perpetrator, the Slovak 'nation' became the main victim after the uprising, and the Jews ended up on the opposite side as co-perpetrators. The transformation cannot, however, be interpreted as meaning that the Jews began to be judged by what they had done instead of who they were. Ďurica made no distinction between those Jews who were killed on the basis of their active participation in or support of the uprising and those who kept themselves outside the conflict but were deported and killed anyway. In the context of the end of the Second World War and the collapse of the Slovak war regime, the national-Catholic narrative perceived Jews as a hostile ethnic group that during the uprising joined Soviet partisans and 'diverse international organisations' against the first Slovak state in history.

Until 1993 the Slovak national-Catholic narrative represented an ideologi-cal use of history, the future dimension of which was solely focused upon the creation of an independent Slovakia, which in practice meant Slovakia's separa-tion from Czechoslovakia/the Czech Republic and the country's opposition to other 'historical enemies' such as the Soviet Union and Hungary. The first Slovak state in history served here as a foundation myth; as a milestone for a Slovak 'ethnic liberation' and for the establishment of a Slovak nation state.

When the Slovak nationalist movement had achieved its historical main goal the narrative was, however, soon confronted by the Slovaks' new expecta-tions regarding the supranational Europe; expectations which in many respects were similar to those existing in the other Central European post-communist countries.[31] The national-Catholic narrative's future main aim had been ful-filled by an independent Slovakia. The future had become the present, and the enemies were eliminated. Without clearly defined enemy images and without distinct future ambitions the narrative lost a large part of its earlier driving force and its credibility was therefore diminished. Because the national-Catholic narrative could not at the same time legitimate Slovakia's existence as a modern democratic state that would correspond to the Western conception of democracy, and which could also be included in Western political, economic and military structures, there was both room and a need for new modifications and narratives.

Against this background, it took considerable time before the *Múzeum SNP* carried out a radical change in its permanent exhibition. This change did not occur until 1998. The museum's transformation in the time in between can, however, be followed via different conferences and publications. The next major conference organised by the museum in April 1994 did not give any indication of how its historians wanted to locate the Holocaust in relation to the SNP. The conference took place exactly fifty years after the Slovak national uprising, but, even more importantly, just a year before the reunited Europe was to celebrate that a half-century had passed since the end of the Second World War. In fact, the Holocaust's position here was wholly marginal. The conference, entitled 'SNP in the nation's memory', focused on how the uprising itself should be remembered in the new Slovakia. That being said, the debate was particularly important for the museum's future in general.

It was the first time since Czechoslovakia's collapse that the museum had organised a conference on the SNP. It was made manifestly clear that motivations for Czechoslovakia's reunification or affiliation to a group of other countries were no longer sought; instead the uprising's position in the new interpretation of Slovak history was examined.[32] Moreover, the museum chose for the first time the memory of the uprising and not a source-critical reconstruction as the main point of the conference. The main emphasis, which had earlier concerned the question of what had actually happened, was now consequently moved towards a new and open search for *meaning*. The organisers underlined this fact in the introduction of the conference book: 'The committee of the organisation demanded that the discussion contributions should touch upon different subjects in a generalising perspective with focus upon connections and continuity, without getting into too many concrete details.'[33]

This new attention directed towards the memory of the uprising did not, however, lead to a manifest turn towards historical-cultural or theoretical questions surrounding the nature of historical consciousness. As became clear, it was rather a question of attempting to create a new methodical guidance for how to correctly understand the SNP in the new Slovakia. The museum's historians were still seeking the collective memory, which with the aid of scientific findings could conceivably explain the uprising and its actors in a uniform, national way. Ladislav Takáč spoke about 'the nation's genes' and claimed that 'the nation often sends its desperate calls to the historians' work rooms: when will you finally publish a qualified objective study that the whole of society can accept as its own?'. Despite him emphasising that 'we are witnessing a struggle between two different conceptions which want to create a picture of the wartime Slovak

Republic in the memory of the nation' – which meant that the museum saw itself as having another historical interpretation than that of the diaspora – he did not move on to questions about why there were different understandings of history in a nation, which factors were behind this and which truth criteria were decisive, but maintained instead: 'now *we* can sift the wheat from the chaff'. The director of the museum distanced himself from the national-Catholic narrative and also from the no longer so present communist narrative, and called for a new interpretation that in *an objective way* could confirm *the whole* nation's new historical memory.[34] The need for a new interpretation that would be neither communist nor national-Catholic was also expressed by other delegates, such as the former dissident, Jozef Jablonický, whose area of expertise was the complex of problems surrounding the uprising in Slovakia. Just after the Velvet Revolution he published a book on the falsification of this history during the communist era.[35] The task of the museum and the historians was, according to Jablonický, to present a non-deformed explanation for the 'nationally straight-backed posture'.[36]

The Holocaust's place in the new, but still not wholly clear SNP version was not yet manifest at the time of the two other conferences that in the mid-1990s were also organised by the *Múzeum SNP* and which focused on the persecution of Jews during the Second World War. The first took place in April 1994 under the name 'The escape from a death camp', and was intended to remind people of Rudolf Vrbas' and Alfred Wetzler's escape from Auschwitz fifty years earlier. The second seminar was about the sixth work-battalion, which consisted of Jews and was the only exception in the Slovak army during the war era. The seminars and these two subjects had, once again, the aim of 'supplementing the collective memory'. Neither Vrbas' and Wetzler's escape nor the sixth battalion would be allowed to be forgotten. But any attempt to include these events in a new historical narrative and give them an explicit, future-orientated meaning was not presented here, either. From the museum's side it was again a matter of mainly descriptive history writing.

By actively controlling the organisation of the other conference, the *Múzeum SNP* was, however, able to meet the wishes of the few Holocaust survivors who were still alive. The event was sponsored by one of them, Tibor Pivko, who after the war had lived in the USA. By organising the conference the survivors wanted to protest against a decision by the Slovak authorities, which after communism's collapse refused to recognise Jewish prisoners from the sixth work-battalion as political prisoners of the Slovak war regime.[37] From the survivors' side it was a case of both existential and moral motives. The museum did not, however, participate in the dialogue between the survivors and Slovak authorities, which took place outside the framework of this conference.

A single attempt to show how the link between the Holocaust and the SNP could become apparent did, however, arise during the November 1995 conference on the work-battalion. 'The start of the uprising in August 1944 became a milestone in the Slovak Jews' position in society. The Jews became once more free and equal citizens in the territory that was controlled by the rebels,' Jozef Jablonický said in his conference speech.[38] Jablonický emphasised that the two concentration camps for Jews in Nováky and Vyhne were within that territory controlled by the rebels, and were therefore opened and ceased functioning during the uprising. To claim that the rebels' 'regime' became totally democratic and that it treated the Jews like everyone else was, however, problematic for several reasons.

None of the three main groups that took part in the uprising – the army, the communists together with partisans, and 'the democrats' (that is to say the non-communists) – had earlier resisted the Holocaust or contributed with other actions that could confirm Jablonický's direct link. There was no visible support for Jews within the army and nothing that could indicate that they were perceived as equals there. Until 1944 the whole army functioned as an organic component of the Tiso regime. Even certain military leaders who were at the forefront of the uprising gained their war experiences when serving the regime and fighting for the official Slovakia's, and thereby even the Third Reich's, strategic interests. At that time it was – excepting the mentioned sixth work-battalion – forbidden for Jews to become soldiers in Slovakia. Jablonický gave no explanation as to why and how these particular revolting soldiers suddenly accepted Jews as equals.

The non-communist group also came from an environment that did not show any explicit sympathies for Jews. Some of its members were from circles which at the start of the war were not unequivocal opponents of the politics of the Hlinka Party and Tiso, or even profited from 'the Aryanisation process' in regard to Jewish property; the process whereby the Jews collectively had their property confiscated between the summer of 1939 and March 1942.[39] There was not any deeper analysis by Jablonický on this matter, either.

The communist resistance had no roots in the Tiso regime. One could therefore expect that this group in particular felt least hostile towards the Jews, especially as many of those Jews who were not deported fought in the uprising alongside partisans close to the communists. The communist leadership organised the partisan brigades and coordinated their activities with representatives of the Red Army. There was, however, a manifest suspicion of Jews even among the highest communist leaders, which was, for example, recorded in a document written by the communist leadership and delivered to the Soviet army during the uprising. In it the Jews were criticised as being unsuitable for illegal tasks because, it was claimed, they could not keep silent, and often even cooperated with the German Gestapo.[40] Jablonický did not attempt to analyse this further.

I am describing all these issues in order to show what historical context those people, who wanted to give both the uprising and the Holocaust a new meaning, needed to take into account. There was no 'natural' connection between the two events. There were no obvious sympathies for Jews in the leadership of the uprising that could prove that their participation in the uprising secured their equality in society. What most clearly united all the resistance groups during the uprising was not respect for democratic principles or conceptions or people's equal value, but the Tiso regime as their common opponent. The same applied also to the uprising's leaders in their relation to the Jews. The uprising lasted such a short time that it was difficult to draw such far-reaching conclusions as Jablonický had done. The SNP leaders indeed declared the racist laws of the Tiso regime null and void. However, some members from all three main groups participating in the SNP against the Tiso regime played an active role in anti-Semitic pogroms that occurred in several Slovak towns shortly after the end of the war.[41] This makes the assertion about the SNP as 'a milestone in the Slovak Jews' position in society' even more problematic and questionable.

The culmination of the museum's exertions to scientifically use modern Slovak history to refute the national-Catholic narrative occurred in September 1996, when the *Múzeum SNP* was host for another major conference, entitled *Nezodpovedané otázky* ('Unanswered questions'), with the significant sub-heading: 'Towards questioning the SNP and the resistance movement in our national history'. The aim of those who initiated the conference was to gather Slovak 'anti-nationalistic' historians working both within and outside the museum and together actively refute the assertions spread by Tiso's supporters and which questioned the uprising and the whole opposition to the Tiso regime. A total of 34 delegates met at Banská Bystrica on this occasion. The need to hold a conference of this kind arose, again, in connection with the successes of nationalist groups at the official political level. An expression of these successes was the aforementioned book, *Dejiny Slovenska a Slovákov*, written by Milan Ďurica, which was published in two editions (1995 and 1996) and distributed in Slovakia as an official textbook for higher secondary schools.

The conference in Banská Bystrica took place before Slovakia was criticised by the EU because the government used EU grants to print and distribute Ďurica's book. Despite the fact that the museum was in the hands of the state, its management and historians wanted to more actively than earlier indicate their distance from the ideological use of history that was being established within the government coalition. The defence against criticism of the uprising and the resistance movement would be based on 'objective historical facts and the newest results from scientific research'. The organisers also stressed that it was 'false and unwarranted' to question the SNP's significance.[42]

When the museum's new director, Ján Stanislav, in the conference's main speech summarised his view of the discussion about the uprising's position in Slovakia's history, he said that 'the Slovak nation', because of the uprising, 'proved that people did not wish to solve the problems concerning their

Figure 14 The statue, 'Victims Warn', made by the sculptor Jozef Jankovič, is situated at the entrance to the museum. It was removed in the early 1970s during the era of the communist 'normalisation' but returned in 2004. The message, stressing the suffering of anonymous victims, did not correspond with the goals of the communist propaganda wanting to emphasise the heroic resistance of the communist and partisan fighters. Photo: Tomas Sniegon

freedom with the help of non-democratic methods'. That Stanislav's point of departure was the present became particularly apparent when he, with history's help, tried to point out the uprising's importance for Slovakia's future:

> Thanks to the uprising Slovakia returned to its place among the democratic countries, and the uprising to a great degree washed away that stain which the persistent cooperation between the Hlinka Party's political leadership with Hitler's Nazi Germany constituted. In the uprising we found our way to democracy. The uprising is one of the greatest national events in our modern history, which in a sense could be called modern only after the uprising – Thanks to the uprising we became brave in the eyes of the world.[43]

Stanislav spoke of a democratic Slovakia that had existed even prior to the Second World War, despite there never having existed a democratic country called Slovakia during the interwar period or earlier. To elucidate the link between the uprising's memory and the conception of Slovakia's future, Stanislav emphasised that the independent Slovakia created on 1 January 1993 was not, and historically could not be, a continuation of the Slovak Republic of the period 1939–1945, either politically, militarily or spiritually.[44]

Among the delegates was Pavol Mešťan, director of the Museum of Jewish Culture in Bratislava. This museum did not focus on the Holocaust, but rather on Jewish culture until the Second World War. That being said, Mešťan used the whole of his speech to analyse the attempts 'to interpret and abuse the Jewish question in Slovakia'.[45] Those who abused or misinterpreted the question were, according to Mešťan, advocates of the national-Catholic narrative. However, he did not examine the use of the Holocaust on the anti-nationalist side, nor did he take up the question of how the Holocaust and the Slovak uprising could be linked together, or what position the Holocaust could have in the interpretation of Slovak history which gave legitimacy to an independent and democratic Slovakia.

Summarising the conference, the organisers mentioned important theoretical historical-cultural problems, but tried to solve them in a simple manner in the same way as previously. Although they called for interdisciplinary cooperation between historians, political scientists and linguists, they explained that cooperation of this type should primarily lead to 'the correct and exact interpretation' of history.[46] Director Stanislav used the term historical consciousness with the same aim in mind: 'A nation's true historical consciousness can only be born from objective and thoroughly researched facts and a professional interpretation of them'.[47] By this he merely demonstrated, however, that historical consciousness in his view was not at all about finding an identity within time. It was rather the case that only one interpretation of history can be accepted as correct, while all the other interpretations must be false.

During the time of the nationalists' participation in the Slovak government the *Múzeum SNP* lost, in 1996, its prominent position as a national museum and became just a regional museum instead. This change also affected a number

of other Slovak museums. It need not, therefore, have been based on the museum's criticism of the national-Catholic narrative.[48] The reform was, however,
only temporary, as the museum's status was once again raised after two years
when the controversial coalition finally fell from power. The *Múzeum SNP* was
then transferred from the control of the regional authorities back to that of the
Department of Culture in Bratislava.

From a Europeanisation perspective this change was important. The new
agreement that once again elevated the museum's status was signed with the
new government and was formulated in accordance with its political priorities.
In the agreement it was emphasised that the museum in its activities had to focus
on 'documenting the anti-fascist and national liberation struggle as well as the
Slovak national uprising as an important part of the European anti-fascist resistance during the Second World War' and to battle against 'contemporary expressions of neo-fascism, racial hatred and intolerance'.[49] The guidelines for the new
period were thus clear and signified that both Europe and the Holocaust would
have more prominent historical-cultural positions in Banská Bystrica.

In another document from 2001 the museum's director, Stanislav, confirmed the decisive role that the direct link to the Slovak state's politics had
played for the *Múzeum SNP*: 'If this organisation is to consistently fulfil all its
tasks with importance for the whole of society and internationally, it can only
do so if it remains under the Slovak culture department's direct leadership as
one of its cultural flagships.'[50]

The Europeanised resistance, the doubtful Holocaust

During the communist era the *Múzeum SNP* modified or changed its permanent exhibitions on important anniversaries, when wanting to again draw
attention to the memory of the uprising. In the 1990s it was decided not to
utilise a similar occasion in 1994 – fifty years after the uprising – or in 1995,
when the whole world celebrated the fiftieth anniversary of the end of the
Second World War. Until 1998, when Slovakia was controlled by a government
which caused the country's international isolation, the uprising's memory was
tolerated rather than highlighted by the political elite. Following the parliamentary election of 1998, a change in government took place in Bratislava and
a new coalition, with membership of both the EU and NATO as its foremost
priorities, came into power. In the same year a new 'permanent' exhibition was
opened in Banská Bystrica. With this the Holocaust – for the first time since
1969 – returned to the museum's exhibition galleries. *Múzeum SNP* thereby
became the first museum in Slovakia that had a long-term inclusion of the
Holocaust in its exhibition activities.[51]

It was, however, only a question of a few square metres, i.e., a fraction
of the museum's total space. Only a few pictures and basic information were

presented. That being said, the focus was primarily upon the first stage of the Holocaust up to 1942, with the question of guilt as the most important. The main text drew attention to the Tiso regime's guilt regarding the deportations of Jews from Slovakia in 1942. The text emphasised that the Slovak government 'of its own free will and with its own bureaucratic means' between March and October 1942 deported almost 58,000 Jews from Slovakia to death camps belonging to the Third Reich. Only a few hundred of them returned after the war.[52] The context of meaning for the Jewish SNP participation, which was also mentioned, was far less clear. The creators of the exhibition in this instance perceived the Jews as an isolated ethnic entity, which was not actually placed closer to the domestic political Slovak context and was by no means heroised in the same way as the other, Slovak resistance men.

The new political tendency that came after the fall of the 'non-liberal democracy' first began to have an historical-cultural impact in Banská Bystrica in 1999. This was characterised by an increased focus on the uprising's international aspects and an intensive emphasis on Slovakia's affiliation to the West. The direct confrontation with the national-Catholic narrative, however, lessened in pace with the weakening of the nationalists' political influence and in pace with the fact that the national-Catholic narrative lost its significance as part of that ideology which gave historical legitimacy to a state-upholding founding myth.

The change was first noticed concretely at a conference the *Múzeum SNP* organised in Banská Bystrica in June 1999. This conference had the significant title *SNP 1944 – Vstup Slovenska do demokratickej Európy* ('The Slovak national uprising of 1944 – Slovakia's entry into a democratic Europe'). The emphasis that Slovakia 'returned to a democratic Europe' was prominent. That the title of the conference was motivated by Slovakia's current and not earlier situation, and that Slovakia rather than Europe was in the centre, became clearer when none of the historians who spoke at the conference found it important to discuss the problem with the main title and the question of which democratic Europe Slovakia entered. Apart from the fact that the uprising failed and Slovakia again came under German control, in 1945 the country reverted to Czechoslovakia and thereby subsequently came completely into the Soviet sphere of influence.

Director Ján Stanislav directly underlined the connection between 'the uprising's meaning' and the contemporary situation when he spoke of the importance of learning from history 'at a time of striving for our old continent's integration'.[53] His colleague Dušan Halaj expressed himself even more explicitly: the striving to highlight the international dimension of the Slovak national uprising, he said, 'has namely a current significance. The contemporary attempt to integrate the European states also starts from the common fight against fascism.' According to Halaj, none of the members of the anti-fascist front cared about the others' ethnic origins, religion, nationality or race.[54] This was a new interpretation that completely corresponded to the task the museum had been given in the new agreement with the Slovak government from 1998. Katarina

Zavacká, a political scientist from Bratislava, focused wholly on the present and spoke of the 'SNP's significance for Slovakia's current foreign policy'.[55] Never, after 1989, had the emphasis on the SNP been presented as a 'current' or for contemporary politics 'very significant' event as emphatically as by the Banská Bystrica historians in 1999.

However, the Holocaust did not either fit into this Slovak 'Europeanised' historical picture. As the Israeli-Slovak historian, Akiva Nir, reminded his listeners, anti-Semitism was present in parts of the underground movement – the non-communist and the communist (the army was not mentioned in this context). He even presented explicit instances, such as when the partisans freed political prisoners from the Ilava camp but left a Jewish woman to die there because of her race. In another example he described how Slovak and Russian partisans stole valuables from the Jews and even killed some of them. Nir did not, however, in his mainly factual description, go so far as to directly question the whole anti-nationalist and Europe-friendly interpretation of the SNP.[56] Nonetheless, the museum's conclusion from the conference was that nothing 'can influence or question the SNP's principal and primary significance in Slovakia's modern history as a wholly national and progressive tradition'.[57]

For the first time, in 2000, the museum used the Holocaust in its brochure that served as a guide for the museum's visitors. The new brochure had seventy-five pages and the Holocaust was presented on two of them. In contrast to the earlier presentations of Jews as racist-defined victims of Tiso's Slovak state or as participants in 'the anti-fascist resistance' within the SNP, the Holocaust was here suddenly presented under the heading 'Repressions of the opposition – the Holocaust in Slovakia'.[58] The Holocaust's character was thus transformed from having been a result of a meaningless race oppression to a direct political action. The Jews were understood as being oppressed not for *who they were* but for *what they did*, that is to say opposing the regime. The intentions of the text became even more confusing when it was stated that:

> ... the protective treaties concluded with Germany, the infamous activities of Hlinka Guard together with the arrival of German advisers to Slovakia, increased the fascist character of life in this country. Among other things this enabled the state authorities to use their power to persecute anti-fascists, whether Communists, Protestants, Catholics or Jews.[59]

In this generalising description the Slovak Catholics were suddenly placed at the same level as the Jews, despite it having been the political Catholicism that was the domestic perpetrators' foremost ideological weapon against the Jews. The text continued:

> Any resistance of the part of the population could be suppressed through new law and legal provisions. For example, the Jewish population was particularly harshly stricken by the so-called Jewish Code (in force from September 1941).

This just strengthened the perception of the Holocaust as a reaction to the resistance to the Slovak war state. The ambiguity was finally completed by a picture of a doll made by a prisoner in Theresienstadt. During the war this camp was, in fact, situated outside Slovakia in the Protectorate Bohemia and Moravia.

It can be observed that the clearer the role the *Múzeum SNP* gave the SNP in their new history writing, to fulfil their task and adapt the Slovak resistance against the Tiso regime and Nazi Germany to the European 'anti-fascist' line, the harder it became to give the Holocaust its own place in the historical narrative. The museum's explanations for the Holocaust thereby became difficult to reconcile with those interpretations of the genocide of the Jews that had become rooted in the EU and its related institutions.

The Stockholm International Forum on the Holocaust, which took place in Sweden in the beginning of 2000, was a manifest example of this political striving to put the Holocaust at the centre of the European integration process.[60] In front of representatives from forty-eight countries, Slovakia's President Rudolf Schuster expressed his sorrow about the 'terrible suffering inflicted upon the innocent Jewish people through all the injustice and violence committed against them during the Second World War'. But when he laid the blame for the Holocaust on the contemporaneous Slovak government's official politics he at the same time emphasised that 'Slovakia ranks as the first country among those whose citizens helped the Jewish people in those difficult times. Slovak non-Jews saved no less than ten thousand Jewish lives during the Shoah, while putting their own lives at risk'.[61] The meaning of Schuster's speech was to give legitimacy to the new Slovak political course and show that the oppression of the Jews during the Second World War did not actually fit into 'the Slovak nation's spirit'.

That Slovakia's most prominent representatives, with the president at their head, wanted to use the Holocaust not only for the purpose of Europeanisation but also for their own nation, to 'exonerate the country's name', became even clearer a year later when Schuster spoke at the first occasion of the Day of Remembrance of Holocaust Victims in Slovakia in Kremnička near Banská Bystrica.[62] The date was intended to remind people of the issuing of the anti-Jewish laws in Tiso's Slovakia. Schuster focused his speech on the new Slovakia and emphasised that the way in which the country commemorated the anti-Jewish race laws made Slovakia a positive example for a number of other countries.[63]

The Europeanisation of the Holocaust, which intensified in connection with the EU's expansion and proceeded in parallel with the new nationalisation of Slovakia's history, also came to expression in Banská Bystrica. At the millennium change the *Múzeum SNP* maintained its earlier position as a dominating museum for Slovakia's modern history and the only national museum dealing with the wartime history. The museum had forty staff, and up to 180,000 visitors annually, of whom about 25 per cent were from abroad.

In its capacity as the only Slovak institution systematically dealing with the memory of the Holocaust, the museum in Banská Bystrica developed contacts with several foreign museums which had the Holocaust as their main subject matter: Yad Vashem in Israel, The Holocaust Memorial Museum in Washington, the Anne Frank House in Amsterdam and the museum at Theresienstadt, but also other more broadly orientated war museums such as The Museum of the Great Patriotic War in Moscow. Despite the cooperation with certain special-ised institutions one could not, however, discern any consistent course in the museum's way of using the Holocaust and including it in the new history writing.

In its search for a new role for the new century the *Múzeum SNP* organ-ised a conference in November 2000 entitled *Poslání a profilace múzeí najnovších dejin v 21. storočí* ('What task and profile shall contemporary history museums have in the 2000s?') About 140 people from Slovakia, but also from the Czech Republic, Germany, Poland and France, participated. The museum's manage-ment presented their future plan of activities and asked the delegates for their opinions and comments. The management based their thoughts on the con-viction that the *Múzeum SNP*'s position in Slovakia would remain dominant, which meant that the museum would be allowed to expand its sphere of inter-est in order to 'fill empty areas in the historical memory so as to be able to correspond to a European standard'.[64]

In the text presenting the thought of an expanded concept for the *Múzeum SNP*, the management explained that they wanted to put the focus of the museum's activities on more than just one event. The presentation and research activities should include the complete Slovak history during the Second World War, but also other important historical events both prior to and after the war. Among them would be the Slovak perspective on the 1968 Prague Spring movement and the collapse of communism in 1989. If the plans were success-ful a new exhibition documenting current forms of neo-Nazism, xenophobia, racial hatred and intolerance would be installed as well. The intention, in other words, was to link together historical events and contemporary problems in one and the same 'permanent exhibition' which would expand the new historical national-European narrative; a development of the earlier policy. It was thought that the museum would modify or even change its old name. The sugges-tions mentioned were 'The Slovak national uprising's and the modern history's museum' or 'The newest history's museum'.

The Holocaust in Slovakia was described as 'one of the darkest chapters in Slovakia's modern history' which 'until now has created a sensitive social stigma in the nation's consciousness'. The primary scientific need to 'fill empty areas' in Slovakia's history by continuing to conduct research on the Jews participa-tion in the SNP was still talked about. At the same time a connection was made to a moral history usage when it was said that the intention was to 'pay back the museum's debt to the Jews', primarily by taking part in the creation of a

Slovak national exhibition at Auschwitz-Birkenau, 'where the Jewish participation in the resistance movement, the SNP, the Jewish victims of the Holocaust on Slovak territory and in this concentration camp would come to be documented as thoroughly as possible and presented in a dignified manner'.[65] The reason for actually wanting to continue focusing on the Holocaust in the future was, in other words, unclear even here. A better presentation abroad was consequently a way for the museum and Slovakia to 'pay back its debt'. The situation did not become any clearer in the new 'permanent' exhibition in the *Múzeum SNP*, which at the same time was the first exhibition in Banská Bystrica after Slovakia's EU entry on 1 May 2004.

The exhibition bore the name 'Slovakia in the European anti-fascist resistance movement 1939–1945'. It opened in August 2004, sixty years after the beginning of the Slovak national uprising. Despite it again focusing solely on the war years and not the uprising's memory after the war, its connection to Slovakia's EU membership was obvious. In the text to the exhibition, written before Slovakia had become a member of the EU, it was stated:

> Even today when Slovakia is striving to take part in the European integration process the anti-fascist resistance and the SNP have significance as political capital which cannot be lost. Following Slovakia's entry into the EU in May 2004 the value of this aspect of Slovak military and democratic traditions will increase even more. This will increase the chances of the Slovak Museum of the National Uprising of presenting the anti-fascist resistance and the SNP as part of the European anti-fascist resistance during the Second World War. Even the West European democratic countries constructed their progressive democratic traditions on the same foundations.[66]

The period of 'Slovakia's participation in the European resistance to fascism' began as early as 1939, instead of the uprising's year of 1944 that was used earlier. In the same way the museum placed Slovakia in a 'European anti-fascist movement' in the introductory period of the war, just when the first Slovak nation state had been created. For the first time an attempt was made in Banská Bystrica in 2004 to encompass a longer period of time than between 1939 and 1945. The introductory section concerns the period 1918–1939, which covers the years between the formation of Czechoslovakia and the creation of the first Slovak nation state, and the concluding section is about the post-war period until 1954, the era of Stalinism, and in some aspects extends to the 1960s, with its de-Stalinism tendencies. It is not my aim to conduct a deep analysis of the whole exhibition here, but I wish to underline that this was the first time the museum wanted to use such a long time period in order to give the Slovak national-European narrative more distinct contours.[67]

The exhibition is the largest in the museum's history, and conforms to the Slovak national-European narrative. The main text, which introduces the section about the Holocaust and has a prominent position, attempts once again to highlight only the Slovaks' positive relations with the Jews: 'Despite threats of imprisonment and the risk of losing their own life many Slovaks helped to save hundreds of Jews.' It is unclear what is meant by 'many Slovaks', and the information about 'hundreds of Jews' does not accord with the statement made by Slovakia's president at the Holocaust conference in Stockholm. There Schuster spoke of 'no less than 10,000 Jews' who were saved thanks to the Slovaks' help.

The space for the Holocaust is once more very limited. In Slovakia the Holocaust is chronologically divided into three periods: expressions of anti-Semitism in Slovak society; anti-Jewish laws and rules, and two stages of deportations of Slovak Jews to concentration camps. The term 'extermination camp' is never used and the Holocaust is, once again, used only descriptively. Irrespective of all this, the exhibition's conclusion is that Slovakia emerged from the war as a 'democratic winner'.

There are many indications that the museum has as a starting point the state directive from 1998 in its representation, and that it applies the national-European narrative in an unproblematic manner.[68] What is paradoxical is that the *Múzeum SNP* is behind yet another exhibition on the Holocaust in Slovakia outside the Slovak Republic; an exhibition designed in a different way and representing a contrast to the exhibition in Banská Bystrica. It is a question of the 'Slovak national exhibition', held at that location which more than any other has become the Holocaust's main symbol: the former concentration and Holocaust camp of Auschwitz-Birkenau.

Auschwitz–Birkenau as a different Slovak Holocaust

The last exhibition about Slovakia and the Holocaust I wish to mention was opened in the state museum at Auschwitz-Birkenau on 8 May 2002. This was the exhibition organised by the *Múzeum SNP* and which would 'pay the Slovak museum's debt'. It has become the largest and most complex exhibition ever about the genocide of the Slovak Jews. Although organised by the *Múzeum SNP*, this exhibition has a completely different character than all the attempts to present the Holocaust in Banská Bystrica. As with the January 2000 Stockholm conference, the Slovak attitude towards the memory of the Holocaust can be directly compared to other countries that have opened their exhibitions at the same time and in the same place.

Those who produced the exhibition were confronted with a completely different environment at Auschwitz-Birkenau than what they were used to in Banská Bystrica. Instead of a modern building from the communist era, here was an authentic site which, moreover, had become the most symbolic site in the whole world; so symbolic that its name is often used synonymously with the Holocaust. People died and were imprisoned during the war in the place where the memory of the Holocaust was to be presented to both older and younger generations of international visitors. The visiting groups' aims also differed: while, at the *Múzeum SNP*, one could first and foremost learn about the Slovak uprising's history, people came to Auschwitz to honour the memory of the Holocaust's victims and increase their knowledge about this history. Additionally, the texts written in English and a few other languages demanded another vocabulary than texts in Banská Bystrica, which were written in Slovak and intended for a Slovak public. The Holocaust needed, in other words, to be contextualised in a different way. Particularly the Holocaust's Europeanisation – rather than the Europeanisation of the Slovak resistance – and consideration for the Jewish historical culture were, in the direct confrontation with other exhibitions and on the authentic site, much more prominent here than in Banská Bystrica.

For the reasons given, *the Holocaust* and not the Slovak resistance is the main subject in Auschwitz. In its own definition the *Múzeum SNP* describes the exhibition's main aim as being: 'to provide visitors with a historic objective view and course of the Holocaust in Slovakia in the years of the World War II'. The Holocaust is presented 'in causal historic connections with the development of the Slovak society and with the regime of the war Slovak republic in the years 1939–1945'.[69] The focus on the relation between 'ordinary Slovaks' and 'the Slovak society' on the one hand, and the Holocaust on the other, is much more explicit in this case than in the *Múzeum SNP* itself. One half of the Auschwitz exhibition is directly concerned with Slovak society and its attitude towards the Jews.

The exhibition is divided into four thematic sections. The first deals with life of the Jewish minority in Slovakia up to 1938. The second is called 'Slovak society and the solution of the Jewish question, 1939–1945'. In the name itself one can discern a difference compared to Banská Bystrica – Slovak society is focused upon and not only the Slovak state or regime, as has been done in Slovakia. Drawing attention to solely the state or the regime makes it a lot easier to lay the whole blame upon Tiso, the government and a limited number of the most powerful and active officials. Expressed with Raul Hilberg's terminology, this exhibition focuses for the first time not only on *perpetrators* (Tiso, the Hlinka Party) and *victims* (Jews) but also on Slovak *bystanders*. The exhibited pictures indicate a greater support for Tiso than had been shown earlier in the *Múzeum SNP*'s material: smashed windows of Jewish shops and similar images indicate that anti-Semitism was present to a large extent in Slovakia as early as 1938 and 1939, i.e., before the Jews began to be deported to the death camps. This portrayal connects to the same one that commenced as early as the mid-1960s with the film, *The Shop on Main Street*, but cut short after the collapse of the Prague Spring movement at the end of the 1960s, and ignored until the exhibition in Auschwitz-Birkenau itself.

The third section illuminates the problem of thefts of Jewish property – 'Aryanisations' – in Slovakia. The picture screens give concrete figures on Aryanised Jewish companies. As the number of such companies exceeded

10,000, it is clear that many Slovaks were needed to take them over. At the same time attention is drawn to the question of whether the Jewish owners stolen from were a potential social problem for Slovak society – clearly, if the power balance changed and the Jews survived the oppression and the war, they would demand their companies and other property back and at the same time strive for justice against those who had received Aryanised Jewish property. This leads thoughts to the conviction that there must have been a lot of people in society who had reason to wish that the Jews never returned.

The fourth and final section has been given the name 'Holocaust – never again!' and focuses on the Jews' lives in the first Slovak nation state – on the killing, the deportations and testimonies from the few who managed to survive. Rudolf Vrbas' and Alfred Wetzler's escape from Auschwitz-Birkenau is presented as an important action in the history of the Holocaust.

The exhibition has been 'Americanised' in a similar way to the reconstructed museum in the former Holocaust camp of Belzec in today's Poland, or the new Holocaust monument in central Berlin. This Americanisation reflects the feeling of empathy at least as much as the exhibited objects' authenticity, evoking in the audience an understanding of the feelings of the prisoners on their way towards death. Between the two main halls that the Slovak exhibition is situated in, one is forced to pass through a long, dark corridor leading to a symbolic cremation oven. Also this aspect is completely new in Auschwitz compared to Banská Bystrica, as no similar 'emotional authenticity' as a complement to, or replacement of, 'document authenticity' is used in either the case of the SNP or the Holocaust at the latter museum.

How can the presentations of the Holocaust in Auschwitz and Banská Bystrica be so different when it is a case of one and the same museum being responsible for both? Apart from those aspects already mentioned – which could be summarised as different degrees of adaptation to different environments and historical cultures meeting in the former extermination camps on Polish territory – there are two other aspects that have an important role. Firstly, the historical-cultural freedom of choice is far more limited in Auschwitz, as it is necessary to adapt to a number of given directions not present in Banská Bystrica. Secondly, the *Múzeum SNP* is not the only organisation behind the Auschwitz exhibition, despite it being the main organiser on the Slovak side. Apart from the *Múzeum SNP*, the Museum of Jewish Culture in Bratislava, the Slovak National Archive, the Slovak Film Institute and even Yad Vashem in Israel also contributed.[70] Particularly the latter institution's influence appears to be much greater here than at the various conferences in Slovakia and the design of the *Múzeum SNP*'s own exhibitions there.

While the background to the presentations of the Holocaust in Auschwitz-Birkenau and Banská Bystrica are different, the presentation of the Slovak uprising in Auschwitz is identical to that in Banská Bystrica. The uprising is described in both places as 'the Slovak nation's' revolt. Because Slovak society is problematised in the exhibition far more than earlier, in relation to both Tiso and the Holocaust, the assertion about the uprising's 'wholly national' character is even more full of contrasts at Auschwitz. But as the uprising is contextualised as an action carried out to stop the Nazis' regime and thereby also the Holocaust, and not as an action that would first and foremost exonerate the Slovak nation, the ethnic nuances in this main interpretation remain unresolved and marginal.

Europeanisation at the cost of the Holocaust

The post-communist development of the Museum of the Slovak National Uprising can be divided into three different periods: the first commencing just after communism's collapse and ending with Czechoslovakia's partition in 1993; the second from 1993 and until the first major change of government in independent Slovakia in 1998, and the third from 1999 until Slovakia's EU entry in 2004. The periodisation indicates that the museum has focused on three different primary tasks.

During the first period the museum concentrated on jettisoning the legacy of its communist past. Its permanent exhibition was reorganised and came to include subjects earlier tabooed or ignored. Here the Holocaust also entered the picture, however without its history being placed in any clear context. That being said, the *Múzeum SNP* gave the Israeli historians the opportunity to present their contributions in Slovakia without them needing to confront the diaspora's foremost representatives, while the 1992 Bratislava Tiso conference was of another nature altogether. In contrast to the national-Catholic narrative's proponents, the museum did not otherwise react directly to the current political questions and did not get involved in the ongoing political discussions on Slovak history. In its striving to distance itself from the earlier communist ideological use of history, the museum at this time showed an increased interest in using history scientifically. The staff underlined the need to reconstruct and discover new historical facts, which was done in a traditional, descriptive way. An objective source-critical survey was the main aim – the past was in the centre when both the current and future dimensions were uncertain.

The second period placed new demands upon the *Múzeum SNP*. Above all a new position was needed, this time no longer in the Czechoslovak but instead in the Slovak context. More distinctly than earlier the museum tried to refute the dominating Catholic-nationalist narrative's main foundations; a refutation in which the Holocaust was also included. The striving towards supplementing the collective memory continued, but it was indicated more clearly that the museum wanted to place the Holocaust in direct opposition to the extreme nationalism – without, however, managing to establish a connection of meaning between the Slovak national uprising as the new, democratic Slovakia's founding myth, and the Holocaust, which still appeared as a 'by-product'.

The nationalist ideological history usage was fought against during this time with a use of history that also included manifest ideological aspects, as its spokespeople struggled for a united Slovak nation and, moreover, used at least partly the same categories that in the communist history usage were utilised in opposition to other historical narratives and ideologies, including the national-Catholic. The intention was to construct new connections for the interpretation of the uprising and the Holocaust in order to legitimise 'a positive Slovak-ness' in post-communist Slovakia. However, the ideological struggle still proceeded mainly on the domestic front.

The third period involved the museum's main focus being redirected once more. The increasingly intensive Europeanisation of the Slovak national uprising became the museum's new task and priority, which extended to the perception of the Holocaust. On the one hand, the Holocaust's placement in the museum's own permanent exhibition, or even at the international level, would be 'proof' that Slovakia now highlighted the Holocaust in the same way as the other candidate countries and the rest of democratic Europe. On the other hand, the Second World War and the European resistance to Nazism were nationalised at the expense of the Holocaust. Among all the uses of history characterising the museum's activities during these years, the political use was particularly important: the Holocaust came to emphasise Slovakia's affiliation to the 'anti-fascist coalition'.

The varying uses of history and the expectations confirm the important role of historical consciousness during the whole of the studied period, from 1990 to 2004. That the Holocaust has never attained a clear position in the Slovak 'anti-nationalist', post-communist writing of history, which was presented here by the *Múzeum SNP* as its most prominent representative, can to a great extent be attributed to the fact that the attempts to see the Slovak nation as a united, collective hero have never been abandoned. Neither Jews nor the Holocaust have fitted into the picture of the active Slovak resistance to 'fascism'. The museum's historians have never ceased to use the same concepts as those present during the Cold War, when Jews in the communist narrative were turned into perpetrators instead of victims. At the same time the Jews' activity during the SNP was never allowed to challenge the conception of the active, heroic Slovak collective resistance, which – as during the communist epoch – continued to legitimise the *Múzeum SNP*'s existence even after the fall of communism and partition of Czechoslovakia.

The emphasis on the active resistance in August 1944 almost completely overshadowed the discussions on who were actually whose victims in the 'anti-nationalist' interpretation of modern Slovak history. The Holocaust was used as proof against Tiso and his government, but the Jews' role as one of the foremost groups of victims during the Second World War was never drawn attention to. 'The risk' of giving the Jews a status of this kind was manifestly apparent in the exhibition at Auschwitz-Birkenau, as it would at the same time be necessary to intensify the discussion about definitions of perpetrators and 'bystanders'.

The lack of a historical context of meaning for the Holocaust in the *Múzeum SNP* during essentially the whole period of 1990–2004, but especially between the years of 1998 and 2004, indicates that it could primarily have been external, international factors that maintained the Holocaust interest even in Banská Bystrica. That the Holocaust became part of the historical-cultural agenda in Slovakia appears to have been more a reaction to the international situation, above all the Europeanisation process, than those demands and needs emanating from within Slovak society.

Notes

1. Ivan Kamenec, 'Dvojsečnosť mýtov o Slovenskom národnom povstaní", in Krekovič, Mannová and Krekovičová, *Mýty naše slovenské*, 199–202.
2. See, for example, Silvia Miháliková, 'Politický obraz Slovenska: medzi krížom a európskou hviezdičkou', *Sociológia – Slovak Sociological Review*, Volume 37(6), 2005, 529–54.
3. See Cohen, *Politics Without a Past*, 177–78.
4. The diaspora's reaction was very influential. Representatives of two of its co-organisations, the Canadian Slovak League and the foreign, Matica Slovenská, wrote a letter that they sent to Slovakia's president, the prime minister and parliament's speaker. In the letter they wrote, for example: 'As a sly and treacherous avalanche, news arrived that shook us, the news that the anti-national coup of August 1944, which was a knife against the first Slovak independent state's throat, was forced upon Slovaks both at home and abroad by a decision from Slovakia's highest representatives as the most important national day'. Cited by Ladislav Takáč, 'Vojnové roky v pamäti slovenského národa', in Lipták, *SNP v pamäti národa*, 76.
5. See Zora Bútorová and Martin Bútora, 'Možno súčasne chváliť vojnový Slovenský štát i SNP?', *Národná obroda*, 8 August 1994.
6. For more about this, see, for example, Kováč, *Dějiny Slovenska*, 238.
7. Ivan Kamenec, 'Civilný sektor a každodenný občiansky život na povstaleckou Slovensku', in Katarína Kováčiková and Dezider Tóth, Eds, *SNP 1944: Vstup Slovenska do demokratickej Eurόpy. Materiály z medzinárodnej konferencie k 55. výročiu SNP*, Banská Bystrica: Múzeum SNP, 1999, 129–44.
8. The so-called Vrba-Wetzler report was at its time the most detailed report on life in Auschwitz-Birkenau. See, for example, Hilberg, *Destruction of European Jews*, 322.
9. Pierre Nora, 'Between Memory and History: Les Lieux de Memoire', *Representations* 26, Special Issue: Memory and Counter-Memory, Spring 1989, 7–24.
10. Kristian Gerner, 'Historien på plats', in Karlsson and Zander, *Historien är nu*, 168.
11. Rüsen, *Berättande och förnuft*, 160–77.
12. See: Eyal, 'Identity and Trauma', 5–36, quote p. 19. Quoted from: Jozef Jablonický, 'Boj za pravdu o povstaní', *Parlamentný Kurier* 7–8, 1994. Eyal sees a sharp difference between how 'Slovak historians' and 'Czech dissidents' use history – the former in order to strengthen the national narrative and the latter to defy forgetting and challenge the conscience. As is apparent from the earlier chapters, I do not, however, share his sharp categorisation – in my view the ideological use of history is also present among those Czechs he studied. On the other hand, the moral use of history is far more manifest in the Czech case.

13. A description of the museum's history in English can be found on its homepage: http://www.muzeumsnp.sk/english/index.htm

14. *Múzeum SNP: Sprievodca po expozícii*, Banská Bystrica, 1977, 7.

15. Múzeum SNP:s archive, document AVS.

16. *Múzeum SNP: Sprievodca po expozícii*, Banská Bystrica, 1977, 5.

17. Vnuk, *Dedičstvo otcov*, 81 and 84.

18. Milan Ďurica, 'Slovenský národný odpor voči nemeckému nacizmu', in Gabriel Hoffmann, *Zamlčaná pravda o Slovensku*, 107–8.

19. Priatelia prezidenta Tisa na Slovensku a v cudzine, 'Po povstaní prezident Tiso diplomaticky zachránil celé Slovensko pred zúriacimi Nemcami od úplného zničenia a zmasakrovania', in Hoffmann, *Zamlčaná pravda o Slovensku*, 234.

20. Ján Mikula, 'Pravda o povstaní alebo Povstanie s jednou legendou', in Hoffmann, *Zamlčaná pravda o Slovensku*, 221.

21. Fascism was still defined in the closing phase of communism as 'the most reactionary product of the imperialist period'. Further, above all fascism's anti-proletarian character was specified, which coincided with the official ideological picture of the working class as the war's greatest victim: 'Fascism represents the mono-political bourgeoisie's openly terroristic dictatorship and is its last and final means to suppress the revolutionary workers' movement'. The definition of Nazism was far more limited, as it was described as 'a political movement in Germany'. See *Ilustrovaný encyklopedický slovník*, Prague: Academia, 1980, Vol. I, 628, and Vol. II, 604.

22. *Tragédia slovenských židov*, Banská Bystrica 1992. Ten years later a selection of these contributions was published in English. This publication was a joint work of the Banská Bystrica museum and the Auschwitz-Birkenau State Museum in Poland. See *The Tragedy of the Jews of Slovakia*, Auschwitz-Birkenau State Muzeum, Muzeum of the Slovak National Uprising, 2002.

23. Katarina Hradská, 'The Influence of Germany on the "Solution of Jewish Question" in Slovakia', in *The Tragedy of the Jews of Slovakia*. Auschwitz-Birkenau State Muzeum, Muzeum of the Slovak National Uprising, 2002, 92.

24. Yashayahu Jelinek, 'The Catholic Church and the Jews in the Period from Spring 1942 to Spring 1944 in Slovakia', *The Tragedy of the Jews of Slovakia*, 164.

25. Akiva Nir, 'The Zionist Organisations, Youth Movements and Emigration to Palestine in 1918–1945', *The Tragedy of the Jews of Slovakia*, 37–57.

26. Rüsen, *Berättande och förnuft*, 136–37.

27. See Yehuda Bauer, 'The Tragedy of the Slovak Jews within the Framework of Nazi Policy towards the Jews in Europe in General', *The Tragedy of the Jews of Slovakia*, 76.

28. Ivan Kamenec, 'Reflections of the Holocaust in Slovak Society and Literature', in Karlsson and Zander, *Holocaust Herritage*, 165–66. See also Deborah Lipstadt, *Denying the Holocaust*, New York: Plume, 1994, 7.

29. The description proceeds from Fareed Zakaria's definition of 'illiberal democracy' in such regimes whose leaders had been elected in a democratic way (often via a referendum) but later to a great extent ceased to respect the citizens' rights and freedom. For more on this, see Fareed Zakaria, *Budoucnost svobody*, Prague: Academia, 2005, 122–23. See also Fareed Zakaria, *The Rise of Illiberal Democracy*, http://www.fareedzakaria.com/ARTICLES/other/democracy.html; and Kopeček, *Od Mečiara k Dzurindovi*, 22–28.

30. Ďurica, *Dejiny Slovenska a Slovákov*, 200.

31. Leff, *The Czech and Slovak Republics*, 265–69.

32. See 'Introduction' by Ladislav Takáč, director of the Múzeum SNP, in Lipták, *SNP v pamäti národa*, 5–6.

33. Ibid., 5.

34. Ladislav Takáč and Milan Gajdoš, 'Rezistencia a vojnové roky v pamäti slovenského národa', in Lipták, *SNP v pamäti národa*, 70–83.

35. Jozef Jablonický, *Glosy o historiografii SNP. Zneužívanie a falšovanie dejín SNP*, Bratislava: NVK International, 1994.

36. Jozef Jablonický, 'Slovenské národné povstanie v historiografii v rokoch totality', in Lipták, *SNP v pamäti národa*, 97. In the foreword to the second edition of his book on the 'falsification' of the uprising, which was also published in 1994 in connection with the SNP's fiftieth anniversary, Jablonický also wrote that 'there are citizens who from consideration of the current situation will discredit and mock the uprising. There is a tendency to interpret 29 August 1944 in a way that does not unite Slovaks and does not remind them of their democratic traditions'. He then claimed that 'the Slovak national uprising placed Slovaks among those nations and states that fought against Nazi Germany and its satellites'. See Jablonický, *Glosy o historiografii SNP*, 5–6.

37. For more on this, see Bernard Knežo-Schönbrun's speech from the introduction of the conference: Bernard Knežo-Schönbrun, 'Na úvod', in Bernard Knežo-Schönbrun, ed., *Pracovné jednotky a útvary slovenskej armády 1939–1945. VI. robotný prápor*, Banská Bystrica and Bratislava: ZING Print, 1996, 6–10.

38. Jozef Jablonický, 'Židia v rezistencii na Slovensku', in Knežo-Schönbrun, *Pracovné jednotky a útvary slovenskej armády 1939-1945*, 162.

39. For more on this matter, see Nižňanský, *Židovská komunita na Slovensku medzi československou parlamentnou demokraciou a slovenským štátom v stredoeurópskom kontexte*.

40. See, for example, Mlynárik, *Dějiny Židů na Slovensku*, 301–2.

41. Ibid., 305–44.

42. Dušan Halaj and Dezider Tóth, *Nezodpovedané otázky. K spochybňovaniu odboja a SNP v našich národných dejinách*, Banská Bystrica: Múzeum SNP, 1996, 5.

43. Ján Stanislav and Dušan Halaj, 'K deformáciam interpretácie protifašistického odboja na Slovensku a SNP', in Halaj and Tóth, *Nezodpovedané otázky*, 18–19.

44. Ibid., 10.

45. Pavol Mešťan, 'Snahy o nové interpretácie a dezinterpretácie židovskej otázky na Slovensku', in Halaj and Tóth, *Nezodpovedané otázky*, 57–63.

46. Ibid., 6.

47. Stanislav and Halaj, 'K deformáciam interpretácie protifašistického odboja na Slovensku a SNP', 9–10.

48. See https://interoperabilita.kultury.sk/drupal/files/Stratmuzgal.doc.

49. Doc. nr. MK 2217/98-1 och 1244/2002-1 från 21.12.1998, 15.8.2002, see: www.muzeumsnp.sk

50. Ján Stanislav, 'Koncepcia Múzea Slovenského národného povstania', in *Museologica* II/2001, Banská Štiavnica: Univerzita Mateja Bela, 2001, 92.

51. The Museum of Jewish Culture in Bratislava did no open its own permanent exhibition on the Holocaust until September 2005, viz., after Slovakia's entry into the EU in 2004. The exhibition is in a synagogue in the town of Nitra and entitled 'The Slovak Jews' fate' (*Osudy slovenských židov*).

52. From the exhibition's 1998 text *Scénár stálej expozície Múzea SNP v Banskej Bystrici*, júl 1998, zostavila Mgr. Katarína Kováčiková, 20–21.

53. Kováčiková and Tóth, *SNP 1944*, 13.

54. Dušan Halaj, 'Medzinárodný rozmer SNP–súčasný stav, možnosti a perspektivy výskumu', in Kováčiková and Tóth, *SNP 1944*, 250.

55. Katarína Zavacká, 'Význam SNP pre zahraničnú politiku Slovenskej republiky v súčanosti', in Kováčiková and Tóth, *SNP 1944*, 20–24.

56. Akiva Nir, 'Slovenskí Židia v odboji a Slovenskom národnom povstaní, in Kováčiková and Tóth, *SNP 1944*, 265–75.

57. Kováčiková and Tóth, *SNP 1944*, 497.

58. *The Slovak National Uprising Museum, Exposition Guide*, Banská Bystrica: Múzeum SNP, 2000, 14.

59. Ibid., 15.

60. Karlsson, 'The Uses of History', 38–55.

61. *The Stockholm International Forum on the Holocaust. Proceedings*, Stockholm: Svensk Information, 2000, 73. Schuster did not, however, state from where he got the figure of 10,000 saved Jews.

62. Even the decision to make the day when the anti-Jewish laws were introduced in wartime Slovakia into the Day of Remembrance of Holocaust Victims in Slovakia (which first took place in 2001) coincides with the European wave. The decision was taken one year after the Stockholm conference and after the EU had begun to note the candidate countries' attitudes to the Holocaust.

63. *ČTK*, 9 September 2001.

64. Stanislav, 'Koncepcia Múzea', 95.

65. Ibid., 108.

66. Ján Stanislav and Dezider Tóth, *Libreto stálej expozície Múzea SNP k 60. výročiu SNP*, Banská Bystrica, 2003, 7.

67. For further details, see www.muzeumsnp.sk

68. Cf: Barbara Lášticová and Andrej Findor, 'From regime legitimation to democratic museum pedagogy? Studying Europeanization at the Museum of the Slovak National Uprising', in Barbara Lášticová and Andrej Findor, eds, *Politics of Collective Memory: Cultural Patterns of Commemorative Practices in Post-War Europe*, Vienna and Berlin: LIT Verlag, 2008, 237–57.

69. http://www.muzeumsnp.sk/index.php?a0=expozicie&a1=osviencim

70. It was still, however, Ján Stanislav, Dezider Tóth and Stanislav Mičev who were the main actors. All three came from Banská Bystrica.

CHAPTER 7

The Holocaust – lacking historical cultures in Slovakia and the Czech Republic

In this study I have presented four cases in which historical consciousness in the Czech and Slovak societies was activated to the highest degree during the 1990s and the early twenty-first century in connection with the memory of the Holocaust. It has, however, also been necessary to expand the chronological framework of the analysis to include the post-war era's communist decades. During the whole communist period up to 1989, the memory of the Holocaust in the Czechoslovak historical culture was influenced in a decisive way by the communist ideological use of history. In the 1970s and 1980s this was expressed by a non-use of the Holocaust history. The period was characterised by a lack of freedom to give history another meaning than that which had been decided at the official level.

The Velvet Revolution of 1989 brought in its wake the return of a pluralistic historical interpretation. However, the return of the Holocaust in the post-communist Czechoslovak historical culture and in its two national components proved to be both complicated and problematic. Neither for the Czech nor the Slovak historical consciousness did the Holocaust come to be what Jörn Rüsen has called a 'borderline event', a milestone that is indispensable for the construction of independent national historical narratives.[1] In neither the Czech nor the Slovak historical culture have I found any proof that the Holocaust was perceived as a trauma or, in Rüsen's words, a 'catastrophic historical experience' for the majority populations of the respective states.

Rüsen claims that historical experiences become either normal, critical or catastrophic – that is to say, traumatic – in people's historical consciousness.

Notes for this section begin on page 209.

In a normal historical experience the given historical event is understood and explained within already existing historical narratives and already existing historical-cultural frameworks, while in a critical experience it must be transformed though not radically reshaped. In a catastrophic or traumatic experience, however, a radical change is forced upon the historical consciousness. A new narrative must be created to make it possible for painful experiences and memories to be worked out and overcome.[2] In the Czech case the historical experience of the Holocaust never exceeded the 'normal' level, while in the Slovak case it reached the critical level, meaning that a certain adjustment of the narratives was demanded in order for them to be included in people's historical consciousness. However, neither the Czech nor the Slovak comprehension of the Holocaust stimulated any need for traumatic processing: a confrontation with the already existing national-historical narratives and a compulsion to find a new meaning.

The Holocaust's marginal position in the Czech and Slovak post-communist historical culture is too problematic to be explained as solely the result of a legacy from the communist ideological usage of history. It should not be forgotten how the Holocaust was perceived before the communist era and how the perception of it in the Czech Republic and especially Slovakia was influenced by certain specific groups, as well as by general trends beyond the national borders. In my analysis I therefore try to show how broader historical-cultural developments have influenced the Czechs' and Slovaks' historical consciousness and determined which role the past in general and the Holocaust in particular are given.

The 'Jew-free' Czech victim role

The Holocaust attained no clear meaning in most Czechs' historical consciousness in the new Czech Republic. On the contrary, it was essentially portrayed as an external phenomenon that did not concern the Czechs at all. This fact was nothing new, however, as similar tendencies could be traced back even to before the communist takeover of power in 1948.

Discussion of the Nazi genocide of Jews, Roma and other groups during the Second World War was marginalised immediately after the war's end, when the Holocaust had an unobtrusive position in contrast to the conflict between Czechs and Germans over events during the war itself and in connection with the forced expulsion of Germans immediately afterward. The Czech majority population saw itself as the war's greatest victim, and this sentiment was just as pronounced half a century later. The Czechs were the first non-German-speaking people to be affected by Nazi Germany's plans of expansion when they were forced to leave the Sudetenland. A broader German occupation of Bohemia and Moravia, which represented the whole Czech portion of Czechoslovakia, followed soon thereafter. The fact that Czechoslovakia was given to Hitler in Munich in front of the whole world and without resistance, and that this occurred before the industrial genocide of Jews commenced, only strengthened the Czechs conviction of their role as victims. It influenced the Czech and Czechoslovak writing of history during the whole post-war period, particularly as the communist interpretation of the victim role placed special emphasis on Germany having planned to exterminate the whole Slavic population in Europe. According to this interpretation, the Nazis would have been successful in this had not Hitler been confronted by heroic Soviet resistance. The Jews were, by this account, neither the first nor unique victims of the Nazi aggression.

Emphasis on the Slavic ethnic groups as the main target for the Third Reich's racial policies was frequent in the Slavic countries of Eastern Europe during the whole post-war era. The Soviet-communist ideology used simple figures as proof of the Slavic main victim role: in the Soviet territories, more ethnic Russians or Ukrainians died during the war than Russian or Ukrainian Jews. However simplified this 'comparative mathematics of victims', it had a significant influence on all of the mentioned historical cultures.[3] That being said, both Czech and the Slovak historical culture were very special and could not seek support from such simplified mathematical comparisons.

Both in the Protectorate of Bohemia and Moravia and in the Slovak Republic, the Jews during the Second World War comprised the largest single victim group, which – especially in the Slovak case – was hit harder than the local Slavic majority population. In the Slovak case it was a matter of a few thousand Slovaks compared to more than 70,000 Slovak Jews – only counting the territory that belonged to Slovakia during the entire war. If Ruthenia and the south Slovak regions occupied by Hungary after the start of the war are added, the proportions are even more convincing. In the Czech case the number of Czech victims was higher, but the situation was nonetheless similar. Here as well it depended on how the victims were counted, i.e., if victims from the Sudetenland were included, and here as well more complex calculations of the Jews' total over-representation in the statistics must be taken into account. In total, as much as 75–80 per cent of all war victims in Czechoslovakia were Jews.

The memory of the Holocaust could, even so, never compete in the Czech historical culture with the memory of the Czech suffering during the German occupation. This was demonstrated particularly clearly when the 1942 assassination of the deputy Nazi Reichsprotektor, Reinhard Heydrich, was highlighted. Regardless of Heydrich's direct connection to the Holocaust and the genocide's intensification following his death, later Czech and Czechoslovak history writing always focused exclusively on the Czech, non-Jewish dimension, on acts such as the terror strikes in the villages of Lidice and Ležáky. These villages were razed to the ground as direct revenge for Heydrich's death, accompanied by the murder of all village men over the age of sixteen and the deportation of the women and children. Attention was turned away from the Holocaust and towards the suffering of the Czechs, even in cases that for the rest of the world became milestones for the understanding of the Holocaust, such as the film *Schindler's List*.

Czech self-reflection in relation to the Holocaust was not generally regarded as necessary; during the Second World War the Jews were not the victims of the Czechs, but of the Germans or 'the fascists'. Those who in relation to the Holocaust could be characterised as 'bystanders' were, moreover, not perceived as belonging to any special category. During the entire post-war period, and even in the post-communist 1990s, there were no revelations about Czech anti-Semitism that could have dislodged the foundations of the Czech historical narrative. There was no massacre that could provoke the Czech historical consciousness in a manner similar to the Polish debate about Jedwabne, nor were there any signs bearing witness to ethnically motivated violence against Jews just after the 1945 liberation, as in the case of the 1947 pogrom in Topolčany, Slovakia. When the communist anti-Semitism at the end of the 1940s and beginning of the 1950s could also be explained as a product of the Soviet-dominated Stalin epoch, there was really little after the fall of communism that was able to provoke Czech historical self-reflection.

An important background to the scant interest in the Holocaust in the Czech Republic of the 1990s was the fact that there were no important actors who could place the Holocaust at the centre of the national historical culture in the same way that Jan Gross did in the already noted Polish case of Jedwabne.[4] The intellectual and political elites linked important questions concerning people's individual morality or the collective Czech morality exclusively to events and situations from the communist epoch. The Jewish minority was too small and too invisible to gain a hearing for its existential use of the Holocaust at a national level. Despite the Roma minority being much larger, it had few of its own prominent representatives who were publicly visible and also utilised history. In the case of the Roma, there was also the lack of a historical culture that could ascribe a special meaning to the Holocaust/Porrajmos for the Roma identity.

In the Czech cultural sphere the lack of Holocaust perspectives seems especially unfathomable when comparing the situation in the 1990s with the literary and film production from the period between the end of the 1950s and 1968. The relatively long list of books and films about the Holocaust, which between 1956 and 1968 attracted national attention, had an exceptionally modest continuation in the 1990s. The first Oscar-winning Czechoslovak film with the Holocaust in the main role, *The Shop on Main Street* from 1966, was a climax in Czech and Slovak filmmaking during the period of reform-communism. However, the most recent Czech film on the subject to be nominated for an Oscar, *Musíme si pomáhat* ('Divided we fall'), from 2000, appears to be something of an exception. Nevertheless, this film was not primarily understood as a film about the Holocaust by the public since the Holocaust was just one of the events mentioned there; as a comedy with a high grade of irony the film did not present any clear ambition with regards to Czech history either.[5] Another widely discussed film about the Holocaust, *Protektor*, came first in 2009. Book production was rather more comprehensive, primarily due to a number of survivor memoirs being printed in new editions after having been published abroad during the Cold War, most of which did not gain much attention on the national level. The factors behind this difference are difficult to explain. The artists no longer needed to struggle for their individual and artistic freedom against the political power, especially because there was no longer any oppression similar to that during the de-Stalinisation period. Additionally, several of the most prominent cultural personalities, with Václav Havel at their head, had now become the foremost representatives of the new establishment. As a theme the war does not seem to have been as relevant as communism and the present: the most successful film of all was *Kolja*, about the consequences of the 1968 Soviet occupation, which in 1997 was awarded an Oscar for best foreign film. Knowledge about what happened to the Czech and Slovak Jews is still fragmentary among those generations that did not directly experience the war. Concerning the Holocaust's place in the Czech narratives, it is paradoxical that it was exactly during the de-Stalinisation period and not during the post-communist era that the Holocaust was most used, and that the genocide was used as both a Jewish and a Czech trauma. The common enemy was the totalitarian power, that is to say, not only Nazism and not only communism. It was then that the Holocaust was transformed into a narrative about people's powerlessness against the great machine of totalitarian power.

The Czech historical culture was not unique in its 'resistant' relationship to the Holocaust, or rather its marginalisation of the Holocaust up until the beginning of the 1990s. Leaving aside the Eastern and Central European countries, whose development in the post-war era was similar to that in Czechoslovakia, a similar situation can be found even in Western European countries like France, where prominent attention to the Holocaust was also given only after the end of the Cold War.[6] In contrast to Western European societies, however, the Czech historical culture was influenced only to a very limited extent by the Americanisation of the Holocaust, as is demonstrated both in the *Porrajmos* debate and in the reactions to *Schindler's List*.

The 'Jew-free' Slovak heroisation

As opposed to the Czech historical culture's preoccupation with its own victim role, the Slovak post-communist historical culture was dominated by the heroisation of the Slovak role during the Second World War. This was clearly shown in both the war accounts I have analysed: the national-Catholic narrative and its 'anti-nationalist' and European-orientated opposite. While 'national leaders', who were claimed to have been successful in realising 'the nation's everlasting dream' and creating the independent Slovak state, were lifted up in the first case, 'the entire nation's' active heroic role in the fight against fascism was emphasised in the second case. But no clear position was given to the Holocaust here either.

The Slovak historical culture could not ignore the Holocaust as easily as its Czech counterpart could. Because of its specific character during the Second World War in Tiso's Slovakia, the Holocaust had a more central role in the Slovak historical consciousness. Yet its concrete position in the Slovak historical culture nonetheless remained diffuse in the post-communist Slovak writing of history, in which the Holocaust became a weapon in the conflict over which Slovaks were heroes and which were villains during the war. In the national-Catholic case the Holocaust was used to explain away the Slovak guilt, while in the 'anti-nationalist' case it was used to compromise the group of people that had managed to assume power over the Slovak state and the nation. They were, however, presented as a deviating minority whose guilt could not call into question the heroism of the Slovak nation.

The need for national self-reflection was impeded by the fact that Slovakia to a great degree could hide behind the whole of Czechoslovakia's status as the victim of Hitler and the Third Reich during the war. Slovak society was thus never forced into a confrontation of its own with both the Holocaust of Slovak Jews and with its war relationship to Germany. Because the punishment of the Tiso regime's primary actors was left to Czechoslovak authorities as a more or less internal Czechoslovak affair, the task of calming the inflamed Czech–Slovak ethnic relations became as important to the official Czechoslovakia as bringing the perpetrators to justice. Together with the communist ideological usage of history, this can explain the absence of self-reflection between 1945 and 1989.

Nor did national self-reflection appear when the opposition to the national-Catholic narrative began to formulate its own 'anti-nationalistic' narrative. On the contrary, this opposition sketched a new collective, national heroic image. That even the 'anti-nationalistic' historians who used the Holocaust in a scientific way – along with the intellectual elites – did not utilise the Holocaust to directly call into question the picture of the Slovak nation as a collective hero is somewhat surprising. It may have been due to the individual actors' own communist backgrounds and the way that the communist historical narrative, the development of which several of them had contributed to, interpreted the heroic Slovak resistance to the Tiso regime and to 'fascism'. The postcommunist Slovak identity may have been too young and unstable to be questioned within its foundations.

The respective nation's emphasis on the victim role in the Czech case and on the hero role in the Slovak case meant that the interpretation of war events in both of the Czechoslovak federal republics did not automatically lead to a conflict. There was no competition between the two nations concerning these roles. There was certainly bitterness on the Czech side about the leading Slovak nationalists having exploited the situation and reached a settlement with Germany after the Munich Agreement, but Slovakia's position never challenged Germany's role as main perpetrator. The Czechs, as the larger nation, still felt themselves to have been the victims of the Germans and not the Slovaks. No Slovak murders of Czechs were mentioned in Czech historical writing. The Holocaust, which would probably also have been mentioned in a murder discussion of this kind, remained 'forgotten'. In this lies an important reason for the Holocaust remaining unmentioned even during Czechoslovakia's division.

Cultural Europeanisation as a determining factor

It is important to point out that none of the main impulses for the most significant individual debates about the Holocaust in Czechoslovakia and later the Czech Republic and Slovakia came from within the Czech or Slovak historical cultures themselves. In the Czech case, the Schindler debate was initiated by an American film and the debate on the *Porrajmos* by an American researcher and activist, whose activities received support from American institutions. In the Slovak case, reactions were provoked by the activities of the Slovak World Congress and the diaspora's dominance in the Slovak debate over the Holocaust before Czechoslovakia's dissolution. However, the Slovak World Congress, which had its centre in North America, cannot be viewed as either the American or the domestic Slovak historical culture's typical representative. In spite of this – as I have shown – the consequences of the Americanisation during the first part of the 1990s were far from as obvious as the consequences of the Europeanisation process at a later stage, when both the Czech Republic and Slovakia applied for membership in the European Union and when the EU was seriously preparing its expansion – one that for the first time would include former communist countries from Eastern and Central Europe.

In his book on European post-war history the historian, Tony Judt, writes that the Holocaust has already become a part of the common European identity created after the Cold war. He bases his observation on the conviction that the renewed memory of the dead European Jews has become the actual definition of and the guarantee for the continent's renewed humanism.[7] Although the situation presented by Judt is without doubt the foremost goal of the Europeanisation process, I have not been able to confirm that the development in the post-communist Czech and Slovak historical cultures has come this far. This applies especially to those cases where the European conception of the Holocaust's role in the future European historical culture collides with the traditional self-images in the particular national historical narratives of the two countries I have studied. This relationship confirms the tension between Europeanisation and nationalisation in turn-of-the-century Europe that research on the Holocaust has pointed to.[8]

The main aim with the concept of the Holocaust as a foundation stone for the construction of the new European identity has, judging by all accounts, been to lessen the significance of nationally and ethnically dominated historical narratives and to create a European narrative that can point to the Holocaust as a warning example of hate and non-tolerance, using it to foster respect, humanity and tolerance between individuals, ethnic groups and nations. This intention has hardly been realised in the Czech Republic or Slovakia, however. The boundaries that have characterised and defined ethnic, national, religious or other groups have, rather, been strengthened by the latest decades' discussions regarding the history of the Holocaust.

When following how attention was drawn to the Holocaust after the Czech Republic and Slovakia had applied for EU membership in the mid-1990s, one finds that the initiative to steer the memory of the Holocaust in a desired 'European' direction usually came from high-ranking politicians and the official representatives of the countries, not from intellectuals or other 'ordinary citizens'. This reflects first and foremost a political striving towards an increased European cultural integration, which after the Cold War would complete the hitherto mainly economically and politically directed integration process. One can take as an example the Czech Republic's President, Václav Havel, who until the mid-1990s was not particularly active in connection with the Holocaust debate. During both Czechoslovakia's division and later in the 'Lety debate's' introductory phase, he used the Holocaust more or less formally and sporadically, without consistently including it in those speeches, publications and actions which had to do with his support for human rights. His clearest engagement in relation to the memory of the Holocaust was not demonstrated until 1999, when in cooperation with the Czech Department of Culture he initiated the conference, *Fenomén Holoucastu,* which was followed by a project called *Zmizelí sousedé* ('Vanished neighbours'). The project's goal was that young Czechs between the ages of twelve and eighteen would begin to remember their vanished neighbours who were deported and murdered during the Second World War. The students were to describe their search for the Holocaust's victims in different articles and papers.[9] The moment at which 'Vanished neighbours' took place corresponded to the time when the Czech government institutions were to adapt their activities to the demands of the European authorities. Thus the project can, in Havel's case, be seen as a political activity, and bears witness to the young Czech democracy respecting the principles of the European Union. Slovakia's President, Rudolf Schuster, also began suddenly paying attention to the link between the Holocaust and the Europeanisation process during the end-phase of the expansion process after the Stockholm International Forum on the Holocaust, despite the fact that both he and his predecessor, Michal Kováč, had more or less ignored debates about the Holocaust during practically the whole of the 1990s.

Actions of this kind actually confirm the disproportion Klas–Göran Karlsson has pointed out between, on the one hand, the Holocaust's political 'canonisation' (*von oben*) by European political institutions and, on the other, a significantly more complicated use of the Holocaust from below that does not as unequivocally reflect the image of the Holocaust as being at the centre of the particular historical cultures in Europe.[10] The question therefore remains as to whether the Holocaust's Europeanisation can really be seen in this way as the Europeanisation of the Czech Republic and Slovakia.

It is namely beyond all doubt that a historical culture – especially a national one – changes considerably slower than contemporary politics. The creation of a historical culture includes far more people than just politicians and reflects significantly more varied interests than just political ones. The mental consequences of the ideology that influenced the Czech and Slovak societies for more than four decades could not disappear as quickly as the communist power structure. As I have shown, the long-term continuity in the relationship between the national self-image and the Holocaust was manifest in both the Czech and the Slovak historical cultures.

The politicians' reactions indicated not only that they had joined the new European direction, but also that they feared potential negative reactions from the EU if their countries did not comply with the demands placed upon them. Despite the fact that the Holocaust's place in the respective historical cultures never changed substantially, there did not arise – with the exception of the reaction to Milan Ďurica's book, *Dejiny Slovenska a Slovákov* – a strong, public 'European' criticism of how the memory of the Holocaust was treated in the Czech Republic or Slovakia. Both countries became members of both the EU and NATO and are today considered to be democratic and Europeanised, despite the fact that during the whole post-communist period they never consistently confronted and settled disputes regarding their own war history, including the Holocaust. The Czech Republic has never admitted to any Czech guilt concerning the Holocaust of Czech Jews, and *Slovenská národná strana*, which still sees the first Slovak state from the period of 1939–1945 as a progressive expression of 'the Slovak nation's free will', became once again a part of the Slovak government coalition after the 2006 parliamentary election.

Notes

1. Jörn Rüsen, 'Holocaust, Memory and Identity Building: Metahistorical Considerations in the Case of (West) Germany', in Michael S. Roth and Charles G. Salas, eds, *Disturbing Remains: Memory, History and Crisis in the Twentieth Century*, Los Angeles: Getty Research Institute, 2001, 232–53.

2. See Jörn Rüsen, 'Interpretting the Holocaust: Some Theoretical Issues', in Karlsson and Zander, *Holocaust Heritage*, 46.

3. See, for example, Klas-Göran Karlsson, 'The Holocaust and Russian Historical Culture: A Century-Long Perspective', in Karlsson and Zander, *Echoes of the Holocaust*, especially 209–15.

4. Jan Gross, *Neighbours: The Story of the Annihilation of a Small Jewish Town*, New York: Penguin Books, 2002. See also Barbara Törnqvist-Plewa, 'The Jedwabne Killings – A Challenge for Polish Collective Memory', in Karlsson and Zander, *Echoes of the Holocaust*, 141–76.

5. See: Blahoslav Hruška, 'Okupace a válka v českém filmu po roce 1945 jako téma kultury vzpomínání', in Cornelissen, Holec and Pešek, *Diktatura – válka – vyhnání*, 272–73.

6. Judt, *Postwar: A History of Europe*, 815–20.

7. Ibid., 804.

8. Karlsson, *Folkmordet som spegel och symbolpolitik*.

9. http://www.zmizeli-sousede.cz/aj/index.html

10. Karlsson, 'The Uses of History', 38–55.

Conclusion

In a broad sense, this study is an analysis of how the Holocaust has been incorporated into the Czech and Slovak historical consciousness since the end of the Second World War. Its main focus, however, is the place of the Holocaust in the Czech and Slovak historical cultures during 'the long 1990s', which refers to the period between the fall of the communist regime in Czechoslovakia at the end of 1989 and the entry of both the Czech and Slovak Republics into the European Union in 2004.

From the Czech and Slovak points of view, 'the long 1990s' represent an unprecedented transformation from communist dictatorship to parliamentary democracy and market economy. At the end of 1992, Czechoslovakia ceased to exist as a federative state of Czechs and Slovaks, becoming instead two new nation states within the same territory. New Czech and Slovak democratic and national values needed to be defined at a time when both of these newly born democracies were facing various international processes, including globalisation and Europeanisation.

In post-Cold-War Europe, the Holocaust has become one of the main historical warning signs: a bleak symbol of where the collapse of respect for democracy, tolerance and human rights can lead. When morality and conscience have been placed in the centre of new European politics instead of ideology, the Holocaust has had a great political-symbolic importance. *Europeanisation*, in particular, has put the Holocaust right in the centre of a search for a new, all-European democratic identity, at least as seen by the leading authorities of the European Union. Even in the United States, where interest in the Nazi genocide first arose during the 1970s, the Holocaust has played an increasingly important role after the fall of the Iron Curtain. However, the Holocaust was more or less completely ignored in Czechoslovak communist historical culture before 1989. As this study shows, its 'return' into the post-Communist historical cultures of Czechoslovakia's descendent states was far from self-evident.

The central theoretical concepts of this analysis are *historical consciousness, historical culture* and the *use of history*. *Historical consciousness*, as introduced by Karl-Ernst Jeismann in 1979, reflects the ability of every individual to search after his or her own identity relative to time. It is a mental capacity that helps human beings to orientate themselves temporally in life and to create meaning out of their experience of the past and expectations for the future. Historical consciousness contributes to the development of moral and existential values, principles and attitudes. Its activation is related to the experience of dramatic changes such as the end of the Cold War or the collapse of an existing state, as is the case in this study. In connection with human societies, collective manifestations of historical consciousness are especially important. Historical consciousness provides a mental foundation for *historical culture*, which can be seen as a materialised and visualised manifestation of collective historical consciousness. Historical culture thus illustrates how different groups and societies define their priorities with the help of history and what parts of the past they consider most important for both the present and the future. Historical culture includes a number of historical artefacts, including scholarly monographs, textbooks, museum exhibitions, films and public debates – to name those that have been analysed in this book.

Since neither historical consciousness nor historical culture can be analysed as such, they need to be operationalised. In the case of this study, this has been done by focusing on the *use of history*, a concept introduced by the Swedish historian, Klas-Göran Karlsson, in connection with his research of the *Perestroika* period in the Soviet Union. Use of history refers to the activation of historical consciousness for concrete action. In accordance with Karlsson's typology, several uses of history are shown here in practice, such as existential, moral, political, ideological and scientific. Also illustrated is non-use, a special form of ideological use that deliberately avoids the use of history in order to achieve certain ideological goals.

The Czech and Slovak historical cultures and the place that they give to the Holocaust are analysed through four dominant Czechoslovak, Czech and Slovak historical narratives that were developed by leading history users during the post-war period, all of which first appeared in open competition in Czechoslovakia and in the Czech and Slovak Republics during the 1990s. In these historical narratives, selected events from Czech and Slovak history were organized into various chains in order to provide history with special meanings. Those events that supported the meanings were emphasised, while those that did not fit were either downplayed or ignored.

The four Czech and Slovak historical narratives that dominated 'the long 1990s' were:

- The *Czechoslovak communist historical narrative*, which was common to both Czechs and Slovaks. This was a dominant official historical

narrative already during the period 1948–1989, with the 1960s as a
certain exception.

- The *Czech national-liberal historical narrative*, which presented the
  Czech society as 'traditionally democratic' and at the same time superior to other Central and East European post-communist societies,
  including the Slovak society. Supporters of this narrative saw the first
  Czechoslovak Republic from the interwar period as the peak of Czech
  historical development and wanted to build the new post-communist
  regime in this tradition. The first president of Czechoslovakia, Tomas
  Masaryk, was particularly glorified in this context. The narrative was
  created already during the 1970s and 1980s in opposition to the official
  Czechoslovak communist narrative. After the fall of communism, this
  narrative became dominant in the Czech part of Czechoslovakia and
  later in the new Czech Republic.

- The *Slovak national-Catholic historical narrative*, whose supporters saw
  history's first Slovak nation state in the years 1939-1945 as a pattern
  for future Slovak post-communist development. The main hero here
  was Jozef Tiso, a Catholic priest and the President of wartime Slovakia.
  Even this narrative was already created before 1989. It began to dominate Slovak historical culture during the early 1990s and continued
  until 1998. During the Cold War, it was supported mainly by the Slovak
  diaspora in exile and unofficially by some parts of the Catholic Church
  in Slovakia.

- The *Slovak national-European historical narrative*, which was developed
  first during the 1990s in Slovakia in opposition to the Slovak national-
  Catholic, Czechoslovak communist and Czech national-liberal narratives. The Slovak entry into the European Union was presented as the
  meaning of Slovakia's historical development, while the first Slovak
  Republic from the wartime period was rejected because of its totalitarian character and its subordination to Nazi Germany. The core of
  this narrative was the Slovak National Uprising in 1944, which was
  seen as the beginning of the Slovak path to democracy and 'common
  Europe'.

In each narrative, one period of Czechoslovakia's development after 1918
was seen as especially important. All the narratives, however, were used as ideal
cases; the borders between them were not always fully clear and there were also
alternative Czech and Slovak historical narratives that were less dominant than
these four.

In all the dominant historical narratives, the Second World War played a
central role. In the Czech case, it buried the interwar Czechoslovak parliamentary democracy, whereas in the Czechoslovak communist case, it ended the
development towards capitalism. In the Slovak cases, it allowed the first Slovak

nation state in history to be created in 1939 or it showed the Slovak 'democratic spirit' in the uprising against the Tiso regime.

Since both Czech and Slovak Jews were among the victims of the Holocaust – the number of Czech and Slovak Jews that perished during the Holocaust was as much as seventy-five per cent of the total number of Czechoslovak victims of the Second World War (270,000 out of 360,000) – one could easily expect that the Holocaust would be among the events that were important for historical consciousness in both the Czech and Slovak cases. However, the place the Holocaust was given in the respective historical cultures during the 1990s was more problematic. Since the Czechoslovak communist historical narrative and Slovak national-Catholic historical narrative each supported totalitarian and anti-Semitic regimes, the problems inherent in their treatment of the memory of the Holocaust were less surprising than those in both of the remaining cases. This analysis shows that even the Czech national-liberal narrative and the Slovak national-European narrative gave the Holocaust only a marginal place.

The empirical part of this study focuses on four case studies that show great difficulties with the efforts to incorporate the Holocaust into the Czech and Slovak historical cultures. The first empirical chapter, for example, analyses the role of the Holocaust in Czech-Slovak debates during the process of the Czechoslovak dissolution.

The second empirical chapter presents Czech discussions about the film *Schindler's List*, which became one of the main focal points in the global discussion of the Holocaust during the 1990s and one of the main symbols of 'the Americanisation' of the Holocaust. Because Oskar Schindler was a so-called Sudeten German and at the same time a citizen of interwar Czechoslovakia, Steven Spielberg's attempt to show this man as a German hero of the Holocaust was found to be very problematic, especially from the Czech point of view. The main reason for this was that Schindler had worked as a German agent against Czechoslovakia during the late 1930s.

The third empirical chapter deals with the Holocaust of the Romanies, the *Porrajmos*. In the Czech Republic during the 1970s, a pig farm was built on the site near Prague where a concentration camp for the Czech Romanies had been situated during the Second World War. Several protests from abroad in the early 1990s led to a debate which revealed that the personnel in the Romany camp in Lety were Czech, and that a number of Czechs collaborated with the Nazi regime in the Protectorate of Bohemia and Moravia during the war. The Czech participation in the *Porrajmos* proved too difficult to handle for the Czech historical culture of the 1990s.

The last empirical chapter analyses the representation of the Holocaust of the Slovak Jews in the most prominent Slovak museum of the Second World War – the *Museum of the Slovak National Uprising* in Banská Bystrica. As both a museum and a scientific institution, this museum and its historians participated in the development of a new, national-European historical narrative. At the same time, the museum was the first museum in Slovakia after the collapse of Communism to incorporate the Holocaust into its permanent exhibition. Since the museum also stood behind the Slovak national exhibition in Auschwitz-Birkenau, the analysis shows that the Holocaust of the Slovak Jews was presented differently in each of these cases, one inside and one outside Slovakia, and that the differences were caused both by the place where the exhibition took place and by the audience being addressed.

The main conclusion of this work is that neither in the Czech nor the Slovak historical cultures has the Holocaust became what German historian, Jörn Rüsen, calls a *borderline event*, a trauma considered necessary for the construction of historical narratives that make sense of national history. According to Rüsen, historical events are categorised in our historical consciousness as normal, critical and catastrophic or traumatic. While normal and critical events are usually explained within frameworks of already existing historical narratives, which remain untouched in the 'normal' case and are only partly adjusted in the 'critical' case, catastrophic or traumatic events force our historical consciousness into radical changes. In order to be able to understand and explain 'catastrophic' or 'traumatic' events, people who are affected by them have to create a new historical narrative.

In the Czech case, the Holocaust remained on a 'normal' level, while in the Slovak case it reached a 'critical' level. Thus it hardly affected the dominant Czech historical narratives analysed in this study and it required only partial changes in the Slovak historical narratives. Neither the Czechs nor the Slovaks found a need to radically change their historical consciousness and create a new historical narrative that would make new sense of the Holocaust within their respective historical cultures.

In the Czech case of the 'long 1990s', the Holocaust continued to be presented as an external phenomenon that had nothing do to with the Czechs. The memory of the Holocaust was overshadowed by the memory of the conflicts between the Czechs and Germans that occurred before, during and immediately after the Second World War. The fact that the Czech nation became the first victim of the Third Reich in Munich in 1938 (while Austria, in fact, was not considered to be a victim), that it was given to Hitler quite openly and without any resistance, and that all this happened already before the genocide of the Jews actually started, strengthened a predominant Czech feeling that the Czech nation was the main victim of Nazi Germany. In this respect, the Jews were neither the first victims nor unique victims of Hitler. The dominant focus on Czech suffering as compared to Jewish suffering was especially evident in the Czech debate over the film *Schindler's List*.

Slovak historical consciousness during the 'long 1990s' was instead dominated by efforts to stress Slovak heroism during the Second World War. The 'Slovaks' were heroes in both of the dominant Slovak historical narratives studied here: the Slovak national-Catholic and the Slovak national-European.

In the first case, the real heroes were the 'national leaders' headed by Jozef Tiso, a Catholic priest and Slovak president during the war. According to supporters of this narrative, these leaders managed to realise the 'eternal' dream of the entire Slovak nation when they created the first Slovak nation state in history. In the second case, the real heroes were those Slovaks who took part in the 'Slovak National Uprising' in the late summer of 1944, as well as those who revolted against Tiso's wartime state, which was, in fact, only a Nazi satellite with a totalitarian regime. Opponents of the Tiso regime were marginalised or labelled as non-Slovaks in the national-Catholic narrative, whereas in the national-European narrative, it was Tiso and his supporters who were described as a minority while the 'Slovak nation' remained morally clean and democratic.

During the Second World War, Tiso's Slovakia – although unoccupied until the summer of 1944 – deported more than 70,000 of its Jewish citizens to their deaths. Tiso's regime even paid Germany in order to facilitate the deportation of Jews. Thus it was impossible for Slovak historical culture to ignore the Holocaust the same way that Czech historical culture had due to the fact that the German Nazis carried the responsibility for the deportations and killings in Czech territory. The supporters of the Slovak national-Catholic narrative, however, claimed that the deportations and killings happened without Tiso's knowledge, thus using the Holocaust in order to clear Tiso's name. In their conviction, as soon as Tiso learned about the real nature of the deportations, he did his best to stop them. All evidence proving the opposite was rejected and denied. The supporters of the Slovak national-European narrative, in contrast, used the Holocaust in order to prove Tiso's guilt and the guilt of the limited group of people who – with the help of Adolf Hitler – had managed to assume absolute power over the Slovak nation.

It is important to point out that none of the great debates about the Holocaust during the 1990s started within the Czech and Slovak historical cultures. In the Czech case, both the debate about Oskar Schindler and the discussions regarding the *Porrajmos* of the Czech Romanies were initiated by American influences: Steven Spielberg's film *Schindler's List* and the American activist and historical researcher Paul Polansky, who was supported by a number of institutions from the United States. In the Slovak case, the initiative to challenge the Czechoslovak communist narrative and the Czech national-liberal narrative with the Slovak national-Catholic narrative came from the Slovak World Congress, an organisation established within the Slovak diaspora in several Western countries during the Cold War. The Slovak national-European narrative, on the other hand, was in large part a reaction to the activities of the European Union and its institutions. This 'European' influence was evident in the Czech debate about the *Porrajmos* as well. While the effects of the 'Americanisation' of the Holocaust were ambiguous, the political effects of the 'Europeanisation' of the Holocaust were obvious. However, the general impact of the EU's efforts on Czech historical consciousness was much more doubtful.

The results of this study clearly show that the main goal of the Europeanisation of the Holocaust – to make the Holocaust one of the key building blocks of a new common European identity, in which old, nationally and ethnically framed historical narratives would be seriously challenged and subsequently replaced by a new common European historical narrative that could be used against ethnic violence, racism and non-tolerance – was reached in neither the Czech nor the Slovak historical cultures. On the contrary, boundaries between ethnic, national, religious and other groups were emphasised in all of the analysed cases. Despite the effort of some politicians to speed up the process of European integration, both historical cultures showed much less flexibility and much more rigid continuity with previous periods (such as the continuous influence of communist interpretations of history) than these politicians, and especially the European institutions, might have expected.

This confirms the fact that historical cultures develop much more slowly than the politics of the moment. Historical culture is created by many more people than just politicians and reflects many more factors, interests and needs than just those of a political nature. Thus the mental effects of the communist ideology, which influenced both the Czech and Slovak historical cultures during most of the post-war period, could not be removed as quickly as the communist structure of political power.

Bibliography

Newspapers and Periodicals

Český deník
Dějiny a současnost
Haló noviny
Historický časopis
Katolícke noviny
Lidové noviny
Mladá fronta Dnes, MF Dnes
Národná obroda
Práca
Pravda
Právo, Rudé právo
Reflex
Republika
Respekt
Roš Chodeš
Sme
Soudobé dějiny
Špígl
Týden
Týdenník
Výber
Zemské noviny

Books and Articles

Adams, Bradley, *The Struggle for the Soul of the Nation*, Lanham, MD: Rowman and Littlefield Publishers, 2004

Adams, Bradley, 'The Politics of Retribution: The Trial of Jozef Tiso in the Czechoslovak Environment', in István Deák, Jan Gross and Tony Judt, eds, *The Politics of Retribution in Europe*, Princeton: Princeton University Press, 2000

Albright, Madeleine, *Madam Secretary*, New York: Miramax Books, 2003

Alm, Martin, *Americanitis: Amerika som sjukdom eller läkemedel. Svenska berättelser om USA åren 1900–1939*, Lund: Lunds universitet, 2002

Alm, Martin, 'Historiens ström och berättelsens fåra', in Klas-Göran Karlsson and Ulf Zander, eds, *Historien är nu*, Lund: Studentlitteratur, 2004

Altman, Ilya, 'The History and Fate of The Black Book and The Unknown Black Book', in Joshua Rubenstein and Ilya Altman, eds, *The Unknown Black Book: The Holocaust in the German Occupied Soviet Territories*, Bloomington: Indiana University Press in association with the United States Holocaust Memorial Museum, 2010

Antohi, Sorin, Balász Trencsényi and Péter Apor, eds, *Narratives Unbound: Historical Studies in Post-Communist Eastern Europe*, Budapest: Central European University Press, 2007

Bakke, Elisabeth, *Doomed to Failure? The Czechoslovak Nation Project and the Slovak Autonomist Reaction 1918–1938*, Oslo: University of Oslo, 1999

Bakke, Elisabeth, 'The Making of Czechoslovakism in the First Czechoslovak Republic', in Martin Schulze Wessel, *Loyalitäten in der Tschechoslowakischen Republik 1918–1938. Politische, nationale und kulturelle Zugehörigkeiten*, Munich: R. Oldenbourg Verlag, 2004.

Barany, Zoltan, *The East European Gypsies: Regime Change, Marginality and Ethnopolitics*, Cambridge: Cambridge University Press, 2002

Barša, Pavel, *Paměť a genocida. Úvahy o politice holocaustu*, Prague: Argo, 2011

Bauer, Yehuda, 'Jews, Gypsies, Slavs: Policies of the Third Reich', in *UNESCO Yearbook on Peace and Conflict Studies 1985*, Paris: UNESCO, 1987

Bauer, Yehuda, 'Correspondence: "Gypsies and the Holocaust"', *The History Teacher* 25(4), August 1992

Bauer, Yehuda, 'The Tragedy of the Slovak Jews within the Framework of Nazi Policy towards the Jews in Europe in General', in *The Tragedy of the Jews of Slovakia.*, Auschwitz-Birkenau State Muzeum, Muzeum of the Slovak National Uprising, 2002

Beneš, Zdeněk, *Historický text a historická kultura*, Prague: Karolinum, 1995

Beneš, Zdeněk, and Václav Kural, eds, *Rozumět dějinám*, Prague: Gallery, 2002

Bernstein, Michael Andre, 'The Schindler's List Effect', *American Scholar Magazine*, Summer 1994.

Blažek, Petr, ed., *Opozice a odpor proti komunistickému režimu v Československu 1968–1989*, Prague: Dokořán, 2005

Blodig, Vojtěch, ed., *Fenomén Holocaust / The Holocaust Phenomenon. Sborník mezinárodní vědecké konference*, Terezín: Památník Terezín, 1999

Blodig, Vojtěch, 'Památník Terezín v minulosti a současnosti', in Christoph Cornelissen, Roman Holec and Jiří Pešek, *Diktatura – válka – vyhnání. Kultury vzpomínání v českém, slovenském a německém prostředí od roku 1945*, Ústí nad Labem: Albis International, 2007

Blodigová, Alexandra, 'Státní příslušnost – úprava státního občanství v Československu do roku 1942', in Helena Krejčová and Jana Svobodová, eds, *Postavení a osudy židovského obyvatelstva v Čechách a na Moravě v letech 1939–1945. Sborník studií*, Prague: Ústav pro soudobé dějiny, 1998

Braxátor, František, *Slovenský exil 68*, Bratislava: LUČ, 1992

Broklová, Eva, and Jan Křen, Eds, *Obraz Němců Rakouska a Německa v české společnosti 19. a 20. století*, Prague: Karolinum, 1998

Bryant, Chad, 'Whose Nation? Czech Dissidents and History Writing from a Post-1989 Perspective', *History & Memory* 12(1), Spring/Summer 2000

Bubeník, Jaroslav, and Jiří Křesťan, 'Zjišťování národnosti a židovská otázka', in Helena Krejčová and Jana Svobodová, eds, *Postavení a osudy židovského obyvatelstva v Čechách a na Moravě v letech 1939–1945. Sborník studií*, Prague: Ústav pro soudobé dějiny, 1998

Büchler, Robert, Gila Fatranová and Stanislav Mičev, *Slovenskí Židia*, Banská Bystrica: Múzeum SNP, 1991

Bugge, Peter, 'The Use of the Middle: Mitteleuropa vs. Střední Evropa', *European Review of History* 6, 1999

Bugge, Peter, 'Příběh, prostor, konec – středoevropská literatura jako téma v české kulturní debatě osmdesátých let', in Daniel Vojtěch, ed., *Česká literatura na konci tisíciletí*, Prague: Ústav pro českou literaturu AV ČR, 2001

Bútorová, Zora, and Martin Bútora, 'Wariness towards Jews as an Expression of Post-Communist Panic: The Case of Slovakia', *Czechoslovak Sociological Review* 28, 1992

Bútorová, Zora and Martin Bútora, 'Možno súčasne chváliť vojnový Slovenský štát i SNP?', *Národná obroda*, 8 August 1994

Bútorová, Zora, and Martin Bútora, *Attitudes Towards Jews and the Holocaust in Independent Slovakia*, New York: American Jewish Committee, 1995

Bystrický,Valerián, and Štefan Fano, eds, *Pokus o politický a osobný profil Jozefa Tisu. Zborník materiálov z vedeckého sympózia Častá-Papiernička, 5.–7. mája 1992*, Slovak Academic Press, Bratislava, 1992

Čapková, Kateřina, *Češi, Němci, Židé? Národní identita Židů v Čechách*, Litomyšl: Paseka, 2005

Čapková, Kateřina, *Czech, Germans, Jews? National Identity and the Jews of Bohemia*, New York and Oxford: Berghahn Books, 2012

Čapková, Kateřina, and Michal Frankl, *Nejisté útočiště. Československo a uprchlíci před nacismem, 1933–1938*, Prague and Litomyšl: Paseka, 2008

Čarnogurský, Ján, *Videné od Dunaja,* Bratislava: Kalligram, 1997

Čarnogurský, Pavol, *14 marec 1939*, Bratislava:Veda, 1992

Čermáková, Radka, 'Poválečné Československo. Obnovený stát ve střední Evropě', in Blanka Soukupová, Peter Salner and Miroslava Ludvíková, eds, *Židovská menšina v Československu po druhé světové válce. Od osvobození k nové totalitě*, Praha: Židovské muzeum v Praze, 2009

Cieslar, Jiří, *Kočky na Atalantě*, Prague: AMU, 2003

Císařovská, Blanka, and Vilém Prečan, *Charta 77: dokumenty*, Prague: Ústav pro soudobé dějiny AV ČR, 2007

Cohen, Robin, *Global Diaspora: An Introduction*, Seattle: University of Washington Press, 1997

Cohen, Shari J., *Politics Without a Past: The Absence of History in Postcommunist Nationalism*, Durham, NC and London: Duke University Press, 1999

Cole, Tim, *Selling the Holocaust*, New York: Routledge, 2000

Cornelissen, Christoph, Roman Holec and Jiří Pešek, *Diktatura – válka – vyhnání. Kultury vzpomínání v českém, slovenském a německém prostředí od roku 1945*, Ústí nad Labem: Albis International, 2007

Crowe, David, *Oskar Schindler: The Untold Account of His Life, Wartime Activities, and the True Story Behind the List*, Boulder, CO: Westview Press, 2004

Cuhra, Jaroslav, 'Katolická církev a odpor vůči normalizačnímu režimu', in Petr Blažek, ed., *Opozice a odpor proti komunistickému režimu v Československu 1968–1989*, Prague: Dokořán, 2005

Čulen, Konstantin, *Po Svätoplukovi druhá naša hlava. Život Dr. Jozefa Tisu*, Middletown, PA: Slovak League of America, 1947

Davidová, Eva, *Cesty Romů. Romano Drom 1945–1990*, Olomouc: Vydavatelství univerzity Palackého, 1995

Deák, István, Jan Gross and Tony Judt, *The Politics of Retributions in Europe*, Princeton: Princeton University Press, 2000

Dějiny KSČ v datech, Prague: Svoboda, 1984

Dietsch, Johan, *Making Sense of Suffering: Holocaust and Holodomor in Ukrainian Historical Culture*, Lund: Lund University, 2006

Dinuš, Peter, *Vyrovnávanie sa s minulosťou?* Bratislava:Veda, 2010.

Ducháček, Milan, 'Pražský květen 1945 očima Otakara Vávry', in Petr Kopal, ed., *Film a dějiny*, Prague: Nakladatelství Lidové noviny, 2005

Ďurica, Milan, *The Political Activities of Dr. Jozef Kirschbaum in 1939–1945 as Described in Secret German Documents*, Abano Terme: Piovan Editore, 1988

Ďurica, Milan, *Slovenský národ a jeho štátnosť*, Padova: Cleup; 1989

Ďurica, Milan, 'Dr. Jozef Tiso v hodnotení Hitlerových diplomatov a tajných agentov', in Valerián Bystrický and Štefan Fano, eds, *Pokus o politický a osobný profil Jozefa Tisu. Zborník materiálov z vedeckého sympózia Častá-Papiernička, 5.-7. mája 1992*, Bratislava: Slovak Academic Press, 1992

Ďurica, Milan, *Jozef Tiso – slovenský kňaz a štátnik I, 1887–1939*, Martin: Matica slovenská, 1992

Ďurica, Milan, *Dejiny Slovenska a Slovákov*, Bratislava: SPN, 1996

Ďurica, Milan, 'Dr. Jozef Tiso a problém Židov na Slovensku', in Gabriel Hoffmann, ed., *Zamlčená pravda o Slovensku*, Partizánske: Garmond, 1996

Ďurica, Milan, 'Slovenský národný odpor voči nemeckému nacizmu', in Gabriel Hoffmann, ed., *Zamlčená pravda o Slovensku*, Partizánske: Garmond, 1996

Ďurica, Milan, 'Slovenský podiel na európskej tragédii Židov', in Gabriel Hoffmann, ed., *Zamlčená pravda o Slovensku*, Partizánske: Garmond, 1996

Ďurica, Milan, *Jozef Tiso 1887–1947. Životopisný profil*, Bratislava: LÚČ, 2006

Edelheit, Abraham, and Hershel Edelheit, *History of the Holocaust*, Boulder, San Francisco and Oxford: Westview Press, 1994

Eyal, Gil, 'Identity and Trauma: Two Forms of the Will to Memory', *History & Memory* 16(1), Spring/Summer 2004

Fabricius, Miroslav, and Katarína Hradská, *Jozef Tiso. Prejavy a články, zv. II, (1938–1944)*, Bratislava: AEP, 2007

Fabricius, Miroslav, and Ladislav Suško, *Jozef Tiso. Prejavy a články (1913–1938)*, Bratislava: AEP, 2002

Fatranová, Gila, 'K deportáciam slovenských Židov v roku 1942', in Robert Büchler, Gila Fatranová and Stanislav Mičev, eds, *Slovenskí Židia*, Banská Bystrica: Múzeum SNP, 1991

Fatranová, Gila, 'Slovensko-židovské vzťahy', *Acta Judaica Slovaca* 4, Bratislava, SNM – Múzeum židovskej kultúry, 1998

Fatranová, Gila, 'The Viability of Anti-Semitic Manifestations', in Raphael Vago, ed., *Anti-Semitism at the End of the 20th Century*, Bratislava: Judaica Slovaca, 2002

Fawn, Rick, 'Czech Attitudes towards the Roma. "Expecting More of Havel's Country"?' *Europe–Asia Studies* 53(8), December 2001

Fiala, P., and R. Herbut, a kol., *Středoevropské systémy politických stran. Česká republika, Maďarsko, Polsko a Slovensko*, Brno: Masarykova univerzita, 2003

Fikejz, Radoslav, *Oskar Schindler (1908–1974)*, Svitavy: Městské Muzeum a galerie Svitavy, 1998

Flanzbaum, Hilene, ed., *The Americanization of the Holocaust*, Baltimore, MD: The John Hopkins University Press, 1999

Frajdl, Jiří, 'Schindlerovské mýty ukončeny', *Nový zítřek-Levicové noviny* 12, 1997

Frajdl, Jiří, 'Jak si svitavští radní ušili z ostudy kabát', *Hraničář*, January 1998

Frankl, Michal, 'Holocaust Education in the Czech Republic, 1989–2002', *Intercultural Education*, Vol. 14, No. 2., June 2003

Frankl, Michal, *Emancipace od židů. Český antisemitismus na konci 19. století*, Prague and Litomyšl: Paseka, 2007

Frištenská, Hana, Ilona Lázničková and Andrej Sulitka, *Neznámý holocaust*, Prague: Muzeum romské kultury, 1995

Gadamer, Hans-Georg, *Sanning och metod – i urval*, Göteborg: Daidalos, 1997

Gerner, Kristian, *Centraleuropas historia*, Stockholm: Natur och kultur, 2004

Gerner, Kristian, 'Historien på plats', in Klas-Göran Karlsson and Ulf Zander, eds, *Historien är nu*, Lund: Studentlitteratur, 2004

Gerner, Kristian, 'Hungary, Romania, The Holocaust and Historical Culture', in Klas-Göran Karlsson and Ulf Zander, eds., *The Holocaust on Post-War Battlefields*, Malmö: Sekel Bokförlag, 2004

Gerner, Kristian, and Klas-Göran Karlsson, *Folkmordens historia*, Stockholm: Atlantis, 2005

Gjuričová, Adéla and Michal Kopeček, eds, *Kapitoly z dějin české demokracie po roce 1989*, Prague and Litomyšl: Paseka, 2008

Gjuričová, Adéla, Michal Kopeček, Petr Roubal, Jiří Suk and Tomáš Zahradníček, *Rozděleni minulostí*, Prague: Václav Havel Library, 2011

Glejdura, Štefan, 'Dejinné metamorfózy Slovenska v rokoch 1945–1975', in Jozef Rydlo, ed., *Slovensko v retrospektíve dejín*, Lausanne: Liber, 1976

Gregorovič, Miroslav, *Kapitoly o českém fašismu*, Prague: Nakladatelství Lidové noviny, 1995

Greguš, Ctibor, *Slovensko – dlhá cesta k suverenite*, Bratislava: Tatrapress, 1991

Gross, Jan T., *Neighbours: The Story of the Annihilation of a Small Jewish Town*, New York: Penguin Books, 2002

Gruber, Ruth Ellen, *Virtually Jewish: Reinventing Jewish Culture in Europe*, Los Angeles: University of California Press, 2002

Gruntová, Jitka, *Legendy a fakta o Oskaru Schindlerovi*, Prague: Naše Vojsko, 2002

Hahnová, Eva and Hans Henning Hahn, *Sudetoněmecká vzpomínání a zapomínání*, Prague: Votobia, 2002

Halaj, Dušan, 'Medzinárodný rozmer SNP–súčasný stav, možnosti a perspektivy výskumu', in Katarína Kováčiková and Dezider Tóth, eds, *SNP 1944: Vstup Slovenska do demokratickej Eúrópy. Materiály z medzinárodnej konferencie k 55. výročiu SNP*, Banská Bystrica: Múzeum SNP, 1999

Halaj, Dušan, and Dezider Tóth, *Nezodpovedané otázky. K spochybňovaniu odboja a SNP v našich národných dejinách*, Banská Bystrica: Múzeum SNP, 1996

Hancock, Ian, 'Responses to the Porrajmos: The Romani Holocaust', in Alan Rosenbaum, ed., *Is The Holocaust Unique?* Boulder, CO and Oxford: Westview Press, 2001

Hamar, Eleonora, *Vyprávěná židovství. O narrativní konstrukci druhogeneračních židovských identit*, Prague: Sociologické nakladatelství SLON, 2008

Havelka, Miloš, ed., *Spor o smysl českých dějin 1895–1938*, Prague: Torst, 1995

Havelka, Miloš, *Dějiny a smysl*, Prague: Nakladatelství Lidové noviny, 2001

Havelka, Miloš, '"Smysl" a "pojetí" a "kritiky dějin"; historická "identita" a historické "legitimizace" (1938–1989)', in Miloš Havelka, ed., *Spor o smysl českých dějin 1938–1989*, Prague: Torst, 2006

Havelka, Miloš, ed., *Spor o smysl českých dějin 1938–1989*, Prague: Torst, 2006

Havelka, Miloš, *Ideje, dějiny, společnost*, Prague: Centrum pro stadium demokracie a kultury, 2010

Hedbávný, Zdeněk, *Alfréd Radok. Zpráva o jednom osudu*. Prague: Národní divadlo, 1994

Heitlinger, Alena, *In the Shadow of the Holocaust and Communism*, New Brunswick and London: Transaction Publishers, 2006

Herf, Jeffrey, *Divided Memory: The Nazi Past in Two Germanys*, Cambridge and London: Harvard University Press, 1997

Hilberg, Raul, *The Destruction of the European Jews*, New York: Holmes & Meier, 1985

Hlavičková, Zora, 'Wedged Between National and Trans-National History: Slovak Historiography in the 1990s', in Sorin Antohi, Balász Trencsényi and Péter Apor, eds, *Narratives Unbound: Historical Studies in Post-Communist Eastern Europe*, Budapest: Central European University Press, 2007

Hoffmann, Gabriel, ed., *Zamlčená pravda o Slovensku*, Partizánske: Garmond, 1996

Hojda, Zdeněk, and Jiří Pokorný, *Pomníky a zapomníky*, Prague and Litomyšl: Paseka, 1996

Holý, Jiří, ed., *Holokaust – Šoa – Zaglada v české, slovenské a polské literatuře*, Prague: Karolinum, 2007

Holy, Ladislav, *The Little Czech and The Great Czech Nation*, Cambridge and New York: Cambridge University Press, 1996

Hradská, Katarína, 'The Influence of Germany on the "Solution of Jewish Question" in Slovakia', in *The Tragedy of the Jews of Slovakia,* Auschwitz-Birkenau State Muzeum, Muzeum of the Slovak National Uprising, 2002

Hroch, Miroslav, 'Literární zdroje českého historického povědomí v 19. století', in *Polska, Czeska i slowacka świadomość historyczna XIX. wieku*, Warsaw: Zaklad Narodowy im. Ossolińskich, 1979

Hroch, Miroslav, 'Historické vědomí a potíže s jeho výzkumem dříve a nyní', in Jiří Šubrt, ed., *Historické vědomí jako předmět badatelského zájmu: teorie a výzkum*, Kolín: ARC, 2011

Hruška, Blahoslav, 'Okupace a válka v českém filmu po roce 1945 jako téma kultury vzpomínání', in Christoph Cornelissen, Roman Holec and Jiří Pešek, eds, *Diktatura – válka – vyhnání*.

Kultury vzpomínání v českém, slovenském a německém prostředí od roku 1945, Ústí nad Labem: Albis International, 2007

Hübl, Milan, *Svár dvou pojetí českých dějin*, Informace o Chartě 77, červenec-srpen 1984

Hübl, Milan, *Češi, Slováci a jejich sousedé*, Prague: Naše vojsko, 1990

Ilustrovaný encyklopedický slovník I, Prague: Academia, 1980

Ilustrovaný encyklopedický slovník III, Prague: Academia, 1982

Jablonický, Jozef, 'Boj za pravdu o povstaní', *Parlamentný Kurier 7–8*, 1994

Jablonický, Jozef, *Glosy o historiografii SNP. Zneužívanie a falšovanie dejín SNP*, Bratislava: NVK International, 1994

Jablonický, Jozef, 'Slovenské národné povstanie v historiografii v rokoch totality', in Július Lipták, ed., *SNP v pamäti národa. Materiály z vedeckej konferencie k 50. výročiu SNP*, Banská Bystrica: Múzeum SNP, 1994

Jablonický, Jozef, 'Židia v rezistencii na Slovensku', in Bernard Knežo-Schönbrun, ed., *Pracovné jednotky a útvary slovenskej armády 1939–1945. VI. robotný prápor*, Banská Bystrica and Bratislava: ZING Print, 1996

Jančík, Drahomír, and Eduard Kubů, *'Arizace' a arizátoři*, Prague: Karolinum, 2005

Jeismann, Karl-Ernst, 'Geschichtsbewusstsein', in Klaus Bergmann, Klaus Fröhlich, Annette Kuhn, Jörn Rüsen, Gerhard Schneider (Hrsg.), *Handbuch der Geschichtsdidaktik*, Band 1, Düsseldorf: Pädagogischer Verlag Schwann, 1979

Jelínek, Ješajahu Andrej, *Židia na Slovensku v 19. a 20. storočí*, Bratislava: Judaica Slovaca, 2000

Jelinek, Yashayahu, 'The Catholic Church and the Jews in the Period from Spring 1942 to Spring 1944 in Slovakia', *The Tragedy of the Jews of Slovakia*, Auschwitz-Birkenau State Muzeum, Muzeum of the Slovak National Uprising, 2002

Judt, Tony, *Postwar: A History of Europe since 1945*, London: William Heinemann, 2005

Kaleta, Petr, ed., *Národnostní otázka v Polsku a Československu v meziválečném období*, Prague: Masarykův ústav AV, ČR 2005

Kamenec, Ivan, 'Ako sa vidíme sami a ako nás vidí verejnosť', *Historický časopis* 39, 1991

Kamenec, Ivan, *Po stopách tragédie*, Bratislava: Archa, 1991

Kamenec, Ivan, *Slovenský stát*, Prague: Anomal, 1992

Kamenec, Ivan, *Jozef Tiso 1887–1947. Tragédia politika, kňaza a človeka*, Bratislava: Archa, 1998

Kamenec, Ivan, 'Civilný sektor a každodenný občiansky život na povstaleckou Slovensku', in Katarína Kováčiková and Dezider Tóth, eds, *SNP 1944: Vstup Slovenska do demokratickej Európy. Materiály z medzinárodnej konferencie k 55. výročiu SNP*, Banská Bystrica: Múzeum SNP, 1999

Kamenec, Ivan, *Hladanie a blúdenie v dejinách*, Bratislava: Kalligram, 2000

Kamenec, Ivan, 'Problémy asimilácie židovského obyvateľstva na Slovensku', in Ivan Kamenec, *Hladanie a blúdenie v dejinách*, Bratislava: Kalligram, 2000

Kamenec, Ivan, 'Rozdvojená historiografia', in Ivan Kamenec, *Hladanie a bludenie v dejinách*, Bratislava: Kalligram, 2000

Kamenec, Ivan, 'Reflections on the Holocaust in Slovak Society and Literature', in Klas-Göran Karlsson and Ulf Zander, eds., *Holocaust Heritage: Inquiries into European Historical Cultures*, Malmö: Sekel Bokförlag, 2004

Kamenec, Ivan, 'Dvojsečnosť mýtov o Slovenskom národnom povstaní", in Eduard Krekovič, Elena Mannová and Eva Krekovičová, eds, *Mýty naše slovenské*, Bratislava: Academic Electronic Press, 2005

Kamenec, Ivan, Vilém Prečan and Stanislav Škorvánek, *Vatikán a Slovenská republika (1939–1945). Dokumenty*, Bratislava: Slovak Academic Press, 1992

Kaplan, Karel, *Pravda o Československu 1945–48*, Prague: Panorama, 1990

Kaplan, Karel, *Dva retribuční procesy. Komentované dokumenty (1946–1947)*, Prague: Ústav pro soudobé dějiny, 1992

Kaplan, Karel, *Zpráva o zavraždění generálního tajemníka*, Prague: Mladá fronta, 1993

Karlsson, Klas-Göran, *Historia som vapen*, Stockholm: Natur och kultur, 1999

Karlsson, Klas-Göran, 'The Holocaust and Russian Historical Culture: A Century-Long Perspective', in Klas-Göran Karlsson and Ulf Zander, eds, *Echoes of the Holocaust: Historical Culture in Contemporary Europe*, Lund: Nordic Academic Press, 2003

Karlsson, Klas-Göran, 'Historiedidaktik: begrepp, teori och analys', in Klas-Göran Karlsson and Ulf Zander, *Historien är nu*, Lund: Studentlitteratur, 2004

Karlsson, Klas-Göran, 'Russian Nationalism, Antisemitism, and the Ideological Use of History', in Klas-Göran Karlsson and Ulf Zander, eds., *The Holocaust on Post-War Battlefields*, Malmö: Sekel Bokförlag, 2006

Karlsson, Klas-Göran, *Folkmordet som spegel och symbolpolitik. Förintelsens plats i den europeiska historiekulturen*, Stockholm: Forum för levande historia, 2008

Karlsson, Klas-Göran, "The Uses of History and the Third Wave of Europeanisation", in Bo Stråth and Malgorzata Pakier, eds, *A European Memory*, New York: Berghahn Books, 2010

Karlsson, Klas-Göran, and Ulf Zander, eds, *Echoes of the Holocaust: Historical Culture in Contemporary Europe*, Lund: Nordic Academic Press, 2003

Karlsson, Klas-Göran, and Ulf Zander, eds, *Historien är nu*, Lund: Studentlitteratur, 2004

Karlsson, Klas-Göran, and Ulf Zander, eds, *Holocaust Heritage: Inquiries into European Historical Cultures*, Malmö: Sekel Bokförlag, 2004

Karlsson, Klas-Göran, and Ulf Zander, eds, *The Holocaust on Post-War Battlefields*, Malmö: Sekel Bokförlag, 2006

Kárný, Miroslav, *"Konečné řešení": Genocida českých židů v německé protektorátní politice*, Prague: Academia, 1991

Kárný, Miroslav, 'Československé oběti německé okupace 1938–1945', in Ivona Řezanková, ed., *Cesta do katastrofy. Československo-německé vztahy 1938–1947*, Vrůtky, 1993

Keneally, Thomas, *Schindler's Ark*, London: Coronet, 1982

Kirschbaum, Jozef, *Slovaks In Canada*, Toronto: Canadian Ethnic Press Association of Ontario, 1967

Kirschbaum, Jozef, ed., *Slovak Culture through the Centuries*, Toronto: SWC, 1978

Kirschbaum, Jozef, ed., *Desať rokov činnosti Svetového kongresu Slovákov*, Toronto: SWC, 1981

Kirschbaum, Stanislav J., *A History of Slovakia: The Struggle for Survival*, New York: Palgrave Macmillan, 1995

Klaus, Václav, *O tvář zítřka*. Prague: Pražská imaginace, 1991

Knežo-Schönbrun, Bernard, ed., *Pracovné jednotky a útvary slovenskej armády 1939–1945. VI. robotný prápor*, Banská Bystrica and Bratislava: ZING Print, 1996

Knežo-Schönbrun, Bernard, 'Na úvod', in Bernard Knežo-Schönbrun, ed., *Pracovné jednotky a útvary slovenskej armády 1939–1945. VI. robotný prápor*, Banská Bystrica and Bratislava: ZING Print, 1996

Kocourek, Václav, ed., *Populární politický slovník*, Prague: Mladá fronta, 1962

Kolář, Petr and Michal Kopeček, 'A Difficult Quest for New Paradigms: Czech Historiography after 1989', in Sorin Antohi, Balász Trencsényi and Péter Apor, eds, *Narratives Unbound: Historical Studies in Post-Communist Eastern Europe*, Budapest: Central European University Press, 2007

Kopal, Petr, ed., *Film a dějiny*, Prague: Nakladatelství Lidové noviny, 2005

Kopeček, Lubomír, ed., *Od Mečiara k Dzurindovi. Slovenská politika a politický systém v prvním desetiletí samostatnosti*, Brno: Masarykova universita, 2003

Kopeček, Lubomír, 'Proměny moderní slovenské politiky', in Lubomír Kopeček, ed., *Od Mečiara k Dzurindovi. Slovenská politika a politický systém v prvním desetiletí samostatnosti*, Brno: Masarykova univerzita, 2003

Kopeček, Lubomír, 'Stranický systém Slovenska', in P. Fiala and R. Herbut, a kol., *Středoevropské systémy politických stran. Česká republika, Maďarsko, Polsko a Slovensko*, Brno: Masarykova univerzita, 2003

Kopeček, Michal, *Hledání ztraceného smyslu revoluce*, Prague: Argo, 2009

Korbel, Josef, *Twentieth Century Czechoslovakia: The Meanings of Its History*, New York: Columbia University Press, 1977

Koura, Petr, 'Obraz nacistické okupace v hraném českém filmu 1945–1989', in Petr Kopal, ed.,
    Film a dějiny, Prague: Nakladatelství Lidové noviny, 2005
Koura, Petr, 'Obraz holokaustu v českém hraném filmu', in Jiří Holý, ed., Holokaust – Šoa – Zaglada
    v české, slovenské a polské literatuře, Prague: Karolinum, 2007
Kováč, Dušan, Dějiny Slovenska, Prague: NLN, 2002
Kováčiková, Katarína, Scénár stálej expozície Múzea SNP v Banskej Bystrici, Banská Bystrica: Múzeum
    SNP, 1998
Kováčiková, Katarína, and Dezider Tóth, eds, SNP 1944: Vstup Slovenska do demokratickej Európy.
    Materiály z medzinárodnej konferencie k 55. výročiu SNP. Banská Bystrica: Adade, 1999
Kozlíková, Daniela, Romská otázka – překážka vstupu České republiky do Evropské unie?, Prague:
    Sociologický ústav ČSAV, 2001
Králová, Štěpánka, 'Jeden ze šestatřiceti spravedlivých', MFDnes, 12 March 1994
Kraus, Ota, and Erich Kulka, Továrna na smrt, Prague: Naše vojsko – SPB, 1959
Krejčová, Helena, 'K některým problémům židovské menšiny a českého antisemitismu po roce
    1945', in Jerzy Tomaszewski and Jaroslav Valenta, eds, Židé v české a polské občanské společnosti,
    Prague: Karlova univerzita, 1999
Krejčová, Helena, 'Židovská komunita v moderní české společnosti', in Václav Veber, ed., Židé v
    novodobých dějinách, Prague: Karolinum, 1997
Krejčová, Helena, and Jana Svobodová, Postavení a osudy židovského obyvatelstva v Čechách a na
    Moravě v letech 1939–1945. Sborník studií. Prague: Ústav pro soudobé dějiny, 1998
Krekovič, Eduard, Elena Mannová and Eva Krekovičová, eds, Mýty naše slovenské, Bratislava:
    Academic Electronic Press, 2005
Křen, Jan, Bílá místa v našich dějinách, Prague: Lidové noviny, 1990
Křen, Jan, 'K diskusím o pojetí českých dějin', in Miloš Havelka, ed., Spor o smysl českých dějin
    1938–1989, Prague: Torst, 2006
Křen, Jan, 'Historické proměny češství', in Miloš Havelka, ed., Spor o smysl českých dějin 1938–
    1989, Prague: Torst, 2006
Kroutvor, Josef, Potíže s dějinami, Prague: Prostor, 1990
Kubů, Eduard, and Jaroslav Pátek, Mýtus a realita hospodářské vyspělosti Československa mezi světovými
    válkami, Prague: Karolinum, 2000
Kulka, Erich, Židé v československé Svobodově armádě, Prague: Naše vojsko, 1990
Kushner, Tony, The Holocaust and the Liberal Imagination: A Social and Cultural History, Oxford:
    Blackwell, 1994
Lášticová, Barbara and Andrej Findor, 'From Regime Legitimation to Democratic Museum
    Pedagogy? Studying Europeanization at the Museum of the Slovak National Uprising', in
    Barbara Lášticová and Andrej Findor, eds, Politics of Collective Memory: Cultural Patterns of
    Commemorative Practices in Post-War Europe, Vienna and Berlin: LIT Verlag, 2008
Lášticová, Barbara and Andrej Findor, eds, Politics of Collective Memory: Cultural Patterns of
    Commemorative Practices in Post-War Europe, Vienna and Berlin: LIT Verlag, 2008
Levy, Daniel and Natan Sznaider, The Holocaust and Memory in the Global Age, Philadelphia:
    Temple University Press, 2005
Lindström, Fredrik, 'The First Victim? Austrian Historical Culture and the Memory of the
    Holocaust', in Klas-Göran Karlsson and Ulf Zander, eds, The Holocaust on Post-War Battlefields,
    Malmö: Sekel Bokförlag, 2006.
Linenthal, Edward T., Preserving Memory: The Struggle to Create America's Holocaust Museum, New
    York: Columbia University Press, 2001
Lipscher, Ladislav, Židia v slovenskom štáte 1939–1945, Bratislava: Print-servis, 1992
Lipstadt, Deborah, Denying the Holocaust, New York: Plume, 1994
Lipták, Július, ed., SNP v pamäti národa. Materiály z vedeckej konferencie k 50. výročiu SNP, Banská
    Bystrica: Múzeum SNP, 1994
Lipták, Lubomír, Storočie dlhšie ako sto rokov, Bratislava: Kalligram, 1999
Loshitsky, Yosefa, ed., Spielberg's Holocaust: Critical Perspectives on Schindler's List, Bloomington and
    Indianapolis: Indiana University Press, 1997

Lukáč, Pavol, 'Historická a politická identita Slovenska na prahu jeho intergácie do EÚ', in László Szigeti, ed., *Slovenská otázka dnes*, Bratislava: Kalligram, 2007

Lukeš, Igor, 'The Rudolf Slansky Affair: New Evidence', *Slavic Review* 1, 1999

Magdolenová, Anna, 'Vznik a vývoj idey Slovenskej štátnosti', in Gabriel Hoffmann, ed., *Zamlčená pravda o Slovensku*, Partizánske: Garmond, 1996

Mann, Arne, *Romský dějepis*, Prague: Fortuna, 2001

Mayer, Peter, Bernard Weinryb, Eugene Duschinsky and Nicholas Sylvian, *Jews in the Soviet Satellites*, Syracuse University Press, 1953

Mendelsohn, Ezra, *Jews of East and Central Europe Between the Wars*, Bloomington: Indiana University Press, 1983

Mešťan, Pavol, 'Snahy o nové interpretácie a dezinterpretácie židovskej otázky na Slovensku', in Dušan Halaj and Dezider Tóth, eds, *Nezodpovedané otázky. K spochybňovaniu odboja a SNP v našich národných dejinách*, Banská Bystrica: Múzeum SNP, 1996

Mešťan, Pavol, *Antisemitizmus v politickom vývoji Slovenska*, Bratislava: SNM-Múzeum židovskej kultury, 1998

Mešťan, Pavol, *Antisemitizmus v politickom vývoji Slovenska 1989–1999*, Bratislava: SNM-Múzeum židovskej kultury, 2000

Miháliková, Silvia, 'Politický obraz Slovenska: medzi krížom a európskou hviezdičkou', *Sociológia – Slovak Sociological Review* 37(6), 2005

Mikula, Ján, 'Pravda o povstaní alebo Povstanie s jednou legendou', in Gabriel Hoffmann, ed., *Zamlčená pravda o Slovensku*, Partizánske: Garmond, 1996

Milton, Sybil, 'Gypsies and the Holocaust', *The History Teacher* 24(4), August 1991

Milton, Sybil, 'Correspondence: "Gypsies and the Holocaust"', *The History Teacher* 25(4), August 1992

Mithander, Conny, John Sundholm and Adrian Velicu, *European Cultural Memory Post-89*, Amsterdam and New York: Rodopi, 2013

Mlynárik, Ján, *Dějiny Židů na Slovensku*, Prague: Academia, 2005

Motl, Stanislav, 'Schindlerův rok', *Reflex* 12, 1994

Munk, Jan, 'Jews of East and Central Europe Between the Wars. The Terezín Memorial in the Year 2000', *Museum international*, LIII, 1, UNESCO, 2001

Munk, Jan, *60 let památníku Terezín/60 years of the Terezín Memorial*, Terezín: Oswald Publishers, 2007

Murín, Karol, *Spomienky a svedectvo*, Hamilton, Ontario, 1987

Múzeum SNP, *Sprievodca po expozícii*, Banská Bystrica: Múzeum SNP, 1977

Navrátil, Pavel a kol., *Romové v české společnosti*, Prague: Portál, 2003

Nečas, Ctibor, *Nad osudem českých a slovenských cikánů v letech 1939–1945*, Brno: Univerzita J.E. Purkyně, 1981

Nečas, Ctibor, *Českoslovenští Romové v letech 1939–1945*, Brno: Masarykova univerzita, 1994

Nečas, Ctibor, *Romové v České republice včera a dnes*, Olomouc: Vydavatelství Univerzity Palackého, 1995

Nečas, Ctibor, *MA-BISTEREN-NEZAPOMEŇME. Historie cikánského tábora v Hodoníně u Kunštátu*, Prague: Muzeum romské kultury, 1997

Nečas, Ctibor, *Holocaust českých Romů*, Prague: Prostor, 1999

Nenadál, Radoslav, 'V osidlech minulosti' (Epilog), in William Styron, *Sophiina volba*, Prague: Odeon, 1995

Nir, Akiva, 'Slovenskí Židia v odboji a Slovenskom národnom povstaní, in Katarína Kováčiková and Dezider Tóth, eds, *SNP 1944: Vstup Slovenska do demokratickej Európy. Materiály z medzinárodnej konferencie k 55. výročiu SNP*, Banská Bystrica: Múzeum SNP, 1999

Nir, Akiva, 'The Zionist Organisations, Youth Movements and Emigration to Palestine in 1918–1945', in *The Tragedy of the Jews of Slovakia*, Auschwitz-Birkenau State Muzeum, Muzeum of the Slovak National Uprising, 2002

Nietzsche, Friedrich, *On the Use and Abuse of History for Life*, Sioux Falls, SD: EZreads Publications, 2010

Nižňanský, Eduard, *Židovská komunita na Slovensku medzi československou parlamentnou demokraciou a slovenským štátom v stredoeurópskom kontexte*, Prešov: Universum, 1999

Nižňanský, Eduard, *Nacizmus, Holocaust, slovenský štát*, Bratislava: Kalligram, 2010

Nižňanský, Eduard a kol., *Holokaust na Slovensku 1–7*, Bratislava: Nadácia Milana Šimečku, Židovská náboženská obec, Vojenský historický ústav, 2001–2005

Nora, Pierre, 'Between Memory and History: Les Lieux de Memoire', *Representations* 26, Special Issue: Memory and Counter-Memory, Spring 1989

Novick, Peter, *The Holocaust in American Life*, New York: Houghton Mifflin, 1999

Novick, Peter, *The Holocaust and Collective Memory*, London: Bloomsbury, 2001

Nyström, Kerstin, 'The Holocaust and Croatian National Identity. An Uneasy Relationship', in Klas-Göran Karlsson and Ulf Zander, eds, *The Holocaust on Post-War Battlefields*, Malmö: Sekel Bokförlag, 2006

Oliveriusová, Eva, 'Úspěšný pokus o fúzi mýtu a literatury faktu', *Světová literatura* 1, 1986

O procesech a rehabilitacích. Prague: Florenc, 1990

Osterloh, Jorg, *Nacionálněsocialistické pronásledování Židů v říšské župě Sudety 1938–1945*, Praha: Argo, 2010

Otáhal, Milan, *Opozice, moc, společnost 1969/1989. Příspěvek k dějinám 'normalizace'*, Prague: Maxdorf, 1994

Otáhal, Milan, *Normalizace 1969–1989: Příspěvek ke stavu bádání*, Prague: ÚSD AV ČR, 2002

Pape, Markus, *A nikdo vám nebude věřit. Dokument o koncentračním táboře Lety u Písku*, Prague: GpluG, 1997

Pavel, Ota, *Smrt krásných srnců*, Praha: Československý spisovatel, 1971

Pavel, Ota, *Jak jsem potkal ryby*, Praha: Mladá fronta, 1974

Pavlát, Leo, 'V muzeu výjimečné historie i současnosti', in Magda Veselská, ed., *Archa paměti. Cesta pražského židovského muzea pohnutým 20. stoletím*, Prague: Academia and Židovské muzeum, 2012

Pasák, Tomáš, *JUDr. Emil Hácha (1938–1945)*, Prague: Horizont, 1997

Pasák, Tomáš, *Český fašismus 1922–1945 a kolaborace 1939–1945*, Prague: Práh, 1999

Pěkný, Tomáš, *Historie Židů v Čechách a na Moravě*, Praha: Sefer, 2001

Pěkný, Tomáš, 'Pavel Tigrid 1917–2003', *Roš Chodeš* 3, 2003

Pilátová, Agáta, 'Tváří v tvář dějinám i sobě samým', *Film a doba*, 1966

Pojar, Miloš, Blanka Soukupová and Marie Zahradníková, *Židovská menšina v Československu ve 30. letech*, Prague: Židovské muzeum v Praze, 2004

Pojar, Miloš, Blanka Soukupová and Marie Zahradníková, *Židovská menšina za druhé republiky*, Prague: Židovské muzeum v Praze, 2007

Polansky, Paul, *Tíživé mlčení*, Prague: GplusG, 1998

Polansky, Paul, *Bouře*, Prague: GplusG, 1999

Poloncarz, Marek, *Internační tábor pro německé obyvatelstvo. Malá pevnost Terezín 1945–1948*, Terezín: Památník Terezín, 1997

Poučení z krizového vývoje ve straně a společnosti po XIII. sjezdu KSČ, Prague: Svoboda, 1970

Prečan, Vilém, 'Zuviel Vergangenheit: ein Bericht aus Prag', in Süssmuth, Hans (Hg), *Transformationsprozesse in den Staaten Ostmitteleuropas 1989–1995*, Baden Baden: Nomos, 1998, pp. 256–71

Probst, Lothar, 'Founding Myths in Europe and the Role of the Holocaust', *New German Critique*, No. 90, Autumn 2003

Proces s vedením protistátneho spikleneckého centra na čele s Rudolfom Slánským, Prague: Orbis, 1953.

Rašla, Anton, and Ernest Žabkay, *Proces s dr. Jozefem Tisom*, Bratislava: Tatrapress, 1990

Rataj, Jan, *O autoritativní národní stát. Ideologické proměny české politiky v druhé republice 1938–1939*, Prague: Karolinum, 1997

Řezanková, Ivona, ed., *Cesta do katastrofy. Česko-německé vztahy 1938–1947*, Vrútky, 1993

Ricoeur, Paul, *Time and Narrative: Volume 1*, Chicago and London: Chicago University Press, 1984

Ricoeur, Paul, *Time and Narrative: Volume 3*, Chicago and London: Chicago University Press, 1988

Rosenbaum, Alan, ed., *Is The Holocaust Unique?*, Boulder, CO and Oxford: Westview Press, 2001

Rosenfeld, Alvin, Ed., *Thinking about the Holocaust after a Half Century*, Bloomington: Indiana University Press, 1997

Rothkirchen, Livia, *The Jews of Bohemia & Moravia: Facing the Holocaust*, Lincoln and Jerusalem: University of Nebraska Press and Yad Vashem, 2005

Rubenstein, Joshua, and Ilya Altman, eds, *The Unknown Black Book: The Holocaust in German Occupied Soviet Territories*, Bloomington: Indiana University Press in association with the United States Holocaust Memorial Museum, 2010

Rucker, Laurent, *Stalin, Israel a Židé*, Prague: Rybka Publishers, 2001

Rupnik, Jacques, *Jiná Evropa*, Prague: Prostor, 1992

Rüsen, Jörn, 'Functions of Historical Narration – Proposals for a Strategy of Legitimating History in School', in *Historiedidaktik i Norden 3*, Malmö: Lärarhögskolan i Malmö, 1987

Rüsen, Jörn, 'Holocaust, Memory and Identity Building: Metahistorical Considerations in the Case of (West) Germany', in Michael S. Roth and Charles G. Salas, eds, *Disturbing Remains: Memory, History and Crisis in the Twentieth Century*, Los Angeles: Getty Research Institute, 2001

Rüsen, Jörn, *Berättande och förnuft*, Göteborg: Daidalos, 2004

Rüsen, Jörn, 'Interpreting the Holocaust: Some Theoretical Issues', in Klas-Göran Karlsson and Ulf Zander, eds, *Holocaust Heritage: Inquiries into European Historical Cultures*, Malmö: Sekel Bokförlag, 2004

Rüsen, Jörn, *History: Narration–Interpretation–Orientation*, New York and Oxford: Berghahn Books, 2005

Rydlo, Jozef, *Slovensko v retrospektíve dejín*, Lausanne: Liber, 1976

Rychlík, Jan, *Rozpad Československa. Česko-slovenské vztahy 1989–1992*, Bratislava: AEP, 2002

Rychlík, Jan, 'Czech–Slovak Relations in Czechoslovakia 1918–1939', in Petr Kaleta, ed., *Národnostní otázka v Polsku a Československu v meziválečném období*, Prague: Masarykův ústav AV ČR, 2005

Rychlík, Jan, 'The Slovak Question and the Resistance Movement during the Second World War', in Mikuláš Teich, Dušan Kováč and Martin D. Brown, eds, *Slovakia in History*, Cambridge: Cambridge University Press, 2011

Salner, Peter, *Prežili holokaust*, Bratislava: Veda, 1997

Salner, Peter, *Židia na Slovensku medzi tradíciou a asimiláciou*, Bratislava: Zing-Print, 2000

Sarauw, Lone, *Together We Part: Collective Memory, Political Culture and Break-Up of Czechoslovakia*, Aarhus: University of Aarhus, 2004

Schmarz, Martin, 'Bez Schindlerů bychom to měli jednodušší', *MF Dnes*, 24 August 1994

Seebauer, F., 'Sowjetische Weltsicht konserviert', *Sudetendeutsche Zeitung*, 6 March 1998

Shandler, Jeffrey, 'Schindler's Discourse: America Discusses the Holocaust and Its Mediation, from NBC's Miniseries to Spielberg's Film', in Yosefa Loshitsky, ed., *Spielberg's Holocaust*, Bloomington and Indianapolis: Indiana University Press, 1997

Šiklová, Jiřina, 'The "Grey Zone" and the Future of Dissent in Czechoslovakia', *Social Research* 57, 1990, No. 2

Skalnik Leff, Carol, *The Czech and Slovak Republics: Nation Versus State*, Oxford and Boulder, CO: Westview Press, 1997

Škorpil, Pavel, 'Problémy vyčíslení životních ztrát u československých obětí nacionálně socialistického Německa v letech 1938–1945', in Ivona Řezanková, ed., *Cesta do katastrofy. Československo-německé vztahy 1938–1947*, Vrůtky, 1993

Škvorecký, Josef, *Zbabělci*, Prague: Nakladatelství Lidové noviny, 2001

Smolec, Ján, 'Slovensko sa na fašismis iba hralo', in Gabriel Hoffmann, ed., *Zamlčená pravda o Slovensku*, Partizánske: Garmond, 1996

Sniegon, Tomas, 'Implementing Post-Communist National Memory in the Czech Republic and Slovakia: Institutes of "National Memory" in Bratislava and Prague', in Conny Mithander, John Sundholm and Adrian Velicu, eds, *European Cultural Memory Post-89*, Amsterdam and New York: Rodopi, 2013

Sommer, Vítězslav, *Angažované dějepisectví. Stranická historiografie mezi stalinismem a reformním komunismem (1950–1970)*, Prague: FFUK and Nakladatelství Lidové noviny, 2011

Soukupová, Blanka, Peter Salner and Miroslava Ludvíková, eds, *Židovská menšina v Československu po druhé světové válce*. *Od osvobození k nové totalitě*, Praha: Židovské muzeum v Praze, 2009

Špetko, Jozef, *Líšky kontra ježe*. *Slovenská politická emigrácia 1948–1989*. *Analýzy a dokumenty*, Bratislava: Kalligram, 2002

Staněk, Tomáš, 'Němečtí židé v Československu 1945–1948', *Dějiny a současnost* 5, 1991

Stanislav, Ján, 'Koncepcia Múzea Slovenského národného povstania', *Museologica* II/2001, Banská Štiavnica: Univerzita Mateja Bela, 2001

Stanislav, Ján, and Dezider Tóth, *Libreto stálej expozície Múzea SNP k 60. výročiu SNP*, Banská Bystrica: Múzeum SNP, 2003

Stanislav, Ján and Dušan Halaj, 'K deformáciam interpretácie protifašistického odboja na Slovensku a SNP', in Dušan Halaj and Dezider Tóth, eds, *Nezodpovedané otázky*. *K spochybňovaniu odboja a SNP v našich národných dejinách*, Banská Bystrica: Múzeum SNP, 1996

Stehlíková, Eva, 'Aktuální kontexty obrazu Němce a Německa v české společnosti', in Eva Broklová and Jan Křen, eds, *Obraz Němců, Rakouska a Německa v české společnosti 19. a 20. století*, Prague: Karolinum, 1998

Steinlauf, Michael C., *Bondage to the Dead*, New York: Syracuse University Press, 1997

Stolarik, Mark, 'Slovak Historians in Exile in North America, 1945–1992', *Human Affairs* 6, 1996

Stříbrný, Jan, 'Rezistence a válka v paměti současné české společnosti', in Július Lipták, ed., *SNP v pamäti národa*. *Materiály z vedeckej konferencie k 50. výročiu SNP*, Banská Bystrica: Múzeum SNP, 1994

Šubrt, Jiří, ed., *Historické vědomí jako předmět badatelského zájmu: teorie a výzkum*, Kolín: ARC, 2011

Šubrt, Jiří and Štěpánka Pfeiferová, 'Nástin teoreticko-sociologického přístupu k otázce historického vědomí', in Jiří Šubrt, ed., *Historické vědomí jako předmět badatelského zájmu: teorie a výzkum*, Kolín: ARC, 2011

Šubrt, Jiří and Jiří Vinopal, *Historické vědomí obyvatel České republiky perspektivou sociologického výzkumu*, Praha: Karolinum, 2013

Szigeti, László, ed., *Slovenská otázka dnes*, Bratislava: Kalligram, 2007

Takáč, Ladislav and Milan Gajdoš, 'Rezistencia a vojnové roky v pamäti slovenského národa', in Július Lipták, ed., *SNP v pamäti národa*. *Materiály z vedeckej konferencie k 50. výročiu SNP*, Banská Bystrica: Múzeum SNP, 1994

Táncoš, Július, and René Lužica, *Zatratení a zabudnutí*, Bratislava: IRIS, 2002

Tesař, Jan, *Mnichovský komplex*, Prague: Prostor, 2000

The Slovak National Uprising Museum, Exposition Guide, Banská Bystrica: Múzeum SNP, 2000

The Stockholm International Forum on the Holocaust. *Proceedings*, Stockholm: Svensk Information, 2000

The Tragedy of the Jews of Slovakia, Auschwitz-Birkenau State Muzeum, Muzeum of the Slovak National Uprising, 2002

Tigrid, Pavel, *Kapesní průvodce inteligentní ženy po vlastním osudu*, Toronto: Sixty-Eight Publishers, 1988

Tomaszewski, Jerzy, and Jaroslav Valenta, *Židé v české a polské občanské společnosti*, Prague: Karlova univerzita, 1999

Tossavainen, Mikael, *Heroes and Victims: The Holocaust in Israeli Historical Consciousness*, Lund: Lund University, 2006

Tragédia slovenských židov, Banská Bystrica: Múzeum SNP, 1992

Törnquist-Plewa, Barbara, 'Contrasting Ethnic Nationalisms: Eastern Central Europe', in Stephen Barbour, Stephen and Carmichael, Cathie, *Language and Nationalism in Europe*, Oxford: Oxford University Press, 2001

Törnqvist-Plewa, Barbara, 'The Jedwabne Killings – A Challenge for Polish Collective Memory', in Klas-Göran Karlsson and Ulf Zander, eds., *Echoes of the Holocaust: Historical Culture in Contemporary Europe*, Lund: Nordic Academic Press, 2003

Vaculík, Ludvík, 'Naše slovenská otázka', *Literární noviny* 5/1990

Vago, Raphael, ed., *Anti-Semitism at the End of the 20th Century*, Bratislava: Judaica Slovaca, 2002

Valenta, Jaroslav, 'Kauza Oskara Schindlera v dvojím pohledu', *Soudobé dějiny* 2–3, 1998

Valenta, Jaroslav, Ctibor Nečas and Oldřich Sládek, *Historikové a kauza Lety*, Prague: Historický ústav ČSAV, 1999

Vašečka, Michal, ed., *ČAČIPEN PAL O ROMA*. *Súhrnná správa o Rómoch na Slovensku*, Bratislava: Inštitut pre verejné otázky, 2002

Veber, Václav, ed., *Židé v novodobých dějinách*, Prague: Karolinum, 1997

Veselská, Magda, *Archa paměti*. *Cesta pražského židovského muzea pohnutým 20. stoletím*, Prague: Academia and Židovské muzeum, 2012

Vnuk, František, *Dr. Jozef Tiso: President of the Slovak Republic*, Sydney, 1967

Vnuk, František, *Dedičstvo otcov. Eseje na historické témy*, Bratislava: Alfa Omega, 1990

Vnuk, František, 'Retribučné súdnictvo a proces s Jozefom Tisom', in Valerián Bystrický and Štefan Fano, eds, *Pokus o politický a osobný profil Jozefa Tisu*. *Zborník materiálov z vedeckého sympózia Častá-Papiernička, 5.–7. mája 1992*, Bratislava: Slovak Academic Press, 1992

Vnuk, František, *Neuveritelné sprísahanie*, Trenčín, 1993

Vnuk, František, 'Slovenské dejiny bez ilúzií a príkras. František Bošňák – slovenský Schindler', in Gabriel Hoffmann, ed., *Zamlčená pravda o Slovensku*, Partizánske: Garmond, 1996

Weil, Jiří, *Život s hvězdou*, Prague: ELK, 1949

Weil, Jiří, *Life with a Star*, London: Penguin Books, 2002

Wiley, Mason and Daien Bona, *Inside Oscar: An Unofficial History of the Academy Awards*, New York: Ballantine Books, 1987

Zakaria, Fareed, *Budoucnost svobody*, Prague: Academia, 2005

Zavacká, Katarína, 'Význam SNP pre zahraničnú politiku Slovenskej republiky v súčanosti', in Katarína Kováčiková and Dezider Tóth, eds, *SNP 1944: Vstup Slovenska do demokratickej Európy*. *Materiály z medzinárodnej konferencie k 55. výročiu SNP*, Banská Bystrica: Múzeum SNP, 1999

Index